# MASTERPIECES OF FRENCH LITERATURE

*Marilyn S. Severson*

Greenwood Introduces Literary Masterpieces

GREENWOOD PRESS
Westport, Connecticut • London

**Library of Congress Cataloging-in-Publication Data**

Severson, Marilyn S.
    Masterpieces of French literature / Marilyn S. Severson.
        p. cm. — (Greenwood introduces literary masterpieces, ISSN 1545–6285)
    Includes bibliographical references and index.
    ISBN 0–313–31484–5 (alk. paper)
    1. French fiction—19th century—History and criticism. 2. French fiction—20th
century—History and criticism. I. Title. II. Series.
PQ651.S48 2004
843'.709—dc22        2003059635

British Library Cataloguing in Publication Data is available.

Library of Congress Catalog Card Number: 2003059635
ISBN: 0–313–31484–5
ISSN: 1545–6285

First published in 2004

Greenwood Press, 88 Post Road West, Westport, CT 06881
An imprint of Greenwood Publishing Group, Inc.
www.greenwood.com

Printed in the United States of America

The paper used in this book complies with the
Permanent Paper Standard issued by the National
Information Standards Organization (Z39.48–1984).

10  9  8  7  6  5  4  3  2  1

For my family and friends, without whose encouragement and support this project would not have been completed.

# Contents

# Preface

*Masterpieces of French Literature* provides a critical introduction to landmark novels in nineteenth- and twentieth-century French literature. These novels are masterpieces in the sense that they continue to be widely read outside their native land and their authors' insights into humanity and universal themes easily cross linguistic and cultural boundaries. Through their masterly skill in crafting their works, these authors integrate themes and characters into interesting and readable stories that engross their readers.

The eight novels discussed in *Masterpieces of French Literature* have been the subject of much literary criticism since their publication. Such criticism is often directed toward graduate students or specialists in literature. However, this series focuses on enabling nonspecialist and general readers to gain a deeper understanding of each novel, of the author, and of the environment that produced it. The goal is to help the reader develop the ability to analyze literature through easy-to-use, yet challenging literary criticism that focuses on plot and character development, themes and style, as well as the biographical and historical context in which each author wrote.

Librarians and teachers of English and French were consulted, along with curriculum lists, about the choice of novels to include in this volume. The works included cover a time period of over 100 years and reflect both the development of the French novel during the era as well as themes, characters, and plots that appeal to readers in the twenty-first century. Although discerning readers can find masterpieces in poetry, essays, and plays as well as novels, novels are the focus of this volume; these works of fiction can engage readers immediately, making them think, feel, and reflect upon all manner of human questions from the first page to the last.

During the more than 120 years between Hugo's *The Hunchback of Notre-Dame* (1831), the earliest novel among the eight, and Camus's *The Plague* (1947), the final work of the time period discussed, French literature moved from romanticism and its interest in individual emotions, history, and exoticism to a more specific concern with humanity facing an indifferent universe and choosing ways to confront modern plagues, alienation, and solitude. In between were such literary movements as realism, symbolism, naturalism, surrealism, and existentialism. The novels discussed in this volume are not easily confined to one movement or another, however; they include historical novels, portraits of society, and allegories.

The nineteenth-century novelists discussed in this volume are Alexandre Dumas, Gustave Flaubert, and Victor Hugo. Other novelists of the time period such as Honoré de Balzac, Henri Beyle (known by his pseudonym Stendhal), and Emile Zola also remain major figures in the nineteenth-century French novel. Balzac and Stendhal published at the same time as Dumas, Flaubert, and Hugo; Zola's principal works appeared during the last decades of the nineteenth century. Balzac is best known for his efforts to embrace the social, sentimental, and economic life of a whole generation in a multivolume series, *La Comédie humaine* (*The Human Comedy*). However, he is perhaps too overwhelming in scope and prone to exaggeration in his characters to appeal to current young readers. Stendhal was most interested in the psychology of his characters, and his portrayal of the rise and fall of Julien Sorel in *Le Rouge et le Noir* (*The Red and the Black*) has not often appealed to readers outside of France—the writer himself dedicated the novel to the happy few, realizing that his emphasis on analysis and his intervention in the narrative might not be appealing to the public in general. As part of the literary current called naturalism, which emphasized meticulous descriptions and did not shy away from the seamy side of life, Zola presents unforgettable narratives of crowd scenes and events involving working-class people. Yet, he may appear dated to modern readers.

Dumas, Flaubert, and Hugo appeal more easily to twenty-first-century readers as they interweave story, character, and theme to create a fictional reality that entertains while it analyzes, that presents human nature in recognizable aspects, and that uses narrative forms to present its story.

The two twentieth-century authors discussed in this volume were familiar with their predecessors and were influenced by their accomplishments even as they found their own way of creating a fictional reality. Camus and Saint-Exupéry were part of the variety of the French novel characteristic of the first half of the twentieth century. Other important novelists of the time period include Marcel Proust, André Gide, André Malraux, and Jean-Paul Sartre.

Proust has left a gallery of characters reflecting the variety of their author's view of humanity in his multivolume novel *A la Recherche du temps perdu* (*Remembrance of Things Past*). His writing can be obscure as well as fascinating, but his emphasis on abnormality as the norm makes his vision of the world difficult to absorb at times. André Gide used the novel as well as plays and essays to explore ethical and aesthetic solutions to human problems. He received the Nobel Prize for literature in 1947, and the whole of his literary output has influenced other writers in their attempts to find their personal voice. André Malraux, adventurer, novelist, art critic, and minister of culture under President Charles de Gaulle from 1960–1969, was a writer whose life also reflected activism similar to that of Saint-Exupéry. He also understood the efforts of Camus to make sense of the absurdity of life and urged the publication of the young writer's short novel, *The Stranger*. Malraux's own novels as translated into English have not found a wide public, except for perhaps *La Condition humaine* (*Man's Fate*). Jean-Paul Sartre, a Nobel Prize winner in 1964 although he refused to accept the honor, is an important literary figure whose novels and plays were for the most part contemporary with Camus and Saint-Exupéry. Saint-Exupéry, busy with his career as an aviator, did not often frequent Parisian literary circles, but Camus associated closely with Sartre during the war years after the former arrived in Paris. Their close contacts ended after a disagreement about the philosophical ideas Camus expressed in *L'Homme révolté* (*The Rebel*), published in 1951. Sartre's important ideas and his role as an existentialist thinker do not make his novels easy to read because of their density and emphasis on thought rather than story. Writers such as Camus and Saint-Exupéry are more approachable as they try to make sense in their fiction of what is important in the imperfect world of the first half of the twentieth century.

As this very brief overview of the French novel from 1831 (*The Hunchback of Notre-Dame*) to 1947 (*The Plague*) indicates, novelists were influenced by each other as well as by events in their world. The novels chosen for this volume are both representative and exemplary in the history of French literature and illustrate the novels' contribution to readers' understanding of how human beings act in relationship to the world and their place therein.

*Masterpieces of French Literature* is organized alphabetically by author. When two novels by one author are included, the earlier novel is discussed first. Each chapter deals with one novel and begins with a biographical context section outlining what was happening in the writer's life during the composition of the particular novel. Each novel is examined critically from the standpoint of plot development, characters, themes, and style. Each chapter concludes with a discussion of the historical context in which the novel was written. What was happening in the writer's world politically, socially, and culturally often had an effect on the development of his or her fiction.

France in the nineteenth century underwent numerous political, social, cultural, and economic changes following the Revolution of 1789 which had swept away the Old Regime. These changes impacted writers and their works. Victor Hugo, for example, was a child during the Napoléonic era which followed the Revolution and was writing *The Hunchback of Notre-Dame* as the July Revolution of 1830 was taking place virtually under his windows. This short-lived revolution marked a change in regime from the last Bourbon king to more of a constitutional monarchy. In his historical novel, Hugo writes about an earlier change: the political development in fifteenth-century France of a more centralized monarchy under Louis XI. He also develops the idea that cultural change takes place in fifteenth-century France because the written or printed word becomes more influential on ideas than architectural creations such as the cathedral of Notre-Dame. Hugo's other novel discussed in this volume, *Les Misérables* (1862), is a portrait of his own century that emphasizes social injustices and suggests possibilities for social progress. Alexandre Dumas, on the other hand, reflects his era's interest in the historical past by telling about swashbuckling heroes performing glorious deeds in *The Three Musketeers* (1844), rather than emphasizing a world changing politically and culturally. The next year Dumas gives his readers a portrait of his own time in *The Count of Monte Cristo* (1845). However, this portrait focuses on individual injustices, individual vengeance, and a somewhat equivocal redemption. Gustave Flaubert presents in *Madame Bovary* (1857) his century as he sees it: mediocre people living mediocre lives in a mediocre time and place. These three writers published within a 30-year period, yet all three were affected in different ways by what they saw happening. They influenced each other in that they read each others' works, interacted from time to time in Parisian literary and social circles, and wrote letters to each other, commenting on their fellow authors' publications.

The two twentieth-century authors, Camus and Saint-Exupéry, were also influenced by the world around them—the disillusionment that followed World War II. Camus chose two ways to confront the instability of his time: the emphasis on the absurdity of life in *The Stranger* (1942) and a shift in focus from the indifference of Meursault in *The Stranger* to unceasing effort against life's absurdities shown by important characters in *The Plague* (1947). Saint-Exupéry chose to distance himself from his time in *The Little Prince* (1943), a story whose protagonist teaches the narrator the importance of love and friendship in a setting remote from the death and destruction sweeping the world in which the author and his first readers were living.

All five authors were interested in themes of human values and how humans might make sense of their world. The optimism of Hugo that suffering and poverty could be alleviated, if not eradicated, by people of good will (*Les Misérables*) and the efforts of Dumas to show that an exceptional man can achieve revenge and most likely redemption (*The Count of Monte Cristo*) give way to Flaubert's disillusionment about human capacity to find meaning and happiness. Camus does not share Hugo's optimism but does find meaning in human solidarity and effort to combat that which causes suffering. Saint-Exupéry chooses to emphasize individual values of love and friendship in his story which underscores what is really important in life. Although each author illustrates themes and gives them meaning in different ways, the human condition remains the basic link between the novels discussed in *Masterpieces of French Literature*.

*Masterpieces of French Literature* includes a selected bibliography which notes the English editions used for this study, the original French editions, works that offer biographical information about the authors and general criticism, and reviews from the time of publication.

I wish to thank especially Bitsy McCready Ostenson who read each chapter and provided valuable criticism, suggestions, and insight.

# 1

## Albert Camus
## *The Stranger*
### 1942

### BIOGRAPHICAL CONTEXT

Writing, studying, working with theatre groups, adjusting to his tuberculo-sis—Algerian-born Albert Camus carried on many activities during the 1930s while supporting himself by a series of odd jobs in Algiers, capital of French-controlled Algeria. A brief marriage to Simone Hié in 1934, a short membership in the Communist Party, and trips to Europe, including a stay in Paris, were also part of the decade. By 1937 Camus was seriously seeking a full-time job and began working at the local meteorological institute in December. His assignment was to make an inventory of 25 years of weather data from the 355 weather stations in Algeria (Lottman 163).

The job enabled him to spend his free evenings working with the Théâtre de l'Equipe, a group whose goal was to present the best contemporary theater with a new look at old plays and to create a theater of ideas rather than ide-ology (Lottman 165). In addition he was working on his novel, *La Mort heureuse*, and publishing a book of essays, *Betwixt and Between*, in 1937. His notebooks reflect the ideas he was considering on the absurd; an undated pas-sage just before a December 1938 entry would later be the opening paragraph for *The Stranger* (*Notebooks, 1935–1942* 105).

In 1938 Camus was also involved with a project for a literary magazine that was to showcase the Mediterranean spirit in literature. For the contributors, chiefly young Frenchmen born in French-controlled North Africa, this spirit implied literature influenced by the sun and warmth, which they felt characterized the North African lands bordering the Mediterranean Sea. In a talk on Mediterranean culture given in 1937, Camus emphasized that this culture expressed a "certain taste for life" (Lottman 131). In the first issue, Camus wrote that a movement of youth and passion for man and his works had been born. He added that the journal would attempt to define itself and a culture that exists in countries bordering the Mediterranean Sea (Lottman 178).

*Rivages* was to be published from Edmond Charlot's bookstore in Algiers. The first issue appeared in December 1938 and the second in May 1939. With the outbreak of World War II and the occupation of France, the next issue, including a tribute to Spanish author Garcia Lorca, was halted by censorship; Garcia Lorca was considered an opponent of Francisco Franco, leader of Spain, and the Vichy government of France ordered the type for the issue destroyed (Lottman 179). The Vichy government came to power after France capitulated to Germany in June 1940. Seeing collaboration with Germany as the only way to keep any independence for France, the Vichy officials made every effort to forestall possible problems with the Nazi regime. Since the Nazis had supported Franco during the Spanish civil war, the issue of *Rivages* was seen by the Vichy officials as an attack on a person and a regime that these officials felt should be supported, not criticized.

The literary magazine was not Camus's only project. In his *Notebooks* a June 1938 entry outlines summer literary plans: rewriting his novel, working on his first play (*Caligula*), beginning a book-length essay on the absurd (*The Myth of Sisyphus*), and writing essays on Florence and Algiers (*Nuptials*) (Lottman 181). In addition, during the summer of 1938 Camus was getting acquainted with Francine Faure, a young woman from Oran. Since she visited Algiers only from time to time, their friendship continued through letters.

In July 1938 Camus met the brother of one of his friends, Christiane Galindo. She was part of Camus's circle in Algiers and typed several of his manuscripts for him. Her brother Pierre, a partner in a grain-exporting business, would serve as somewhat of a matchmaker, persuading Francine Faure's mother and sisters that Camus was more than a starving actor. Pierre is alleged to be the source of an element of the plot of *The Stranger*: the encounter with an Arab on the beach (Lottman 184–85).

Camus's journalistic endeavors also began in 1938 with the founding of the *Alger Républicain*, a newspaper dedicated to the ideology of the left. Pascal Pia, hired by the paper's founder to be editor, was a journalist from mainland France and well acquainted with the Parisian literary scene. He was to be influential in Camus's life until a disagreement separated them after the end of World War II. Camus's first assignment for the paper was city news; his beat included police stations, law courts, the city council, and the legislature when it was in session. He also did literary reviews. Camus won a name as a court-room reporter, covering the important trials of the time and taking sides in his bylined articles. Knowledge of the French judicial system and his opinions of this system as reflected in *The Stranger* would come from his experience on the *Alger Républicain*.

Personal writing projects occupied part of Camus's free time, and his journal in late 1938 indicates the writing strategy he was to pursue. On a given theme he would work simultaneously on three different works in three different genres: a play, a novel, and a philosophical essay. Camus chose the absurd for his first theme and noted in early 1939 that reading about the absurd was a priority for the year, although he did not indicate sources for his reading. For him the absurd meant the contradiction between man's longing for life to last and the inevitability of his death. Camus noted that the world is not reasonable, but "what is absurd is the confrontation of this irrational and the wild longing for clarity whose call echoes in the human heart. The absurd depends as much on man as on the world" (quoted in Rhein 27). He began *Caligula*, *The Stranger*, and *The Myth of Sisyphus* at approximately the same time, working on them together, and hoped to publish them at the same time (Lottman 194). A completed project was published in 1938: *Nuptials*, a slim volume of essays.

Along with his reporting and writing, Camus found time to resume his theatrical activities, performing in the Théâtre de l'Equipe's presentation of *Playboy of the Western World*, by the Irish playwright John Millington Synge (Lottman 200–201).

In September 1939 Camus wrote in his *Notebooks*, "War has broken out. But where is it? Where does this absurd event show itself, except in the news bulletins we have to believe and the notices we have to read? It's not in the blue sky over the blue sea, in the chirring of the grasshoppers, in the cypress trees on the hills" (*Notebooks*, *1935–1942* 137–38). No battles were yet being fought on Algerian soil, but the colony was treated more as a military district than as part of metropolitan France. Before war was declared the government had banned a political party headed by an Arab (Parti du Peuple Algérien) as well as the Algerian Communist Party. Camus commented in August 1939 that each time this PPA was attacked, it grew a little more: "The rise of Algerian nationalism is accomplished by the persecutions carried out against it" (Lottman 205).

During the summer of 1939 Camus continued work on his trilogy of the absurd. A first draft of *Caligula* was completed, and the writer made progress on *The Stranger*. However, when war was declared, Camus attempted to enlist in spite of his health, but was rejected. Camus continued with the *Alger*

*Républicain* as long as the newspaper existed. With less advertising and fewer contributions from the shareholders, the paper's financial situation was precarious. The strict censorship in Algeria and the difficulties of printing and distribution caused Pascal Pia to begin a two-page afternoon edition, called *Le Soir Républicain,* on September 15, 1939 (Lottman 210). Pia and Camus baited the censor with unidentified quotations from French classical authors such as Pascal and Hugo. Camus and Pia could not accept the local officials' notion of patriotism. When the newspaper was suspended on January 10, 1940, Camus countersigned the notice at the demand of the policeman delivering the notice. Shortly thereafter, the remaining members of the paper's board censured Camus for pursuing his private policies. The original publisher was to regret later that the paper was closed down before taking a strong stand against fascism, but felt that the closure was preferable to publishing a paper without character (Lottman 214–15).

These events did not keep Camus from his personal projects, and his journal has many comments regarding the horror of the war. However, his employment difficulties continued, and he investigated job possibilities in both Algeria and Paris. In March 1940 Pascal Pia notified Camus that a position was available in Paris with the *Paris-Soir,* a mass circulation daily paper, if he could get there. Camus started on March 23 as *secrétaire de rédaction,* which meant that he was basically responsible for the paper's layout (Lottman 219).

Even with his duties at the paper, Camus was finishing *The Stranger.* In early April he sent the first half of the manuscript to Christiane Galindo for typing (Lottman 222). A terse journal entry in May 1940 states, "*The Stranger* is finished" (*Notebooks, 1935–1942* 181). In a letter to Francine he reflected, "I've just reread all that I've written of my novel. I was seized with disgust and it seemed to me a failure from the ground up, that *Caligula* was hardly better and that my initial plans had been stymied by the limits of what I had managed to do." However, he continued more positively, "I live alone and I am weary, but I don't know if it's despite all this or because of it that I am writing all I wanted to write. Soon I will be able to judge what I'm worth and decide one way or another" (quoted in Todd, 108–9).

When the staff of *Paris-Soir* had to leave Paris ahead of the German army in June 1940, Camus drove one of the cars to Clermont-Ferrand. On arrival he suddenly was afraid he had forgotten to pack the manuscript of *The Stranger,* but later found it in the car's trunk. The paper's staff was sent on to Lyon in September 1940, the same month that Camus's divorce from his first wife, Simone Hié, was final. Francine Faure arrived in Lyon in December 1940, and she and Camus were married there on December 3. However, by the end of the month Camus had been laid off from his job with the paper.

The couple returned to Oran in January 1941, where they attempted to find work. Camus began to teach French, French history, and geography at two private schools in Oran, and his wife found some work as a substitute teacher. In addition to his tutoring and teaching work during 1941 and the early months of 1942 Camus continued as an editor for the publishing firm Editions Charlot, run by his friend Edmond Charlot. Camus was choosing books for a series called Poésie et Théâtre, as well as seeing other books through the publishing process.

Camus asked Charlot in 1941 if the publisher could publish his three works on the absurd in a single volume. Charlot replied that the project was impossible given its cost and added that the works should be published in France for maximum impact (Lottman 248). In April 1941 Camus sent the manuscript of *The Stranger* to Pascal Pia, who sent it on to well-known author André Malraux. Because both Algeria and the southern half of France were under the control of the Vichy government, mail was easily sent between the two regions. The publishing firm of Gallimard overcame the difficulties of sending packages between France's two zones by using a courier from a Gallimard address in Cannes to the firm's address in Paris (Lottman 249). Malraux sent the manuscript, with his enthusiastic recommendation, to Gaston Gallimard, head of the publishing house, although he did indicate that *Caligula* should be published after the public got to know Camus's work: "*L'Etranger* is obviously an important thing. The power and simplicity of the means which finally force the reader to accept his character's point of view are all the more remarkable in that the book's destiny depends on whether this character is convincing or not. And what Camus has to say while convincing us is not negligible" (quoted in Todd 131).

Although the difficulties of communication between Oran and Paris meant that Camus could not control the movements of his manuscript between the various readers solicited by the publisher, he realized what was happening under Nazi control in the northern part of France. Gallimard's prestigious literary journal, *La Nouvelle Revue Française*, was not attracting as many quality submissions, and reorganization was considered. Camus was asked to permit *The Stranger* to appear in the journal. Camus refused the offer, having already decided not to seek publication in a magazine published with Nazi approval (Lottman 251). The book was published by Gallimard on June 15, 1942, with a printing of 4,400 copies; Camus had received an advance for both *The Stranger* and *The Myth of Sisyphus* in April. *The Myth* would appear in October 1942 in a printing of 2,750 copies (Lottman 252).

Positive reviews were printed in publications owned by Gallimard, although a negative one appeared in *Le Figaro* (Todd 131). Jean-Paul Sartre wrote a long essay called "Explication de l'Etranger" that appeared in *Cahiers du Sud,* a magazine published in the Vichy-controlled free zone of France. Sartre understood the connection between *The Stranger* and *The Myth of Sisyphus,* noting that the theory of the absurd novel outlined in *The Myth* would help the reader understand the novel (Lottman 253). Camus confided his feelings, especially about the negative criticism, to his journal: "Three years to make a book, five lines to ridicule it, and the quotations wrong" (*Notebooks, 1942–1951* 20). He included a long response to the critic from *Le Figaro* that he would never send, commenting on what he considered misinterpretation of both text and intentions and refusing to permit the critic the right to say whether a book served or harmed the country: "For you have taken a moral point of view that prevented you from judging with the lucidity and the talent you have been known for. There is a very vague frontier between your criticisms and the judgments that may soon be made by a dictatorship…as to the moral character of this or that work" (*Notebooks, 1942–1951* 22).

Shortly after *The Stranger* was published, Camus was in France, coming to Le Panelier, a hamlet near Le Chambon-sur-Lignon, in August 1942 in an attempt to recover his health. A setback in January required a period of rest, and his doctors felt leaving the damp climate of North Africa would help. Camus and his wife applied for a travel permit in May that was granted in August. They chose Le Panelier, located in the Vivarais mountains of the Massif Central, as it was run by the mother of Francine Camus's uncle by marriage and suited the couple's limited financial means. Camus was thereby enabled by circumstances to start the reading, reflecting, and writing process that would result in his next theme, revolt, and eventually in *The Plague* (cf. chapter 2).

## PLOT DEVELOPMENT

A short novel, *The Stranger* is divided into two parts: part one presents the events in the main character's life from the death of his mother to his act of shooting an Arab at the beach. Part two covers his life in prison, including his trial, his reflections on his life and situation, and his reactions to the court's judgment.

*The Stranger* opens with one of the most well-known short sentences in French literature: "Maman died today" (3). The chapter relates how Meursault, the main character known only by his last name, receives the news. It continues by recounting his trip by bus to the old people's home where his mother had lived, his interactions with personnel at the home, the overnight vigil by the coffin, and the walk to the church and the cemetery. The first-person narrative presents Meursault's impressions as received through his senses. He notes the heat, the light, the clarity of the colors, and his own fatigue; the entire experience remains with him as a series of impressions. When he returns to Algiers, his principal emotion is relief that he can now go to bed and sleep for 12 hours.

Somewhat shorter, chapter two recounts Meursault's swim at the public beach and his encounter with Marie, a former coworker. After their night together Meursault spends Sunday alone at home, watching from his window as people pass by, involved in their Sunday rituals.

Monday finds Meursault back at work, engaging in his usual routine. Two residents of his apartment building figure in this chapter: Salamano and his scruffy dog; and Raymond Sintès, a person of doubtful reputation. Raymond tells Meursault the story of a fight, speaks of his relationship and quarrels with his mistress, and finally comes to the reason he needs to talk to Meursault. Raymond wants Meursault to write a letter to the woman that will make her feel sorry for her actions. Meursault agrees to help Raymond because he "didn't have any reason not to please him" (32). Now Raymond says they are pals, which Meursault accepts.

After working hard all week, Meursault spends Saturday and Sunday morning with Marie. Enjoying her company, Meursault nevertheless responds somewhat indifferently when Marie asks if he loves her: "I told her it didn't mean anything but that I didn't think so" (35). Their lunch preparations are interrupted by female screams and sounds of hitting from Raymond's room. The building residents all come to see what is happening. Marie thinks Meursault should go for a policeman, but he replies that he doesn't like cops. Another tenant brings a policeman who sends the girl away and tells Raymond to wait until he's summoned to the police station. Everyone goes away, Marie and Meursault resume lunch, and after Marie's departure, Meursault sleeps for a while. Raymond appears later, saying that Meursault must be his witness. They go out, have a drink, shoot some pool, and Meursault enjoys the companionship. On their return home they find Salamano searching for his dog. Salamano comes to Meursault shortly to ask if the dog will be given back to him if it is found in the pound. Meursault doesn't know and later hears the sound of crying through the wall.

Events of the next week include Raymond's invitation to the beach for the following Sunday and his report of being followed by a group of Arabs, including his mistress's brother. At work, Meursault's boss offers to send him to Paris, but Meursault lived there as a student and sees no reason to change his current situation. Marie brings up the subject of marriage; Meursault is indifferent but says that they can get married if she really wants to. A strange woman shares Meursault's table as he eats dinner at his usual restaurant. That evening Salamano comes by again, this time to tell how he acquired his dog, which is still lost. He also comments that some people thought badly of Meursault for sending his mother to the home. Meursault explains that he didn't have the money to care for his mother properly.

Part one concludes with the events of the day at the beach. Walking along the beach after lunch, Meursault, Raymond, and Raymond's friend encounter a group of Arabs. Raymond is cut on the arm during the confrontation. After Raymond receives medical treatment, he and Meursault return to the beach. They meet two of the Arabs near some rocks and a spring of water. Raymond wants to shoot them, but Meursault asks to take the gun and says he will shoot only if one of the Arabs pulls out a knife. The Arabs leave, and Raymond and Meursault return to his friends' bungalow. Then, Meursault, his head "ringing from the sun" (57), starts back along the beach. When he arrives at the rocks, the man who knifed Raymond is there. Meursault realizes that he could turn around and "that would be the end of it" (58). However, the burning sun forces him forward: "The scorching blade slashed at my eyelashes and stabbed at my stinging eyes. That's when everything began to reel" (59). Meursault pulls the trigger and realizes that he has "shattered the harmony of the day, the exceptional silence of a beach where I'd been happy" (59). He fires four more times at the motionless Arab: "And it was like knocking four quick times on the door of unhappiness" (59).

Part two opens with Meursault undergoing the investigation and interrogation part of the pretrial process, according to the French system of justice. He finds it convenient that the court should take care of appointing an attorney for him. During their first conversation the attorney tries diligently to bring Meursault to an expression of normal sensitivity regarding his mother's death—the investigators had learned that Meursault had shown insensitivity at the funeral (64). Meursault replies that he has not been in the habit of analyzing his feelings but that he would rather his mother hadn't died. When the lawyer leaves, looking angry, Meursault wishes he could have persuaded the man of his ordinary nature: "I felt the urge to reassure him that I was like everybody else, just like everybody else. But really there wasn't much point, and I gave up the idea out of laziness" (66).

The conversation with the examining magistrate follows similar lines. This official wants to understand Meursault, especially why he paused between the first shot and the other four. Meursault finds it impossible to explain and remains silent; to him this pause doesn't really matter. The magistrate then asks if Meursault believes in God. When Meursault answers "no," the magistrate, shouting, asks if Meursault wants the magistrate's life to become meaningless. Again, Meursault does not see why the magistrate's beliefs have anything to do with him or his shooting the Arab. Their conversations last over 11 months, but the magistrate never again reaches the intensity of the first meeting: "The magistrate seemed to have lost interest in me and to come to some sort of decision about my case" (70).

The second chapter in part two presents Meursault's adaptation to prison life. He receives a visit from Marie. Aware of his own physical sensations, Meursault notes that he has the thoughts of a free man, wanting suddenly to take a walk on the beach. However, after a few months, his thoughts are those of a prisoner, living by the daily routine and learning to kill time by remembering. The more he thinks, the more he remembers. And sleep plays an important role in passing time, once Meursault overcomes those thoughts and desires characteristic of a free man. He even finds a scrap of newspaper between his mattress and the bed planks. The article tells of a man who returns home after a long absence. He is unrecognized and killed for his possessions by his mother and sister, who are running the inn where he stays. Camus will use this true crime anecdote as the basis for his play *The Misunderstanding*. Meursault will read and reread the article, reflecting that one shouldn't play games; the traveler, refusing to reveal his identity, deserved his fate. Meursault may have adapted, but the chapter ends with his statement that no one can imagine what nights in prison are like (81).

The trial begins in the next chapter. Meursault is well aware of the sun glaring through the window. He notes all the concrete details of the courtroom, including the jurors, whom he compares to a row of passengers on a streetcar (83). He observes the reporters speaking with one of them, and even feels he is seeing a reflection of himself in a young reporter who is examining him with "his two very bright eyes" (85). When the questioning begins, Meursault is led through the events culminating in the Arab's death. He is also questioned about his mother and why he moved her to the home. After the noon recess, the procession of witnesses begins: everyone from the director of the home to Marie and Raymond. Meursault's lawyer tries to ask if Meursault is on trial for killing a man or for burying his mother. The prosecutor's reply that Meursault buried his mother with crime in his heart makes the man on trial realize that things are not going well. The trip back to prison as the afternoon fades into evening reminds Meursault of the time of day when he used to be happy (97).

Meursault's predominant reflection as the prosecutor and his lawyer sum up their arguments the next day is how both seem to be arguing as if the whole event has nothing to do with him, the prisoner, the man on trial. The essence of the prosecutor's argument is that Meursault is a man without a soul who has never expressed remorse about his action. Meursault realizes that, due to his position, he must refrain from pointing out that remorse for the past is not part of his makeup. He has always thought about what is happening now or coming in the future (100). When Meursault is given the chance to speak and asked the reason for his act, he responds that it was because of the sun. This remark evokes laughter. His lawyer, giving the argument for the defense, uses the first person pronoun, "I," in his summation. Meursault is told that all lawyers do this but feels that, yet again, he is excluded from the case (103). The heat and the length of the day remove Meursault even farther from what is taking place, but eventually, the verdict is given. In the name of the French people, Meursault is to be executed for his crime.

The concluding chapter recounts Meursault's interest in discovering if there's any way out of the inevitable machinery of justice. He remembers that his father had seen an execution and realizes that the guillotine gives the condemned man no chance as its machinery never fails. Happiness becomes the dawning of a new day with no footsteps coming to get him. He has no more interest in remembering Marie. Meursault refuses to see the chaplain, but the latter finally arrives without announcement. The two have no common ground, and their discussion leads nowhere until Meursault angrily bursts out that nothing really matters since all are condemned to die. With the chaplain's departure and the calm respite of evening, Meursault feels purged of anger and realizes that he is ready to live life all over again; he opens himself to the "gentle indifference of the world" (122). And, in order to feel less alone, he has only to wish for a large crowd of spectators at his execution, "and that they greet me with cries of hate" (123).

## CHARACTER DEVELOPMENT

Meursault, the youngish clerk condemned to be executed for killing an Arab, is the focal point of *The Stranger*. But who is this character? What influences have formed this man who appears emotionally indifferent to human relationships? Camus never explains what has formed Meursault's character; he shows it through what takes place during the time period of the book. Physical sensations and reactions govern Meursault's passage through the portion of his life revealed to the reader. He is very much aware of light, heat, and tactile sensations of all types; for example, his principal reaction to the death of his mother appears to be the fatigue caused by his bus trip to the town where she has been living, by the customary vigil by the casket overnight, and by the heat of the long walk to the cemetery. He is not antisocial as much as he is indifferent to the rituals of social interactions. He is involved in Raymond's dispute with his mistress and the latter's brother through no particular interest in Raymond or his problems but through a vague wish to be agreeable. His relationship with Marie means physical pleasure, not emotional fulfillment. His murder of the Arab is triggered by no animosity toward another human being but by an overwhelming physical reaction to the sun's glaring light and searing heat. It is not until he is imprisoned for this act that Meursault begins to think, to remember, to reflect. His reflections and memories center on himself, and he considers that he has been happy. Yet he remains a stranger to the end, unable to care about the codes others in his world find important and necessary for existence, disinterested in examining reasons for his actions.

This disinterest makes Meursault's motivations for the things he does remain unclear throughout the book. He establishes a relationship with Marie based on her physical attractiveness. She is a pleasant enough addition to his life that he will accept marrying her if that is what she wants. Meursault appears to have no professional ambitions, reacting with indifference to his employer when the latter suggests a move to Paris. Paris, he says, is dirty and gray, unappealing to someone who loves sea, sand, and sun. Human contacts are based on proximity rather than choice. Raymond lives in the same building. Celeste is the owner of the restaurant where Meursault eats often. He realizes that he has taken another human life but never carries his reflections about life to wondering about the Arab's life or its individual value. Is he a sympathetic character? Readers will find their own answers to the question, but Camus has succeeded in creating a memorable character, one who illustrates in a believable, and yes, human, way that life will always end in death.

The other characters in *The Stranger* are developed insofar as they touch Meursault's life and are presented through his observations. The reader learns a bit about Marie, her laughter, her dresses, the salty smell of her hair after swimming, but this information is all concrete. She evidently cares for Meursault—she asks him if he wants to marry her, if he loves her, but doesn't seem all that upset at Meursault's indifference to the whole idea. Marie visits Meursault in prison and testifies at the trial but is no more able than his other witnesses to articulate her understanding of Meursault or his crime. Her role in the story is to be part of the agreeable activities Meursault enjoys, such as swimming, sex, and companionship. However, Marie's ideas about life or even marriage are not evident to the reader and a matter of unconcern to Meursault. He is somewhat sorry about her distress when she visits him in prison, but as the months pass she represents only those pleasures that were part of his existence and soon will exist no more.

Celeste, the restaurant owner, is part of Meursault's daily routine and considers his customer his friend. Yet he cannot explain to the court what he means by saying that Meursault was a man. He does note that Meursault does not speak unless he has something to say. Salamano and his dog live in the same apartment building as Meursault, who observes their love-hate-terror relationship as he does the other ordinary things that happen as the days go on. When the dog is lost, Meursault's recognition of Salamano's distress brings the latter more into focus as a human being, one with emotions and reasons for his behavior. Raymond is also seen in the light of the relationship with Meursault, a relationship that develops more by Raymond's actions than Meursault's will. The reader knows Raymond too through his actions, his dispute with the group of Arabs, his beating of his mistress, and his efforts to gain Meursault's sympathy. Ordinary people leading, on the whole, commonplace lives (although the reader may find Raymond's violence more notorious than ordinary), these secondary characters help center the focus on Meursault and the themes that his story illustrates.

## THEMES

*The Stranger* illustrates the theme that life is absurd; that in an indifferent world, only the act of living gives life any meaning. Yet the character who relates a series of acts from a period in his own life only realizes that living has meaning when he faces a certain death. Camus seems to say that, like many of us, Meursault has lived only for the moment, neither thinking about the past nor planning for the future. And it's that moment that counts, not the meaning of the universe. The universe remains inexplicable; Meursault exists; life is finite; anything else is speculation. However, existence without an ultimate meaning can have its own sort of happiness. When Meursault explores his memories during the months in prison, he realizes his enjoyment of everyday things, such as swimming with Marie and catching a ride on the back of a truck on his lunch break. It takes a catastrophic event such as a trial and a condemnation to make this happiness and this absurdity clear. Awaiting death, Meursault realizes the "gentle indifference of the world" (122), a world where he felt he had been happy and was happy again.

The inherent, essential dignity of a human being and his fundamental solitude are additional themes brought out in Meursault's story, especially in his trial and its aftermath. Meursault is not treated by the court as a person of individual worth but as a hardened criminal, a man without a soul who did not cry at his mother's funeral. But why, indicates Camus, should a man be condemned for refusing to play the game, for refusing to lie? Society's actions are also absurd, as judges and lawyers reduce the accused to a nonparticipant in his own trial and judge him according to standards that seem to have no direct connection with his act. Meursault faces his death alone in his cell, within his world of memory and sleep. The chaplain's visit jolts him from his apathetic sadness, forcing him to realize the worth of life. His indifference to everything but momentary pleasures has brought him to violence and death. He has failed to ask the right questions and now will disappear—yet content with his new realizations, hoping that an audience at his execution will enable him to escape from his solitude.

As a corollary to the theme of the absurd, Camus emphasizes in this compact narrative the value of air and light, sun and sky, sensation and moments of companionship, fleeting as they may be. Life is finite, outmoded social and religious codes may negate the dignity of the individual, but momentary experiences create a certain happiness and give value to the act of living.

The colonial theme in *The Stranger* is never explicit, but the reader may come to certain conclusions regarding Camus's perceptions concerning the French and the Arab inhabitants of Algeria. He grew up among the working-class population of European origin in the Belcourt section of Algiers, impervious to the racial barriers of the more prosperous middle class, according to Germaine Brée, a critic and literature professor who knew Camus (*Camus* 13). Although Meursault becomes involved in Raymond's dispute with the brother of his mistress, his involvement is not because Raymond's adversaries are Arabs; it is because Raymond is Meursault's neighbor, and Meursault has no reason not to help him. The ethnicity of the man Meursault shoots is not the cause of his firing the shots, and the fact that the victim is an Arab plays no apparent role in the trial. However, in a French-governed region in the 1930s, it is highly unusual that a person considered French would be condemned to death for killing an Arab. When Meursault first arrives in prison, he is placed in a common cell where most of the other prisoners are Arabs. They laugh when they see him, a man of evident European origin, but fall silent once he responds to their question about what he has done. Yet, they help Meursault, showing him how to fix his sleeping mat (71). Camus in this scene appears to be showing the underlying humanity that links all humans, even those of different ethnic groups. Again, in the visiting room, Meursault notes that most of the prisoners are Arabs, and that they talk with their visitors in low tones while others are almost shouting to make themselves heard over the physical distance separating prisoner and visitor. The reader catches glimpses of the dual world that is Algeria, but the references in Meursault's story are observations only, never analyses of the colonial situation.

Camus will expand his theme of the absurd in *The Plague*, developing a more thorough questioning of life's lack of ultimate meaning and what to do about it. In *The Stranger* he opens the discussion and conveys the absurd experience through what happens to Meursault. He does not offer definitive solutions to the problem but states it by showing it portrayed through the actions and reactions of one individual.

## NARRATIVE STYLE

Camus chose to write *The Stranger* as a first-person narrative. It is Meursault who recounts what happens, what he feels, and what he sees, expressing himself in short, compact sentences. Jean-Paul Sartre, among other critics, sees a possible comparison with the style of Ernest Hemmingway. In his article "An Explication of *The Stranger*" Sartre notes: "Both men write in the same short sentences. Each sentence refuses to exploit the momentum accumulated by preceding ones. Each is like a snapshot of a gesture or object" (116). By avoiding connecting words such as "because" or "since," Camus highlights Meursault the observer, he who sees the surface but does not analyze the undercurrents. But, as Sartre also comments, Camus's style is not limited to these snapshot sentences. Sentences take on a more continuous movement when the emotional tone heightens as it does during Meursault's outburst to the chaplain.

Mechanics of the sentence structure aside, the use of Meursault as the one who tells his own story is an effective stylistic choice. Unlike many first-person narrators, Meursault makes no attempt to filter his account through an awareness of its meaning. The contrast between his factual commentary and the explosion of his awareness in his vehement refusal of the chaplain's beliefs is striking; the basically impersonal, indifferent tone gives way to one of emotional intensity.

The tempo of the narrative is also important in creating the tone. Those short, unconnected statements of fact at the book's beginning present Meursault's relationship with a series of moments and events. Chronological time is not important to him. Once he shoots the Arab, however, circumstances create a past for him, as the various elements of his trial bring together the events between the death of his mother and the death of the Arab in one condemnatory whole. While in prison he is disconnected from the usual rhythms of his existence and immersed in its current emptiness. Once judgment has been handed down, however, time becomes of utmost importance. It accelerates, bringing Meursault to an awareness that it will end as far as he is concerned. As Germaine Brée notes, "Only with the certainty of death does Meursault become aware of another dimension of time, an inner coherence, rich in beauty, sensation, and feeling, unique and relative, one which cannot be denied; it is the substance of life just as the relentless rhythms of the earth are now the annunciation of death" (108). There is no way out until Meursault's new awareness finds an outlet in a series of vehement questions and comments, tumbling rapidly over one another as they refute and refuse the efforts of the chaplain. The tempo increases through these rapidly expressed sentences until it relaxes into Meursault's final wish for spectators at his execution who will hate him.

The use of the first-person narrator lends itself to the use of indirect speech (he said that he would leave) but also free indirect speech (he wished to leave). Camus uses both types but little direct dialogue (I'm leaving). When it is used, the direct dialogue is not set off from the rest of the narration but often follows smoothly an indirect statement. For example, when Meursault asks a guard why the defense lawyer is using "I" as if he were the accused, the guard replies both indirectly and directly: "He told me to keep quiet, and a few seconds later he added, 'All lawyers do it.'" (103). The spoken phrase doesn't stand out but appears the equal of any other comment, remark, or happening.

Camus's use of description emphasizes the contrast between the ordinariness of Meursault's daily life and the pivotal events that mark his narration. Meursault often finds what he is being told interesting, such as the information about the difference in burial customs between Marengo and Paris (1), but he appears to make no distinction between what is interesting and what isn't, accepting everything with similar reactions. He describes what he sees as it meets his eye: the bright screws on his mother's coffin, the colors of the nurse's clothes, and what the courtroom spectators looks like. The most striking descriptions deal with Meursault's physical reactions to the effects of the sun. He expresses enjoyment of the sunlight at the beach yet is stupefied by its power at various moments: the walk to the graveside at his mother's funeral, the interactions at the beach when the Arab is shot, and the sunlight and the accompanying heat in the courtroom. During the beach scene the sun moves from shining on a "dazzling sea" (49) to causing the sand itself to appear red like blood. Later the beach is "throbbing in the sun" (58), a sun that ultimately causes Meursault's irreparable act of pulling the trigger: "the cymbals of sunlight crashing on my forehead and, indistinctly, the dazzling spear flying up from the knife in front of me" (59). The sun has become a hostile presence. Although those in the courtroom laugh when Meursault says he shot the Arab because of the sun, the reader can accept the only explanation of his act that makes some sense, given the power of the description.

While a good translation can convey the effect of description, sentence flow, and narrative point of view, one of Camus's choices cannot be made clear in English. He uses most often the *passé composé*, or conversational past tense to relate an event that was completed in a definite time in the past rather than the *passé simple*, the literary past tense that is most often used in a literary narrative to set the action in a chronological whole where actions are sequential. Sartre feels that Camus used the *passé composé* in order to emphasize the isolation of each sentence unit (119). Critic Patrick McCarthy, in his book analyzing *The Stranger*, makes a similar conclusion about the choice of tense: "Each act becomes an event that is being lived rather than a segment of a greater whole" (22). English readers will have to be content with the translator's ability to create tempo and tone, both of which bring out clearly the ideas Camus wanted to illustrate in this compact, descriptive, and effective narrative.

## HISTORICAL CONTEXT

The North African country of Algeria, Albert Camus's birthplace and where he spent his formative years, became a French colony in 1830. By 1930 over a million Europeans had settled there with the assurance that Algeria was a part of France and should be developed along modern, that is, western European, lines. "It only remained for the Algerians to become French-enculturated, to abandon their roots in their Islamo-Arabic past, and to enter the French polity as French citizens" (Gordon 1). This vision was prevalent among a minority of tolerant Frenchmen and many of the French-educated Moslem elite. However, during the 1930s the vision of assimilation faded away. The European settlers on the whole gave it only lip service, and in France it lacked government support. The non-European population chafed under the government-imposed restrictions, and various groups formed. The group headed by Messali Hadj promoted the idea of an independent Algeria allied to the Arab world. Another group supported the idea of an assimilation that would be egalitarian and generous to the indigenous peoples. A third group wanted to concentrate on serving Arabs through education while remaining true to the Islamic faith.

The Algerian economy was chiefly controlled by the European population, from agriculture to industry: less than 10 percent of the European population controlled more than half of agriculture. Those of European origin also dominated the managerial and government sectors, supplying nearly all managers, technicians, foremen, and civil servants (Ageron 84–85). Although the Europeans were divided into distinct social classes—Camus's widowed mother earned what she could as a cleaning woman, and he needed scholar-ship help to continue his studies at the high school level—most enjoyed a much higher standard of living than the great majority of native Algerians. Camus would note these differentials in his work for the *Alger Républicain*. For example, his investigative reporting about conditions in the Kabylia area of Algeria provided an account of the poverty and suffering from hunger in the region that was unknown to the urban readers of the paper. Camus did his legwork, supplying facts and figures about food availability and the inade-quacy of the school system and talking with victims of what he considered an unjust system (Lottman 198–99).

It is also helpful for readers to know what was happening in France during these prewar years. In 1936 the Popular Front political group won a majority in the elections for the National Assembly, and certain social reforms were carried out for French citizens. This more left-wing government in metropol-itan France gave new hope to those Algerians wanting more equality. The former governor-general of Algeria, Violette, put forward proposals for electoral reform, and Prime Minister Léon Blum supported the proposed extension of political rights to the Algerian elite, "namely officers and non-commissioned officers, graduates and qualified professionals, and public employees" (Ageron 97). While the bill was supported by some Algerian groups, another saw its aim as creating a privileged minority, and European officials were adamant in their opposition, as were many in France. The bill was never discussed by the Assembly.

Preoccupations in France were focused also on economic recovery after the depression of the early 1930s and the tensions between European countries that erupted into World War II on September 1, 1939. Camus was working on *The Stranger* in a country that was divided politically, economically, and socially in a world soon to be engulfed by war.

Months of what came to be known as the phony war or the *drôle de guerre* followed the fall of Poland, but the Germans began their advance westward in the spring of 1940. Camus arrived in Paris as the French and British were attempting to stop the German advance and was involved in the exodus from Paris with the staff of *Paris-Soir*. On June 16, 1940 a new French government under World War I hero Marshall Philippe Pétain asked for an armistice with Germany. The country was then divided into the occupied section and the so-called free zone. This zone, known as the Etat français or the French State, had its headquarters in the small city of Vichy. The French on both sides of the demarcation line were to undergo four years of wartime conditions, with restrictions on travel, shortages of food and other goods. Yet, as the discussion of the publication of *The Stranger* at the beginning of this chapter indicates, movement was possible, books were published, and many people, including Camus, continued their efforts to make a living and carry out their usual activities.

In Algeria, there was initial support for Pétain's French State, even from Moslems who hated the parliamentary regime of the Third Republic (the French government from 1871 to 1940). Pétain gave equal representation to Europeans and Moslems from Algeria on the National Council he created in January 1941, but the citizenship of Algerian Jews, acquired in 1870, had been revoked in October 1940. The Moslem representatives attempted to gain approval for a program of reforms, but the Vichy government replied only that it would take note of these suggestions (Ageron 98–99).

Camus wrote *The Stranger* in a land where the population was two tiered, divided between the colonizers and the colonized. He wrote at a time when the world was moving, apparently inexorably, toward a cataclysmic war and finished his manuscript with the war taking place all around him. His book was published at a time when his refusal of a transcendent meaning for life struck a chord with readers who had seen their country defeated, who were living a monotonous existence, who had been affected by the cataclysm that was World War I. Many were questioning the meaning of life, and Camus's narrative of one man's experience reflected the concerns and anxieties, the injustices and yes, even the pleasures, of the historical context in which it was written and published.

# 2

# Albert Camus
## *The Plague*
### 1947

## BIOGRAPHICAL CONTEXT

As early as 1938, Albert Camus's *Notebooks* reflect comments on people, ideas, and themes that will appear in his book *The Plague*, published in 1947. In 1938 Camus was living in Algiers and working as a journalist for the *Alger Républicain*. His responsibilities during his time with the newspaper included writing editorials and covering important trials.

When war broke out in Europe in September 1939, Camus attempted to enlist in order to show solidarity; he was turned down because of his long history of tuberculosis. Continuing with the *Alger Républicain*, Camus lost his job when the government suspended the paper in January 1940. The writer went to Oran, the hometown of his fiancée Francine Faure, in search of another job. In March 1940 he was notified that a position was available in Paris with the *Paris-Soir*, if he could get there. Camus started on March 23 as *secrétaire de rédaction*, which meant that he was basically responsible for the paper's layout (Lottman 219).

When the staff of *Paris-Soir* left Paris ahead of the German army in June 1940, Camus drove one of the cars to Clermont Ferrand. The paper's office moved on to Lyon in September 1940, the same month that Camus's divorce from his first wife, Simone Hié, was final. Francine Faure arrived in Lyon in December 1940, and she and Camus were married there on December 3. By the end of the month Camus had been laid off from his job with the paper.

The couple returned to Oran in January 1941 where they attempted to find work. Camus began to teach French, French history, and geography at two private schools in Oran, and his wife found some work as a substitute teacher. A journal entry the same month mentions the little old man who throws paper bits from his balcony to attract cats so he can spit on them, a story that would be part of Tarrou's journal in *The Plague* (Lottman 241). Camus was thinking about his next writing project although *The Stranger* had not been published yet.

In addition to his tutoring and teaching work during 1941 and the early months of 1942 Camus continued as an editor for the publishing firm Editions Charlot, run by his friend Edmond Charlot. Camus was choosing books for a series called Poésie et Théâtre, as well as seeing other books through the publishing process.

Finding life in Oran boring, Camus confessed to friends that he was depressed. His teaching duties, including tutoring, did not bring in much money, and he felt almost imprisoned in Oran. Yet, his journal reflected during 1941 the reading he was doing about the plague, from medical books outlining the symptoms and evolution of the disease to historical works which presented the many epidemics in Europe and Asia. While considering the form his study should take, he read Herman Melville's *Moby Dick* and the *Journal of a Year of the Plague* by Daniel Defoe. Sources closer to home appeared with an outbreak of typhus that struck Algeria in April 1941. His friend the writer Emmanuel Roblès and his wife were living in Turenne, a town some 80 miles from Oran, and Madame Roblès came down with the disease. Her husband was vaccinated and received a medical certificate to travel. He was able to give Camus firsthand information about quarantine and its effects on the sick and their families.

In January 1942 Camus's health worsened. He began spitting up blood one evening, and his doctor discovered that his left lung was now affected and prescribed a long period of rest. It was recommended that Camus leave the damp climate of North Africa, and in May 1942 he applied for a travel permit to go to the mountains of France when his wife's school year ended July 1. The permit was eventually granted in August, and the couple left Algiers on a steamer for Marseilles. Their choice of a destination in France was determined by their lack of financial resources and some helpful family connections. Francine Camus's aunt had married an actor, Paul Oettly, whose mother ran a boardinghouse at Le Panelier, a tiny village near the small town of Le Chambon-sur-Lignon in the Vivarais range of the Massif Central. The area was some 35 miles south of Saint-Etienne, an industrial center about 35 miles south and west of Lyons. Madame Camus's family had been spending summer vacations at Le Panelier since she was a child.

By mid-August the Camus were settled in Le Panelier. Camus's journal mentions early in his stay the ever-present sounds of the springs that were audible at the stone farmhouse (Lottman 261). He went to Saint-Etienne for his pneumothorax injections every 12 days, traveling usually by foot to the train station in Le Chambon-sur-Lignon and then going on via the small, narrow-gauge train. Camus now had the time to concentrate on his writing projects, yet realized that *The Plague* would not be an easy book to write: "'I must stick closely to the idea,' he warned himself." *L'Etranger* describes the nakedness of man faced with the absurd. *La Peste,* the deep identity of individual points of view faced with the same absurd. It is a progression which will become clearer in other works'" (cited in Lottman 262). The other two panels of his current focus were to develop as the play, *Le Malentendu (The Misunderstanding),* and the book-length essay, *L'Homme révolté (The Rebel).*

Camus and his wife had planned that she would return to Algiers ahead of him to search for teaching jobs for the two of them as well as a place to live. By the middle of October 1942 she had reached the Algerian capital city. Camus booked passage on a steamer that was to leave Marseilles November 21. The Allied armies began Operation Torch on November 7, landing on North African shores during the night and moving to control 1,300 miles of coastline within 72 hours. On November 11 the Germans moved to occupy the so-called free zone of France. Albert Camus could not use his passage; he could not even get in touch with Francine now that mainland France was completely under German occupation and Algeria was controlled by Allied forces (Lottman 264–65). Camus would understand personally what forced separation entails: "And one must not forget those for whom . . . the sadness of separation was amplified by the fact that, travelers surprised by the plague and retained in the city, they found themselves removed at once from the person they could not rejoin and from their country" (from "Les Exilés dans la peste," cited by Lottman, 269).

At this point Camus had no income at all, the small stipend he had been receiving from Edmond Charlot in Algeria being cut off by the difficulties in communication by mail between France and Algeria. The publishing firm of Gallimard (publishers of *The Stranger*) put him on the payroll as a reader, paying him a small monthly stipend. Embarrassed by this action, Camus hoped to find a job in Paris and asked Gallimard personnel if there was any chance of work.

Continuing to write, Camus finished the second version of *The Plague* during the winter of 1942–1943; he had completed the first version the preceding winter. A resident of Le Chambon-sur-Lignon later noted that Camus had borrowed local names for several of the book's characters: Father Paneloux from Le Panelier, Dr. Rieux from a local doctor named Riou, Joseph Grand from his neighbors the Grands (Lottman 274). In mid-January 1943

Camus made a two-week visit to Paris. He was a celebrity of sorts, thanks to *The Stranger*. During this visit Camus met with various staff people at Gallimard and also made the acquaintance of Maria Casarès, a young actress with whom he would have a long-standing relationship.

On his return to Le Panelier Camus corresponded with various friends in France, sending food packages as well as letters to such people as the poet Francis Ponge, with whom he had become friends while Ponge was also staying at Le Panelier. He was now able to write to Francine by sending his letters via Portugal. She responded through the same route. While working on his major projects, Camus also wrote an essay on the classical spirit in the French novel that appeared in a literary review published in Lyons and called *Confluences*. He contributed several essays to underground periodicals during his stay in Le Panelier and was in touch with several resistance agents like Francis Ponge and also Pascal Pia, with whom he had worked on the *Alger Républicain*.

June 1, 1943 Camus returned to Paris, in time to attend the opening of Jean-Paul Sartre's play *Les Mouches* and meet its author. Camus would be associated with Sartre and his friends until a definitive rupture in 1952. Also during this visit Camus showed a section of *The Plague* to Jean Paulhan, the chief editorial advisor for Gallimard. Paulhan encouraged the publication of this section on exile and separation in *Domaine Français*, an anthology published in Switzerland and smuggled back into France.

Back in Le Panelier later during the summer of 1943, Camus finished revising his play on the absurd, *Caligula*. He also wrote the first of four letters to be called "Lettres à un ami allemand," in which he spoke about the necessity of resistance. Two of the letters would be published by the underground press and the last two would appear after the liberation of France. The summer would also see the completion of the play *Le Malentendu*. Along with *Caligula* the play was submitted to Gallimard, and the two plays were eventually published together.

After a September 1943 visit to the Dominican monastery of Saint-Maximum, Camus returned to Le Panelier and was finally able to move to Paris on November 1, 1943 to work officially for Gallimard as a reader, although a junior member of the firm. He became more acquainted with Sartre, and the two were members of the jury that was to award Gallimard's new literary prize, Prix de la Pléiade.

After his arrival in Paris, Camus also became involved with the underground newspaper, *Combat*. His friend from Algeria, Pascal Pia, was serving as editor, and had invited Camus to meet with the paper's editorial committee. Since articles in the publication were unsigned to protect the writers from arrest, only two articles have been identified positively as written by

Camus. One in March 1944 discussed a total resistance to total war. The other, published in May 1944, told of German reprisals against a French village (Lottman 304). Camus was now a committed activist in the Resistance, complete with false identity papers, and also part of the group making plans to publish *Combat* as a daily paper in liberated, postwar France.

Camus was also a member of the clandestine Comité National des Ecrivains, a group of patriotic writers complete with an underground publication called *Lettres Françaises*. However, as someone who had opposed the death penalty for years, Camus took a controversial stance when he wrote an article in the May 1944 issue of *Lettres Françaises* criticizing the execution of Pierre Pucheu, a member of the Vichy government who had tried to change sides following the Allied invasion of North Africa. The article, which did not defend Pucheu or collaboration, was unsigned, as was a disclaimer printed below the article. In spite of differences of opinion with his fellow members, Camus remained a member of the CNE board until late 1944.

At the same time as his association with *Combat* and the CNE, Camus was discussing a possible performance of his play *Caligula* and then of *Le Malentendu*. When *Le Malentendu* was accepted for production at the Théâtre des Mathurins, Camus became involved in rehearsals. With all these activities occupying his time, the writer continued working on *The Plague*, writing at night and "without pleasure," according to a letter he wrote to his friend Francis Ponge (note in Lottman 706). He was also doing an essay for an anthology on existence being edited by his former teacher, Jean Grenier.

During the struggle to liberate Paris from the Germans in August 1944, the journalistic activities took first place. Camus worked with his fellow staff members to publish the first public issue of *Combat* on August 21. He would continue the effort to create a new type of newspaper, one with a high moral tone that would call for punishment of collaborators. Yet as time went on, Camus would oppose, once again, the death penalty, even for collaborators.

Francine Camus arrived in France in October 1944 and Camus's personal life made room for his wife, although the night life of Saint-Germain-des-Prés continued to occupy some of his time. By January 1945 Camus's health was affected by all his activities, and he took a temporary leave from *Combat*. He wanted to return to his own writing and his journal entries for this period show many notes for *The Plague*.

By February 1945 Camus was again writing editorials for *Combat*. A trip to Algiers in April to see his mother provided information for a series of articles on the Algerian situation published in the newspaper. In June he went to Germany to inspect the military occupation, wearing a correspondent's uniform. However, by August he was again working on *The Plague*, although spending late afternoons and evenings at *Combat*. Rehearsals for *Caligula* also began the same month. September 1 Camus started to work again at Gallimard as an active employee, having withdrawn from *Combat*. On September 5 the Camus twins, Jean and Catherine, were born.

Work on *The Plague* was suspended when Camus went to the United States, sponsored by the French government, to speak at various universities. Arriving in New York City by ship on March 25, 1946, Camus first spoke at a press conference held at the French Cultural Services. He gave addresses at Columbia University, Vassar, Wellesley, Bryn Mawr, and Brooklyn College during his U.S. stay. A visit to Washington, D.C. and a trip to Montreal, where he again gave a public address, were on his schedule before the return to France in June.

Camus arrived in France to discover that he had been awarded a Resistance Medal. He was a celebrity, though not yet a successful writer from the financial point of view. Writing *The Plague* was still a struggle, and Camus was also working on the essay dealing with revolt. In November 1946 he would contribute a series of articles to *Combat* under the general title "Neither Victims nor Executioners." Yet, in December *The Plague* would finally be sent to the printer. Another phase in the life of Albert Camus had been completed. *The Plague* would be published in June 1947; by autumn nearly 100,000 copies had been sold.

## PLOT DEVELOPMENT

"The unusual events described in this chronicle occurred in 194- in Oran" (3). The opening sentence of *The Plague* states clearly the fictional form chosen by Camus to present certain thoughts and ideas through the medium: a chronicle, a recounting of specific events that take place in a particular geographic location within an established time period. Divided into five parts, the chronicle presents the epidemic in its various phases, from the first dead rat and physical symptoms of the disease, through its takeover of the city and people's lives, across its overwhelming presence and its effect on those who fight it, to its wind down and the opening of the city gates. Within the five sections divisions are indicated by white space separating one from the next.

Part I introduces the city of Oran, a large port on the Algerian coast, focused solely on business, according to the narrator/chronicler, who noted that everyone was bored and devoted to cultivating habits (4). Simpler pleasures are reserved for Saturday afternoons and Sundays. The narrator explains his sources—his personal observations, the accounts of other witnesses/participants, and documents that the narrator was able to consult.

He then begins to recount in detail the events of the first days of what will turn out to be an overwhelming epidemic. Dr. Bernard Rieux, on April 16, steps on a dead rat as he leaves his surgery on the way to visit patients. As the subsequent days unfold, the doctor's wife leaves for a sanatorium in another town where, the couple hopes, she will regain her health and return so that they can make a fresh start. More dead and dying rats appear. Dr. Rieux meets the Parisian journalist, Raymond Rambert, who is in Oran to write about the living conditions of the Arab population. Other characters appear—Cottard, whose failed suicide is discovered by Joseph Grand; Jean Tarrou, whose diaries will be a primary source for the chronicle; Father Paneloux, the priest; and Monsieur Othon, the magistrate. As the epidemic affects more people, perplexity gives way to feelings of panic among the citizenry, but the authorities take no definitive action. The word plague is mentioned for the first time by Dr. Castel, an older doctor who saw the disease during his time in China. Both doctors agree the situation is incredible. The mind cannot accept or visualize the ever-increasing number of dead. Yet, as Dr. Rieux reflects on the situation, he feels that doing one's job as it should be done is the thing to do (39). He urges the authorities to take measures to stop this disease, whatever one chooses to call it; finally the order comes to close the city gates.

Part II opens with reflections on the effect of the unexpected separations caused by closing the town gates. Emotional deprivations are accentuated by the necessary rationing of food and gasoline. Many seek to forget by going to cafés to drink and socialize or to the movies to be distracted. Cottard expresses satisfaction with the situation, Grand shares information about his life, and Rambert feels that he has nothing to do with the situation, since he is not a resident of Oran, and asks Rieux's help to leave.

A week of prayer, called by the authorities, culminates in a special mass where Father Paneloux's sermon accuses the townspeople of deserving their calamity. There is no evident effect from the sermon, but the citizens begin to feel imprisoned, and there are nightly attempts to escape. As spring gives way to the extreme heat of summer, Rambert continues his efforts to persuade town officials that he should have an exit permit.

Tarrou proposes to Dr. Rieux that squads of volunteers be formed to fight the plague. Rieux asks if he has thought through the possible consequences of participation, that is, suffering from the plague himself. Tarrou responds by asking the doctor what he thought of Paneloux's sermon and if he believes in God. Rieux does not, focusing instead on the realization that when there are sick people, they need curing (120).

Grand also prepares to take part in the sanitary squads, noting with surprise Rieux's thanks: "Plague is here and we've got to make a stand, that's obvious"

(127). Rambert, still trying to leave and wanting, above all, to rejoin the woman he loves, now consults Cottard about the possibilities of leaving the city illegally. After his first attempt does not succeed and he learns that Rieux has been separated from his wife by the epidemic, Rambert offers to participate in the squads until he can leave.

Like the build-up in a classical tragedy to the climax of the action, the plague's unrelenting crescendo encompasses and overwhelms the city of Oran in Part III. The wind and heat of summer, the deaths in close communities such as prisons and convents, curfew, martial law, recycled coffins because of a low supply, common graves, and finally mass cremations: the emotional effect of the plague has gone from revolt to a despondent endurance.

Fatigue is the overwhelming emotion of those fighting the plague as Part IV begins; they are too weary to take the ordered precautions as they make their rounds. Rambert gives up his plans to leave, declaring that the plague is everyone's business (194). The new serum Dr. Castel has been working on is ready and tried for the first time on Magistrate Othon's young son. The boy dies, after extreme, drawn-out suffering. Dr. Rieux's anger breaks out as he talks about this death with Father Paneloux: "I shall refuse to love a scheme of things in which children are put to torture" (203). Paneloux's second sermon calls for acceptance of God's will. Yet, one must keep on struggling even while trusting in divine goodness (211). Paneloux refuses all medical help when he is stricken with an illness atypical of the plague; his death follows.

By now, it is autumn. With the shortage of food due to the city's being cut off from the outside world, the gulf between rich and poor widens; the rich can pay the sums demanded on the black market and the poor are limited to the few provisions available in the markets. Many of those whose family members have died of the plague are quarantined in large camps where courage and composure are evident. One evening Tarrou and Rieux have time for talking, and Tarrou tells of his life and why he has come to always take the side of the victims. Their respite from the cares and concerns finishes with a night swim that gives them a sense of "being perfectly at one" (240).

The plague continues and Christmas approaches. Rieux comes across Grand standing in front of a toy store window, in tears: "a loveless world is a dead world" (243). Grand falls ill and asks Rieux to burn all the drafts of the first sentence of the novel he has been working on for years. Grand recovers, the rats reappear, and the mortality figures decrease.

Part V opens with a sense of cautious optimism, as the plague's energy seems to be flagging. Once hope is possible, the plague's dominion is ended. However, Tarrou falls ill, struggles valiantly, but dies, a last gasp of the plague. For Rieux there is no peace, and he then learns that his wife has died. However, the city gates are opening, and the people's mood is euphoric. Reunited lovers, friends, relatives—all have found a long wished for happiness. Rieux reveals that he has been the narrator, sharing with his fellow citizens their commonalities: love, exile, and suffering. He knows the plague will reappear, under new forms and in new disguises, yet "there are more things to admire in men than to despise" (287).

## CHARACTER DEVELOPMENT

The characters in this fictitious chronicle exemplify human attitudes and actions when faced by an extreme situation. Although they illustrate different reactions and points of view, they are believable as human beings.

Dr. Rieux, the narrator, is a doctor who applies all his scientific and medical knowledge to fight this scourge that slowly, and then more and more rapidly, is overwhelming the town where he practices. Adamant that strict measures are needed to conquer the plague, Rieux refuses to judge on the personal level. He will not give Rambert, the journalist who wants to circumvent these measures, a certificate that he is free of the plague since there is no way to determine his condition. Yet, he agrees that Rambert has a certain right to happiness, and he won't denounce Rambert's efforts to leave the city to the authorities. While it may seem that there is a contradiction in Rieux's character, it is also apparent that Rieux, like the majority of human beings, is well aware of the difficulty of finding absolutes in this world where all must die. When the plague victim must be evacuated immediately, Rieux must telephone for the ambulance. Pity cannot keep him from doing what he knows has to be done. Pragmatic, Rieux notes to Tarrou that he has never grown used to seeing people die. He sees his task as a human being, and as a doctor, to cure sick people. He is not interested in sainthood or heroism; he is interested in being a man and bearing witness to their struggles "so that some memorial of the injustice and outrage done them might endure" (286–87).

Rieux the doctor overshadows Rieux the man in this chronicle. No information about his medical education or his family background is given. He has a wife who has been ill for a year and must leave Oran for treatment elsewhere, but the exact nature of the illness is not revealed. The marriage may be going through a difficult phase because Rieux and his wife promise each other a fresh start when she returns, but what difficulties there may be are never specified. As far as friendship and leisure activities are concerned, Rieux has no time to pursue either during the plague. He shares his thoughts about life and death during a conversation with Tarrou and is evidently able to relate to various types of people, feeling a disciplined compassion for such diverse individuals as Grand and Cotteau. Swimming is one activity Rieux enjoys, although there is no time for such pleasure during the plague; his obvious enjoyment during the night swim with Tarrou leads the reader to believe that the sea and being at ease in it have been part of Rieux's prior life. Rieux's view of the world and humanity comes out in conversations throughout the progression of the plague, but his work as a doctor has created this worldview: Rieux believes that man must fight disease, suffering, and death even though all will die eventually.

While Rieux is consistent throughout the chronicle, acting according to the system of values he briefly articulates in interactions with Tarrou and Rambert, the latter changes and develops through his experience in the plague-stricken town. In Oran to write a series of articles on the living conditions of the Arabs, Raymond Rambert is trapped when the city is closed off from the rest of the world. Refusing at first to accept any connection between himself and the place where he finds himself, Rambert's chief concern is to rejoin the woman he loves who is waiting in Paris. He exerts every effort to leave the city, asking Rieux for a certificate that Rambert is free of disease. He also contacts those who will help people escape from Oran for a price and is at first willing to pay whatever it takes to flee. His personal happiness counts more than the public welfare, and he insists that living and dying for what one loves is what interests him. Rambert's thoughts take a new turn, however, when Tarrou tells him that Rieux too is separated from the one he loves. Rambert's subsequent work with the sanitary squads makes him change his mind completely and cease efforts to escape. When Rieux tells him that there is nothing shameful in preferring happiness, Rambert's response reveals his new acceptance of solidarity with his fellow humans: "But it may be shameful to be happy by oneself.... But now that I've seen what I have seen, I know that I belong here whether I want it or not" (194).

Jean Tarrou is another person kept in Oran by the plague. Evidently a man of independent means, Tarrou was staying in a hotel and participating in the normal pleasures of life when rats began dying in the streets. His diaries are a source of information for the narrator, presenting many details that may seem trivial yet have their importance. This man, who wonders constantly if one can become a saint without God, is another who participates directly in the struggle against the epidemic. The determining event in his life proves to have been hearing his father, a prosecuting attorney, seek the death penalty for a criminal. Wanting to fight against death sentences, he became an agitator fighting against the established order until the day when he realized that his group was also responsible for issuing death sentences: the ideal he seeks also risks bringing death to somebody (235). Tarrou has lost his peace and realizes that only by combating plagues and not joining forces with them can a human being reduce the damage done in the world. So Tarrou organizes the sanitary squads and labors on until, with the plague in Oran diminishing, he too succumbs.

Joseph Grand, a timid clerk toiling amid the forms of a municipal government, is the character whom Rieux calls a true hero. His wife had left him years before; he had failed to keep alive in her the feeling that she was loved. Finding the right words remains a problem for Grand; he is writing a novel but has not yet progressed beyond the first sentence. Perfection eludes him. Yet Grand has no second thoughts when it comes to fighting the plague. He embodies the quiet courage of the sanitary squads, agreeing to participate without a moment's hesitation. He relegates his search for literary perfection to his increasingly limited free time. The reader shares with Rieux the concern the latter feels when he finds Grand in tears before the toy shop window, crying for his lost love: "And he knew, also, what the old man was thinking as his tears flowed . . . that a loveless world is a dead world, and always there comes an hour when one is weary of prisons, of one's work, and of devotion to duty, and all one craves for is a loved face, the warmth and wonder of a loving heart" (243). Grand falls sick and asks Rieux to burn all the drafts of his precious first sentence, yet recovers and is determined to begin again. As the book ends, he tells Rieux that he has managed to write to his wife Jeanne and has made a fresh start with his novel's opening sentence: he has left out all the adjectives. He is one of the most human and sympathetic citizens of the plague-stricken world.

Father Paneloux represents a certain Christian attitude when faced with the death that Camus cannot accept. As the writer stated to a group of Dominicans in 1948, he refused to love a creation where children suffer and die (cf. *Essais*, 371–75). In Paneloux's first sermon to the townspeople, the priest declares that the plague is the divine punishment for their sins and the will of God. However, with the spread of the plague, Paneloux joins the fight, serving the sick. After witnessing the tormented death of Magistrate Othon's young son, Paneloux exchanges views with Rieux. The latter cannot accept the priest's God but recognizes that they're allies in this struggle against the plague. His experiences cause Paneloux to change tone in his second sermon. His pronouns are we and us rather than you. His horror and sadness at the death of the child must be accepted by faith, if not understood through reason. Paneloux decides that God's will must be accepted totally, in complete self-surrender. To that end he refuses any treatment when he is struck by what appears to be the plague.

Cottard is the character who thrives on the plague. He remains ambiguous in that the reader never learns why he fears arrest, but he seems to take a certain pleasure in the progress of the plague. All lives, however, are threatened, and Cottard is therefore part of the community, in a certain sense, because he too is vulnerable to the plague. Cottard is involved in the black market as well as escape attempts. When the plague diminishes, his anxiety increases, quite possibly because he fears that his past will catch up with him now that the authorities have more time. After a shoot out with the police, Cottard is dragged away, still incapable of coping with the complexity of human life. Rieux, a witness to the scene, turns his face away as Cottard and his captors pass him. Again, there is no judgment of this character's actions but compassion for his suffering.

Female characters do not play a direct role in this chronicle. The reader is aware of those who are loved: Rieux's sick wife, Grand's long-vanished Jeanne, and Rambert's lover. Rieux's wife leaves for her treatment as the first dead rats appear. He hears from her from time to time and learns of her death just before the city gates reopen. He realizes he will have to make a fresh start alone. For Grand, Jeanne represents failure and a constant sorrow. Grand is able to describe Jeanne in vague terms, telling Rieux that she was so tiny, he feared for her safety when she crossed the street, but he had not been able to assure her she was loved. Jeanne had left with someone else, saying that she needed to make a fresh start. Although Grand is finally able to write about his feelings to Jeanne as the plague leaves, Rambert is the only one who can reunite with his lost love. She is to come on one of the first trains that arrives after the quarantine is lifted. This imminent appearance indicates her faithfulness and wish to rejoin Rambert, but the reader learns nothing more about her as a person. None of the women characters is developed beyond the ideal of human happiness she represents and the illustration she provides of the theme of separation. Even Rieux's mother remains somewhat shadowed. She is a serene presence in his home, there to look after him in his wife's absence. Tarrou appreciates her self-effacement and her way of explaining things simply. Rieux values her unconditional love and her concern, although neither can express this love each feels because love is never strong enough to find the words it needs or deserves. Madame Rieux and the other women are important as part of human life but are seen only through the eyes of the men who love them.

## THEMES

"But what does that mean—'plague'? Just life, no more than that" (285). The old asthmatic, who spends his days transferring peas from one pan to another, summarizes the overarching theme of Camus's chronicle—life, and its inevitable conclusion, death. *The Plague*, which, in Camus's illustration of it, recounts a specific (fictional) epidemic of disease taking place in a particular location at a particular time, is a powerful work that can stimulate the reader to think about the problems of life and ways to confront life in an absurd world. The book can be read on several meaningful levels, however, and the overarching theme has components that may be considered separately.

Separation and exile from loved ones are two related components that illustrate most directly the effects of any pestilence, be it illness or war or tyranny, on those directly involved. Dr. Rieux's wife leaves the city for treatment before the plague takes hold and dies before they can make the fresh start they anticipate at her departure. Grand is able to make a fresh start only because he has written to Jeanne; the act of writing has made him happy. Rambert most directly lives out what separation means. All his actions are directed toward ending his exile from the woman he loves, but, as noted earlier in this discussion, he comes to realize that individual happiness ought not to be realized at others' expense. Rambert is the only one of the main characters who achieves actual reunion as the chronicle comes to a close. These characters are the specific examples of the feeling that permeates this town closed off against its will and against the rest of the world: "It was undoubtedly the feeling of exile—that sensation of a void within which never left us, that irrational longing to hark back to the past or else to speed up the march of time, and those keen shafts of memory that stung like fire" (67). Camus himself knew the feeling well, caught in France by the war, with no evident means of joining his wife in Algeria.

The plague in Camus's chronicle can also be read as a symbol of the Nazi occupation of France, and by extension, of Europe. Those who fight the plague are members of the Resistance. Cottard, with his profit-making ventures, represents black marketers. The efforts to dispose of the ever-increasing number of dead by burning the bodies recall the extermination camps of World War II. Paneloux's first sermon reflects certain official pronouncements of the French Catholic Church that blamed the fall of France on the actions of the French. Yet, such a narrow reading of *The Plague* limits one's understanding of the book's meaning, although Nazi terrorism is indeed a historical event that must not be forgotten. Camus himself recognized the parallels between his book and the events of 1939–1945; in a response to critic Roland Barthes published in the magazine *Club* in February 1955, Camus wrote that while he wanted *The Plague* to be read on several levels, the struggle of European resistance against Nazism was an evident aspect of the work. For him the proof was that readers in all European countries recognized the

unnamed enemy (cf. *Théâtre, Récits, Nouvelles,* 1965). The sense of struggle
and solidarity among those involved in the struggle can apply as well to any
war, government, or event that has an overpowering impact on a population.
As Allen Thiher notes in an essay, "*The Plague* is a metahistorical work
reflecting on the meaning of history and of human experience as described by
history" (Thiher, *Approaches*, 95). And Camus himself said in his response to
Barthes that the plague can serve as a symbol illustrating resistance to
tyranny (*T, R, N,* 1966).

Beyond any understanding of a special historical event, *The Plague* also
enlarges the reader's understanding of human existence with its inevitable
suffering. From the physical suffering of the plague victims to the mental and
emotional distress of all those imprisoned within this closed universe of a city
shut up within its walls, the reader is well aware of the inhumanity of life
when the plague gains the upper hand. Rieux, as narrator, realizes as he
watches the rejoicing at the chronicle's closure that the plague, under whatever form it may reveal itself, is never completely vanquished: "[his tale]
could be only the record of what had had to be done, and what assuredly
would have to be done again in the never ending fight against terror and its
relentless onslaughts, despite their personal afflictions, by all who, while
unable to be saints but refusing to bow down to pestilences, strive their
utmost to be healers" (287). Literary critic, professor, and friend of Camus,
Germaine Brée aptly concludes that the plague, in any context, must sym-
bolize all that which systematically cuts human beings off from life in all its
aspects: "the physical joy of moving freely on this earth, the inner joy of love,
the freedom to plan our tomorrows." Brée notes that there are neither heroes
nor victories in the fight against the plague, only human beings who, like Dr.
Rieux and Grand, refuse to submit to evidence and continue to do what they
can in the struggle. Their reasons are not as important as their allegiance to
humanity rather than to absolutes or abstractions (*Camus* 128–29).

## NARRATIVE STYLE

"Put everything in the indirect style (sermons, newspapers, etc.) and
monotonous relief through pictures of the Plague?" (*Notebooks,* v. 2, 49).
Camus answers this query through the style he chose for his chronicle. He
does turn to dialogue from time to time in *The Plague,* but the indirect narration establishes an objective, somewhat impersonal tone. The narrator
recounts rather than interprets what he observes. His own reflections are
reported with the same concern for objectivity as those remarks he overhears
or the exchanges he has with others. And restrictive phrases such as perhaps,

doubtless, and at least enable the narrator to keep the relatively impersonal distance of the chronicler.

Subtle irony also plays a part in Camus's narrative style, for example in the way in which he describes the administrative structures of Oran. These structures emphasize paperwork and systems, ignoring the human element. When it becomes essential to inform the populace of the dangers of this pestilence, the posters are pasted up in the most remote corners of the city. The military and police officials are more concerned with setting up a system of decorations than finding new and better ways of fighting the epidemic. Even Dr. Richard, a doctor who does not want to admit that the city is dealing with a real plague, is pleased with the system that has been devised to chart the deaths. Immediately after stating his impression that the plague has reached a plateau, Dr. Richard dies—of the plague. The prefect is pleased with the efficiency and speed of the system of burials, an improvement over efforts during previous plagues. Dr. Rieux sardonically comments that although the burials are much the same, careful records are kept. Progress has been made (164). Meanwhile, the plague also progresses.

Setting is another important element in the work's narrative style. Camus chose a city in North Africa where he had been unhappy and bored. Without going into his personal reasons for this choice, it is important to note that Oran, a city set on a cliff near the Mediterranean sea, lends itself in its physical setting to the depiction of the closed-off world of the plague victims. According to the narrator it is located on a bare plateau, surrounded by hills, above a perfectly shaped bay, but with its back to the sea. The elements of Camus's beloved Algerian landscape are there, but influenced by the banality of a modern urban area. The writer has created, through the precise yet concise descriptions of Oran, a mental image against which the reader can watch the plague progress and follow both the events and the characters as they unfold.

Descriptions in *The Plague* can be emotional as well as factual, inviting the reader to share the emotions that the characters experience as well as the physical details of the events taking place. The reader is part of the agony of Magistrate Othon's young son's death and is a member of the audience when the singer playing the role of Orpheus dies on stage during the performance of the opera. He or she is part of the respite Rieux and Tarrou share during their night swim and senses with them the beauty of the night and the feel of the water. As Philip H. Rhein notes in his book on Camus, these moments of complete identification are rare, "for an essential detachment from both the characters and their situation must be maintained in order that the reader can readily transfer his thoughts from the literal to the figurative level of the novel and thereby be constantly aware of the symbolical inferences being made by the author" (Rhein 64). But they occur and enhance the book's impact on the reader.

A discussion of the narrative style of a book originally written in another language must deal with the filter of the translation. Stuart Gilbert's English version appeared in 1948, a year after the original publication in French. For the most part it remains true to Camus's language and tone. On several occasions the translator has added a word or two to a phrase or seemingly changed an emphasis by changing the order of words within a paragraph. A new translation, by Robin Buss, was published in London by Allen Lane–The Penguin Press in 2001, but throughout 2002 it was difficult to obtain a copy in the United States. Buss avoids additions and remains more faithful to the tone of the original French, in this writer's opinion. However, translation concerns do not negate the overall impact of this chronicle of man's awareness that one can resist, if not transform, the absurdity of the world. Victory against the plague is never certain, but Camus's book lets his readers know that the struggle will be carried on "by all who, while unable to be saints but refusing to bow down to pestilences, strive their utmost to be healers" (287). The translators have enabled English-speaking readers to feel the impact of Camus's ideas and sense his use of language to create this impact.

## HISTORICAL CONTEXT

A political plague was covering much of the earth during the time Camus was writing his own chronicle of a plague. World War II was raging over Europe and Asia. The Allied landing in North Africa in November of 1942 kept Camus in France, where he was working on *The Plague*. But in Algeria the landing meant for the Algerian Muslims contacts with the anticolonial declarations of American diplomats and a more vocal reaction against the French policy for Algeria. Many of the Algerian Muslims called for a new political, social, and economic plan for the country. There was no immediate reply from either representatives of the Vichy government or the French resistance that was supporting the allied effort. However, in 1943 General de Gaulle, now copresident of the new free French government, announced that French citizenship would be granted to "some tens of thousands of Muslims who would nevertheless still enjoy their Muslim personal status" (Ageron 100). The Muslim leadership rejected the idea of assimilation, calling instead for independence. Before the liberation of France, on March 7, 1944, de Gaulle signed a decree abolishing the apparatus of administrative and legal discrimination against Muslims. "It conferred upon them instead all the

rights and duties of the French in Algeria, gave them access to all military
and civil positions, and increased their representation in the local Algerian
assemblies from one-third to two-fifths" (Ageron 101). However, the stark
economic conditions worsened by the war and the political intransigency of
many of the European Algerians insured that time for assimilation was past.
Camus himself wrote that the Algerians no longer were interested in such a
policy (Quilliot 43).

The deteriorating situation in Algeria was overshadowed by the develop-
ments of the war in Europe. As noted earlier, Camus was involved in the
underground publication *Combat* as the allied forces landed in Italy and
moved toward France. At the same time, the Resistance became more widespread in his current homeland. With the landings in Normandy in June
1944 and the liberation of Paris in August of the same year, World War II was
going to end with the defeat of Nazi Germany and her allies. All of the battles, the discovery of the death camps in Eastern Europe, the dropping of two
atomic bombs on Japan, and other such events formed a background against
which Camus continued his search for ways to respond to such a universe and
maintain dignity and justice for its individual inhabitants.

At the war's end Camus participated as a journalist in what he hoped
would be France's transformation to a country where the language of ethics
would be essential in the language of politics (Brée 50). Always an opponent
of the death penalty, Camus deplored the executions of collaborators that
took place in France as the war was ending. He also objected to the myth that
most of the French participated in the Resistance, a myth that was growing in
the postwar years. He knew there had been collaborators as well as resisters;
he realized, however, that many tried merely to exist during the war and
occupation and that condemnation was not the answer to the problem of pre-
venting other plagues. When *The Plague* was published in France, the Fourth
Republic's constitution had been ratified, reestablishing a parliamentary form
of government. Women had gained the right to vote for the first time ever in
the October 1945 election that set up the Constituent Assembly. Overseas
possessions, including Algeria, were represented in this assembly and thus
given at least a symbolic share of shaping postwar France (Wright 425). From
its beginning the Fourth Republic was marked by factional politics, and
power was concentrated in the National Assembly with little power given to
the executive branch. To Camus's sorrow, most of the newspapers established
during the Resistance were taken over by powerful economic groups, and the
press became once again a commercial enterprise rather than a public service.
The postwar world was dividing itself into power blocks, procommunist and
anticommunist. France's overseas possessions began to revolt overtly follow-

ing World War II. Although independence for French colonies would not be achieved until the late 1950s and early 1960s, their dissatisfaction was evident during the postwar period in which Camus completed *The Plague*.

French literature and thought reflected the upheaval that World War II had meant in the individual and collective lives of the French. Writers such as Jean-Paul Sartre called for the necessity of commitment in the midst of the disillusionment and anxiety caused by the war and the aftermath of reconstructing national and individual lives. Camus refused the commitment to a particular political cause that was prevalent in France during his work on *The Plague*, being aware of the dilemma between means and ends and the possibility, or even probability, of causing more deaths in attempts to achieve worthwhile objectives. His commitment remained to humanity, and his chronicle would reflect for its first audience their own preoccupations in allegorical form and for its future readers the mid-twentieth-century historical context that colors vividly the human journey into the twenty-first century.

# 3

## Alexandre Dumas
## *The Three Musketeers*
### 1844

With a flamboyant personality and an immense literary output, Alexandre Dumas is a writer whose life story resembles in some ways the lives of the swashbuckling heroes in the romances that would make him famous. His father, like Victor Hugo's, served in Napoléon's army, and the two writers were born in the same year, 1802. Dumas's grandfather, born Alexandre-Antoine Davy de la Pailleterie, spent many years in the French colony of Santo-Domingo (now Haïti), where his children with a black slave known as Marie-Cessette Dumas included Alexandre's father Thomas. When Thomas started his military career in France, his father insisted that he not use the family name. Thomas chose the name of his slave mother.

Thomas married Marie-Louise-Elisabeth Labouret, the daughter of an innkeeper and had a brilliant army career during the First Republic. However, he lost favor with Napoléon after criticizing the general-turned-emperor and died in 1806, leaving his wife and son Alexandre with few financial resources. Alexandre and his mother continued to live in the town of Villers-Cotterets, where she ran a small tobacco shop. Alexandre received a minimum of formal schooling but did have lessons in calligraphy. His beautiful penmanship would enable him to obtain a position as a copyist in the Duc d'Orléans's office in Paris in April 1823.

Once in Paris and copying documents, Alexandre wanted to pursue a writing career. Coworkers advised him to keep silent about such ambitions, and one of his relatives, a department head in the same office, belittled the aspiring writer's lack of education. However, Alexandre began his literary efforts by collaborating with Adolphe de Leuven and Pierre-Joseph Rousseau on a vaudeville sketch. The comedy was a relative success (Hemmings 50).

In 1827 Dumas attended a performance in Paris of Shakespeare's *Hamlet* by an English company and was impressed by the more natural style of the English actors. He also saw a new direction for his own drama and wrote the play *Henri III and His Court*, accepted by the Comédie Française and performed in 1829 to audience acclaim. The play broke with the French classical rules as it ignored the three unities of one main action, one place, and one time period of 24 hours. Its combination of historical and melodramatic elements plus nonstop action held the audience's attention from beginning to end. Dumas was immediately famous.

Dumas continued writing for the theater, finding success with *Antony* in 1831 and *The Tower of Nesle* in 1832. He began to associate with other writers of like mind, including Charles Nodier and Victor Hugo. He also socialized with theater people, including the well-known actress Marie Dorval, and established romantic liaisons with various women.

During the revolution of 1830, which ended in the abdication of Charles X and the establishment of the Orleanist monarchy, Dumas was a curious participant. Going out equipped with a gun and ammunition, Dumas found himself on July 29 leading some 50 men toward the Hôtel de Ville, where the Marquis de Lafayette had set up headquarters as commander of the National Guard. Dumas did not cross the Seine to the Hôtel de Ville when he saw a field gun at the opposite side of the bridge. He returned home under the cover of the smoke from the guns and returned to the Hôtel later in the evening. Overhearing that there was a shortage of gunpowder in Paris, Dumas offered to go to the nearby town of Soissons, where there was a storage depot and obtain a supply. When he returned two days later, he discovered that the insurrection was over and the Duc d'Orléans was established as King Louis-Philippe (Hemmings 66–70).

Street violence during the funeral procession of General Lamarque on June 5, 1832 found Dumas serving as marshall of the detachment of artillerymen who marched behind the coffin. The general had been a friend of Dumas's father. While the funeral orations were going on, Dumas went to a nearby restaurant to rest. On leaving the restaurant he found barricades already up. Dumas rushed to a nearby theater, grabbed guns stored there for a production, and distributed them to nearby insurrectionists. Once this insurrection failed, Dumas was told by a journalist friend that he might be in danger of being arrested for his actions. The threat never materialized, perhaps because the authorities thought Dumas had been killed. However, Dumas took his friends' advice and started off on a trip to Switzerland (Hemmings 86–88).

Dumas developed his storytelling talents with accounts of his travel adventures in Switzerland, publishing six articles in the *Revue des Deux Mondes* between February and November 1833. Between 1833 and 1837 his travel experiences came out in a series of five volumes titled *Impressions de voyage en Suisse*. In addition to describing what he experienced, Dumas devoted entire chapters to retelling local legends, honing his narrative skills (Hemmings 90–91).

The first Dumas novel appeared as a newspaper serial in 1842. Publishing fiction by installments in newspapers started in France in 1836 with Emile de Girardin's paper *La Presse*. Girardin was convinced there was a market for such fiction with the increase of literacy due to the establishment of more schools and the improved standard of living in France. Other newspapers were started, and writers of fiction discovered they could earn a living publishing in these papers. Dumas especially profited during the 1840s, often writing novels for several papers at once (Hemmings 116–17).

Collaboration was Dumas's means of achieving such an extensive output. He had research assistants, secretaries, and copyists, but the most important collaborator was a writer named Auguste Maquet. Originally hoping to become a dramatist, Maquet met Dumas when he showed a play he had written to the author in 1839. Dumas rewrote the play, which was accepted for production at the Renaissance theater.

Their collaboration continued with Maquet's short historical novel, which he left for Dumas to read as the latter was leaving for Italy with his wife, actress Ida Ferrier, in 1840. Dumas liked the story, paid Maquet for the right to rework the novel, and the result, under the title of *The Chevalier of Harmental*, was first of the long series of romances published under Dumas's name but with important contributions from Maquet (Hemmings 120–21).

Dumas's method of working with Maquet usually involved the two talking over the plan for the new work. The collaborator would prepare a preliminary draft of a section of the novel that Dumas would then rewrite, keeping the general lines. Dumas biographer F. W. J. Hemmings calls the collaboration improvisation on a theme worked out in advance. Dumas was spared the work of invention, to a large extent, but could claim, justifiably, that the finished novel was his own, because each page reflected his style complete with dramatic narration, verve, and wit (Hemmings 121–22). Maquet was involved as research collaborator in Dumas's two best-known novels, *The Three Musketeers* and *The Count of Monte Cristo*.

Because Dumas was so prolific and it was known that he used collaborators, the writer was accused often of not writing everything that he signed. Victor

Hugo's son Charles is quoted as saying, "Everyone has read Dumas, but nobody has read everything of Dumas's, not even Dumas himself" (cf. Hemmings 136). Jean-Baptiste Jacquot, who wrote under the name Eugène de Mirecourt, charged Dumas in a pamphlet of running a literary sweatshop. The accusations were so violent in tone that Dumas easily won a libel action. Mirecourt spent 15 days in prison but continued to write against Dumas.

The first segment of *The Three Musketeers* appeared in *Le Siècle*, a newspaper published in Paris, on March 14, 1844. Immediately popular with the newspaper's readers, the novel attracted more and more subscribers to the paper. Directors of other papers visited Dumas, and he promised more novels to various directors even as he continued writing *The Three Musketeers* and began work on *The Count of Monte Cristo* (Schopp 326–27).

On November 30, 2002, to recognize the bicentennial of his birth, Dumas received the ultimate accolade from the French government. His remains were transported to the Panthéon in Paris where they joined the tombs of other important French political figures and writers, including Victor Hugo.

## PLOT DEVELOPMENT

The swashbuckling novel known as *The Three Musketeers* tells the adventures of four young men on the brink of adulthood but still free of its cares and responsibilities. Dumas found the inspiration for his novel in the *Mémoires de M. d'Artagnan* by Courtilz de Sandras. Historical accuracy was not Dumas's objective, but a certain Charles de Baatz d'Artagnan did live between 1611 and 1673, and Sandras's account of the real d'Artagnan's life also mentions three companions known as Athos, Aramis, and Porthos. Using these names from the *Mémoires*, Dumas developed his own heroes and associated their adventures with more well-known historical persons such as the king of France in 1625, Louis XIII; his wife and queen, Anne of Austria; his prime minister, Cardinal Richelieu; and the duke of Buckingham, from the court of England. The novel begins with the introduction of d'Artagnan and continues through 67 chapters and an epilogue to trace his coming of age in the king's service, his friendships, his loves, and his exploits. Dumas relates the story from the standpoint of an omniscient narrator who knows all there is to know about events and characters. However, he is sparing with his comments and interventions as he tells his tale.

In the first chapter, Dumas sets the scene as to time and place—the town of Meung, the first Monday in April 1625—and introduces his 18-year-old Don Quixote, d'Artagnan. The young man is off to Paris to seek fame and glory, preferably through service in the king's musketeers. The young man's impetuous character is revealed through his initial acts. Immediately involved in a fight with a stranger who laughs at d'Artagnan's ugly yellow horse, the young hero is knocked unconscious, but he has remained true to his father's advice: take care of his horse, take no slights from anyone except the king and the cardinal, and follow M. de Tréville as model (2–3). Reviving after the fight, d'Artagnan sees the stranger talking to a beautiful young woman seated in a carriage. When he is about to leave Meung, d'Artagnan discovers that the letter of introduction his father has written to M. de Tréville, in charge of the king's musketeers, is missing. Once in Paris, d'Artagnan sells his horse and hopes to overcome his initial setbacks.

At M. de Tréville's house, d'Artagnan finds a disorderly crowd of members of the king's musketeers. He also has his first views of Porthos and Aramis. D'Artagnan, introduced into M. de Tréville's room, hears de Tréville scold Porthos and Aramis about their altercation with the cardinal's guards the previous day. The ill humor between the two groups of soldiers reflects the tense relationship between the king and his prime minister. The third musketeer involved in the previous day's altercation, Athos, arrives but soon faints due to the wound he received. D'Artagnan tells M. de Tréville of his adventures and desires to become a musketeer and also of his hatred for the stranger in Meung. De Tréville is suspicious that d'Artagnan might be a spy for the cardinal but promises him a new letter of introduction. Always impulsive, d'Artagnan does not wait for the letter but rushes from the house when he sees the stranger across the street. Through his hurried and impetuous actions, d'Artagnan manages to insult Athos, Aramis, and Porthos, separately, and schedules a duel with each of them.

D'Artagnan and Athos agree that they would enjoy each other's conversation if they don't kill each other. Athos appears for the duel, bringing Porthos and Aramis as his seconds. The three are surprised to learn that d'Artagnan had challenged all three, but the duel(s) are stopped when some of the cardinal's guards arrive; duels are illegal. Instead, the musketeers and the guards fight, and d'Artagnan helps the musketeers prevail. He is overjoyed to become an apprentice musketeer.

In the next scene, Louis XIII expresses displeasure about the fights between the musketeers and the guards. M. de Tréville supports his men and is invited to bring his four fighters to meet the king the next day—but the king has gone hunting. M. de Tréville, visiting the guards' commander to complain of their conduct toward the musketeers, is vindicated when one of the guardsmen involved admits that the guardsmen began the fight. Later in the day the four meet the king, who gives d'Artagnan 40 pistoles, a relatively large sum of money. Dumas interjects the comment that in 1625 it was not wrong to accept such a gift from one's sovereign (71).

The following chapter is somewhat of a pause in the ongoing action. D'Artagnan uses the money to buy a good dinner for his friends and acquire a servant, Planchet. The servants of the three are sketched and the mysterious origins of the three musketeers indicated. D'Artagnan, through the efforts of M. de Tréville, secures a place in the guards of M. le Chevalier des Essarts. Although not yet a musketeer, he is part of the king's faction.

The next three chapters add a new thread to the plot. D'Artagnan's landlord, M. Bonacieux, arrives with the story that his wife, one of the queen's attendants, has been abducted. From the description d'Artagnan thinks the abductor is the stranger who insulted him at Meung. Thinking he sees the man across the street, d'Artagnan rushes out to chase him but doesn't find him. The three musketeers arrive, and Aramis mentions that he was mistaken the day before for the duke of Buckingham, an English nobleman visiting the French court. M. Bonacieux hurries in to say that men are coming to arrest him. D'Artagnan says to let Bonacieux be taken. Although Porthos wonders why d'Artagnan accepts this arrest, he agrees with his companions to swear "All for one, one for all" (95). D'Artagnan notes that now they are at war with the cardinal. Madame Bonacieux arrives home, and d'Artagnan, listening from his room, rescues her from the men sent by the cardinal to arrest anyone who comes to the Bonacieux's house. D'Artagnan takes this young, beautiful woman to Athos's apartment and follows her instructions to go to M. de la Porte, the queen's gentleman. M. de la Porte tells d'Artagnan to establish an alibi for himself for the evening.

As impulsive as ever, d'Artagnan goes next to see Aramis to tell him all about this wonderful woman with whom d'Artagnan is now in love. However, instead of finding Aramis, he sees a woman knocking at the shutters and an exchange of handkerchiefs with another woman. The first woman is Madame Bonacieux, who begs d'Artagnan not to meddle. The next news is that Athos has been arrested, mistaken for d'Artagnan. The latter goes to find M. de Tréville and thinks he sees his love, Madame Bonacieux, with Aramis. However, the man is the duke of Buckingham.

Dumas devotes the following chapter to describing the duke, his adventuresome character, and his fixity of purpose in all his endeavors. Smuggled into the queen's apartments, the duke speaks to the queen of his love for her. Anne won't say directly that she loves the duke but states that she is queen and will remain faithful to her marriage vows. She does give the duke a jewel box to remember her by.

The action moves to the opposition side when Monsieur Bonacieux, arrested by officers, is more concerned with his own fate than that of his wife. Finally brought to see Cardinal Richelieu, Bonacieux denies knowing anything about his wife's activities. The man from Meung, in reality the count of Rochefort and one of Richelieu's agents, arrives and reports to Richelieu what he has learned about the queen and Buckingham, including the news that some diamond studs, a gift to the queen from the king, are in the jewel box now in Buckingham's possession. Richelieu pays off Bonacieux, knowing that the money will insure that the husband will now spy on his wife. Next the cardinal sends a messenger off to Milady, his young and beautiful spy, in England with instructions that she obtain 2 of the 12 diamond studs off Buckingham's doublet when she sees him at a ball. M. de Tréville gets Athos's release after a verbal confrontation with Richelieu.

Louis XIII returns to the forefront when he is determined to obtain a letter in the queen's possession, thinking it is a love letter. He sends Chancelor Séguier to take the letter from the queen, who fears that she is lost, given the jealousy of her husband and the hatred of Richelieu. The letter is political, a plan of attack against the cardinal, who offers to resign. The king refuses, knowing he needs a person of the cardinal's abilities in order to govern. The cardinal suggests that the king give a ball and request the queen to wear the diamond studs. Anne is horrified by this request and decides she must trust Madame Bonacieux who offers to help. Madame thinks she can persuade her husband to travel to London and obtain the studs but soon discovers that he is a spy for the cardinal. D'Artagnan, in love with Madame Bonacieux, says he will make the trip. The two take the money the cardinal gave to M. Bonacieux to finance d'Artagnan's voyage to London.

The three musketeers volunteer to help their comrade get to London, and the trip is filled with adventures. D'Artagnan is the only one to reach London and Buckingham. When the duke discovers two of the studs missing, he realizes that Lady de Winter, Milady, is the culprit. He orders new studs and then wants to reward d'Artagnan for his efforts on behalf of Queen Anne. The young man will not accept English gold, since the two countries are at war, but will accept horses. The return to Paris goes well, and the queen wears the right number of diamonds at the ball—to the surprise of the king. D'Artagnan, also at the ball, follows Madame Bonacieux to an antechamber off the queen's apartments. Soon a hand comes through an opening into the room. D'Artagnan kisses the hand and receives a ring.

When d'Artagnan returns to his room, he finds a letter setting up a rendezvous with Madame Bonacieux. He goes to see M. de Tréville, who warns him against accepting presents, especially from women, and says he should find his three companions who have not been seen since they set out with d'Artagnan. D'Artagnan agrees but insists on keeping his rendezvous first. When no one comes to the villa at the set time, d'Artagnan waits an hour and then climbs a tree to look in a lighted window in the villa. All he sees are signs of a struggle. An old man in the neighborhood tells of an abduction he witnessed. Telling the entire story to M. de Tréville later, d'Artagnan accepts his mentor's advice to seek his three companions while de Tréville pursues the matter of Madame Bonacieux's disappearance.

In the next few chapters the reader learns that each musketeer has remained at an inn near the place where each one was forced to stop during the trip to London. And each one is virtually without any money to pay his bills. Porthos is waiting to hear from his lady love, who is to send the needed funds. Aramis is talking of returning to seminary and working on his thesis. He changes his mind when d'Artagnan gives him a letter from the woman Aramis loves. Athos and his servant have retreated to the basement of their inn, locked themselves in, and are busily eating and drinking their way through the innkeeper's supplies. Athos talks about his deceptions in love and about a friend whose wife turned out to be a convicted criminal. Before he and d'Artagnan can leave the inn, Athos has gambled away the horses d'Artagnan brought, and the two go to collect Aramis and then Porthos, riding on their servants' horses. Their major problem now is to acquire enough money to collect their equipment for the siege of La Rochelle. The Protestant-controlled city is attempting to hold out against the king's troops and waiting for help from England that the duke of Buckingham has been working to arrange.

Procuring funds and d'Artagnan's growing involvement with Milady are the subjects of the next several chapters. Dumas weaves the threads of these experiences carefully, and the reader is amused, amazed, and even somewhat appalled as the four companions work their way toward departure for La Rochelle. D'Artagnan traces Milady, and Planchet, d'Artagnan's servant, intercepts a note meant for the Count de Wardes, Milady's current love interest. Next d'Artagnan intervenes when he finds Milady and her brother-in-law, Lord de Winter, in an argument. Challenging Lord de Winter to a duel, d'Artagnan and the three musketeers gain the upper hand against Lord de Winter and his supporters, although d'Artagnan doesn't kill Lord de Winter. Visiting Milady for the first time, d'Artagnan has very mixed feelings, attracted by her beauty but wary of her involvement with the cardinal.

D'Artagnan continues his intrigue with Milady, but her maid, Kitty, tells d'Artagnan that Milady loves the Count de Wardes, not him, and shows him a note meant for the count. D'Artagnan uses Kitty's love for him to hide in her room. He overhears Milady's fury that d'Artagnan didn't kill Lord de Winter. D'Artagnan shudders at this aspect of the woman who both attracts and repels him. However, he seduces Kitty anyway and then writes a note to

Milady, purporting to come from the count, saying that he will visit her at 11 P.M. that evening.

During his visit, d'Artagnan is loved, under his false identity of the Count de Wardes. He both hates and loves this fascinating woman. When Athos sees d'Artagnan's new ring the next day, he recognizes it as one he had given to a woman. He advises d'Artagnan to break off relations with Milady. D'Artagnan agrees and writes a rejection note, signing the name of the Count de Wardes.

It is not easy to be rid of Milady. D'Artagnan visits her yet again and is again enthralled. Milady wants him to avenge her against the Count de Wardes because she thinks the count has rejected her. He agrees but tells himself to be careful. After their night together, d'Artagnan confesses what he has done concerning the count. Milady is furious, and in their scuffle d'Artagnan tears Milady's nightgown from her shoulder. He sees the tattoo of the fleur de lys, the sign of a convicted criminal. D'Artagnan escapes through Kitty's room, and she, in spite of her jealousy, gives him some of her clothes so he can leave the house.

D'Artagnan runs to Athos's apartment and tells him the whole story of his adventures with Milady. Athos's laughter at d'Artagnan's appearance in petticoats soon changes when the two realize that this woman with the tattoo is the one Athos had known also. They discuss selling the ring Milady gave d'Artagnan, although Athos had originally received it from his mother. Ultimately the ring is sold—Athos won't bargain concerning the price, for he is an aristocrat, notes Dumas.

As d'Artagnan is making final preparations to join the French troops at La Rochelle, he receives two letters, one telling him to be on the road to Chaillot and look at the passing carriages without making any sign of recognition. The other letter is an invitation, or perhaps an order, to meet Richelieu. D'Artagnan will follow the instructions in both letters. When the carriage passes, d'Artagnan sees Madame Bonacieux inside but can do nothing. When he goes to Richelieu's residence, the other three wait for him outside the gates. Richelieu knows all that d'Artagnan has been doing and invites him to join the cardinal's guards. D'Artagnan, saying he is not ready, refuses the invitation.

To introduce the action at the siege of La Rochelle, Dumas explains the story behind this French–English conflict, saying it's due in large part to the love both Buckingham and Richelieu have for Queen Anne. D'Artagnan, still in des Essarts's guards, is lonely without his friends and is also ambushed while taking a walk but escapes. When d'Artagnan volunteers for a dangerous mission to see if a certain bastion is occupied, he is again the target of shots. He learns that Milady is behind both assassination attempts. Going to pick up the wounded shooter in order to obtain Milady's letter, d'Artagnan is shot at again from the bastion, but the body of the wounded man which he is carrying saves him.

The next attempt to kill d'Artagnan is with poisoned wine which kills the wounded shooter who drinks it instead. Athos does not want to believe that Milady and his late wife are the same person, but one night he and the other two musketeers meet the cardinal while they are returning from an inn where they have fought to keep three men from forcing a lady's door. With the cardinal they return to the inn. The cardinal goes to speak to the lady, and the musketeers listen to their conversation through a stovepipe. The woman is Milady, and the cardinal is instructing her to go to London and tell Buckingham he has lost. Milady wants written justification for the trip and also vengeance against d'Artagnan.

Later Athos confronts Milady and in the encounter tells her to leave d'Artagnan alone and to give him the cardinal's note. Milady decides to go ahead with the mission to England even without the note and to return to the cardinal afterwards.

Athos wants to consult with his three friends, and they take their breakfast to the Saint-Gervais bastion, vowing to stay there an hour to show their courage under fire. The bastion is within range of the enemy guns, but the four get arms and ammunition from the dead bodies lying in the bastion. During the consultation the four are attacked several times but emerge victorious, using various ruses such as propping the dead bodies up against the ramparts to make it look like more defenders are present. Porthos thinks the queen's ring should be sold to provide funds for the attempt to save Buckingham. The cardinal hears of the exploit in the bastion once the four return and tells M. de Tréville to take d'Artagnan into the musketeers. The ring is sold and Planchet sent to London with a letter to warn Buckingham. Aramis's servant Bazin goes to Aramis's cousin, really his mistress, with a letter to warn the queen. Both emissaries return to La Rochelle with their missions accomplished.

The next series of chapters deals directly with Milady's adventures in England, with one return to the siege at La Rochelle. When the ship carrying Milady approaches Portsmouth, she is removed from the ship and taken to a castle. Her brother-in-law, Lord de Winter, is aware of her trip and responsible for her incarceration. Surprised that Lord de Winter has shown this ability for intrigue, Milady holds her own in their verbal exchange, but de Winter does score by mentioning Milady's French husband, the brand on her shoulder, and her joy in doing evil. He presents John Felton, an officer to whom de

Winter has been almost a father. Felton will be the guard in charge of Milady, and de Winter warns the young man against Milady's powers of seduction.

Back at the siege, the inhabitants of La Rochelle are slowly starving as they wait for the help from England promised by the duke of Buckingham. The cardinal finds the four musketeers playing cards and drinking on the beach as they await the next action. They have also hidden a letter. Once the cardinal leaves they can read the letter, which tells where Madame Bonacieux can be found, information that d'Artagnan has been seeking.

In Portsmouth, Milady is coping with her captivity. Day by day she works on Felton, soliciting his pity for her plight. She ascertains that he is a Puritan and so acts as if she is of the same faith. By the fourth day Felton is no longer listening to Lord de Winter's warnings and cannot decide if Milady is a fiend or Lord de Winter a monster. On the fifth day Milady tells Felton an imaginative version of her life, culminating in the tale that she was seduced by Buckingham. Felton is completely taken in and decides to help Milady escape. He saws through the bars of her window, and the two descend via ropes to the ground. Felton has hired a ship for her but must go into Portsmouth with an order to deport Milady for Buckingham to sign. Milady says she will wait for Felton until 10 P.M. the next night.

When Felton brings the order, he tells Buckingham not to sign it. While Buckingham is distracted by reading a letter newly arrived from France, Felton stabs him. Lord de Winter manages to seize Felton before the young man can escape. The letter is from the queen in France. It urges Buckingham not to send reinforcements to La Rochelle and stop the war. Before he dies, Buckingham hears from Queen Anne's emissary that Anne said to tell him she still loves him. Felton says that his act was due to personal reasons. Then Felton sees the ship leaving with Milady, an hour early, and understands that she has betrayed him.

In France the king has decided to leave the siege, and the musketeers obtain leave. Worried about Madame Bonacieux they set off for Bethune where she is staying in a convent. On the way they see d'Artagnan's original enemy, the man of Meung, that is, the count of Rochefort, and find a slip of paper he has lost with the word Armentières written on it.

Milady is also heading for Bethune after sending a note to the cardinal. After persuading the abbess that she too is a victim of Richelieu, Milady is welcomed and introduced to the other young woman in residence. Milady is clever enough to figure out that the woman is Madame Bonacieux and persuades her that she, Milady, has only been d'Artagnan's friend, never his mistress. Madame Bonacieux, believing she has found a friend, tells Milady of a note that indicates the musketeers' imminent arrival.

The count of Rochefort arrives first, and Milady is able to formulate a new plan of escape. She tells Rochefort to meet her in Armentières. Later, when galloping horses are heard arriving, Milady manages to put a lethal powder in Madame Bonacieux's glass and encourages her to drink. Milady then escapes through the convent garden, and the musketeers arrive to find Madame Bonacieux dying and to learn enough from the abbess to realize that Milady has been at the convent. Athos tells the weeping d'Artagnan to avenge his lost love, and that since Milady was Athos's wife, he is responsible for seeing her captured and judged.

Athos formulates his plan, sending the servants off with specific tasks and finding himself a man who lives alone near the convent. The musketeers set off with the unknown man and Lord de Winter who, by now, has also arrived at the convent. The servants have found Milady at a house in Armentières. When the group of men enters, each one accuses Milady of the deeds she has done against him. The unknown man turns out to be the executioner from the city of Lille whose brother, a priest, was Milady's first victim when she was a young novice. All vote for death.

The execution scene by the banks of a river is very dramatic and visual with lightning striking across the night sky. Milady begs for her life, and when d'Artagnan shows signs of being affected, Athos keeps him away. All Milady's victims forgive her before the executioner takes her across the river and does his work. Milady's body is thrown into the river. Athos tells M. de Tréville that the four have had an amusing leave.

When the musketeers return to La Rochelle, Rochefort arrests d'Artagnan under orders from the cardinal. D'Artagnan informs the cardinal that if the accusation is from Milady, she is guilty of more infamous deeds and is now dead. The cardinal then gives d'Artagnan a blank commission as a lieutenant in the musketeers. The other three have new plans, and Athos writes d'Artagnan's name on the commission, telling him that his bitter memories will have time to change to sweet ones.

A brief epilogue tells what happens to the musketeers: Porthos marries his lady love, now a widow, and his servant achieves his dream of standing behind a gilded carriage. Aramis enters a monastery, and Athos stays in the service for several more years before retiring to his estate. D'Artagnan takes up his commission, fights and wounds Rochefort three times, and they agree to be friends. The three musketeers, with their companion, d'Artagnan, have concluded their adventures.

## CHARACTER DEVELOPMENT

Dumas does not probe the psychological depths of his characters; he lets them present themselves in words and deeds. The heroes are loyal, courageous, and enterprising. The villains are evil, yet attractive and seductive, especially in the case of Milady. All the characters are depicted with broad yet deft strokes and remain vivid in the reader's memory.

D'Artagnan, who rides into Meung seeking adventure, is considered the typical Gascon with the combination of prudence, rashness, courage, ambition, idealism, loyalty, and sentiment. Those who hail from the southwest region of France known as Gascony have long been recognized by these traits in French literature and culture. What happens to the young man in Meung is a first indication of his character: his ugly yellow horse has elicited laughter, and he fights courageously against three men until his sword is broken and he falls unconscious. D'Artagnan does not let this momentary defeat stop his ambitious progress toward Paris and his hope for a career in the musketeers. His love life goes through three women: the lovely Madame Bonacieux, faithful to her mistress, the queen; the sweet and compliant Kitty, maid to Milady; and Milady herself, seductive but treacherous. Swayed by beauty and compliance, d'Artagnan is not above using Kitty to approach Milday, but honorable in his own way, he finds her a safe place once she has helped him escape the siren's clutches. The sentimental side comes to the forefront when Madame Bonacieux dies, and d'Artagnan faints from anguish. Then, weeping bitterly, he is also ready to seek vengeance against Milady and votes for death when she is judged by the group of musketeers—although he is affected by her outcries when she faces execution. True to his galant character, he forgives Milady and says he will weep for her. Saddened by the results of his recent adventures, d'Artagnan takes up his new commission as lieutenant in the musketeers. "Then I will have no more friends, . . . I will have nothing but bitter memories" (624). Like Athos, the reader is sure, however, that this youthful mixture of impetuosity and prudence, who loves not always too wisely, will have time to create sweeter memories.

Athos, Porthos, and Aramis, the three musketeers whom d'Artagnan wants to join, are also made real and believable. Dumas takes their rather vague historical reality as shown in the *Mémoires de M. d'Artagnan* and adds his imagination to make them legendary. Athos, noble and mysterious, reveals his innermost thoughts little by little but only when events force this self-revelation. His closest friends could not remember ever hearing him laugh and had no idea if he had ever had a mistress (73). When d'Artagnan's misadventures with Milady force Athos to accept that this woman is his supposedly dead wife, Athos, as a true musketeer, takes on the responsibility for her judgment, planning and carrying out her trial.

Porthos, a giant of a man, cannot be faulted for any lack of physical action or loyalty to his friends. Athos's opposite in verbal expression, "he talked for the pleasure of talking and the pleasure of listening to himself talk" (73). He usually doesn't understand the plotting of his fellows, but his loyalty makes him follow their lead. His lack of comprehension provides a certain amount of comic relief amidst the shots of the enemy at the bastion of Saint Germain—when it is spelled out to him that the enemy cannot see that the forms against the bastion walls are corpses and their uncertainty will provide the musketeers an opportunity to get away safely, the light goes on: " 'Oh, *now* I understand,' said Porthos, marveling" (456).

Aramis comes across as secretive, never telling his companions the truth about the mysterious communications he receives. "He was the most unusual Musketeer and the most unconvivial companion imaginable" (78). Nothing he says or does during the story goes against this description.

Loyal, true, and brave are the four servants. Planchet tries to counsel prudence to d'Artagnan but follows orders, carrying them out faithfully. Grimaud has been trained by Athos to communicate through gestures rather than words and is punished when he speaks to warn the musketeers that the cardinal is approaching. Bazin, Aramis's servant, dresses only in black, reading pious works during his time off and remaining mute and loyal in all circumstances. Mousqueton likes display as much as Porthos and achieves his heart's desire when Porthos marries the rich widow: he can now wear a splendid costume and ride behind his master's coach. With a few deft descriptions and the dialogues between masters and servants, Dumas creates a memorable set of secondary characters who reflect their adventurous masters.

The three female characters with whom d'Artagnan has relationships are stereotypical in several ways, yet Dumas is able to go beyond the typically feminine traits he gives them and create lively, intelligent, and courageous women. The good ones, Madame Bonacieux and Kitty, think quickly, as their statements and actions indicate. Madame Bonacieux, although her husband says that she isn't clever, develops a plan to save the queen from the king's jealousy. She is bright enough to improvise as situations warrant and to trust d'Artagnan once she realizes that her husband has been paid by Richelieu. She appreciates d'Artagnan's courage and values his loyalty and his love. However, she is more easily fooled by another woman, Milady, and dies of this misplaced trust. Kitty, Milady's maid, also values d'Artagnan, although she realizes his love is not hers to keep. Even though he has just slept with her mistress, she is bright enough and loyal enough to help him escape by giving him her clothes to wear.

All three women are beautiful, but Milady is also evil at heart. Dumas doesn't explain the origin of Milady's villainous nature but shows his *femme fatale* in action. Her beauty attracts d'Artagnan when he first sees her seated in a carriage in Meung. When he learns more of what she has done, he has no respect for Milady, but still feels "an uncontrollable passion for this woman boiling in his veins—a passion heightened by contempt, but passion never-theless" (344). Like d'Artagnan listening in Kitty's room or the musketeers overhearing Milady's conversation with the cardinal through a stovepipe at the inn near La Rochelle, the reader learns of Milady's character from her own lips. Vengeful, ambitious, seductive, and clever, Milady can pace her seduction of John Felton in order to be freed moments before she is to be sent to the duke of Buckingham. An intelligent plotter, she manages to poison Madame Bonacieux and direct the count of Rochefort how to help her escape from the convent before d'Artagnan and his companions arrive. However, in spite of telling Kitty that she won't feel faint as ordinary women might when insulted but will avenge herself (359), Milady cannot overcome the ultimate judgment orchestrated by Athos and carried out by the executioner. The good will ultimately prevail, and this scheming beauty finishes her short life on a dark river bank—dramatic and memorable to the end.

The four major historical characters, King Louis XIII, Queen Anne of Aus-tria, Cardinal Richelieu, and the duke of Buckingham, also come alive through Dumas's skillful use of dialogue. These characters are not cardboard figures in a history textbook but human beings whose conversations show their concerns and emotions.

The king's words reveal him as jealous of what he perceives as the queen's interest in another man and of the cardinal's abilities and power as prime minister. More human than regal, he can also be petulant when he loses at cards, overjoyed when he hears that the musketeers have defeated the cardi-nal's guardsmen, and pleased at the queen's dismay when he directs her to wear his gift of diamond studs at the ball.

The queen's beauty is stressed through the words of those who observe her, but her honor is emphasized in the direct encounter with Buckingham. When the duke reminds Anne of an evening they spent in a garden, she only replies, "But, my Lord, you saw the queen come to the aid of the woman who weakened" (125). As queen, Anne cannot let her personal feelings overcome her royal duty. Horrified that the duke will instigate a war only to see her again when he will negotiate a peace, Anne sees such proofs of love as crimes. Her honor is again seen in her final written message to the duke. She begs him to put an end to the war against France even while she assures him of her regard for his life.

Cardinal Richelieu's character is shown chiefly through his intrigues, both for France and against his personal enemies. He uses the count of Rochefort and Milady among others in efforts to dispose of such enemies as Buckingham and to make sure that he always knows what is happening in France. Dumas puts words in the cardinal's mouth, but they ring true and show Richelieu's ability to adapt to situations and recognize honor in others. First blaming d'Artagnan for Milady's downfall, Richelieu realizes that d'Artagnan's actions were necessary and rewards, rather than punishes, the young man: "[he] thought for the third or fourth time of the future before that twenty-one-year-old youth and what resources his energy, courage, and shrewdness might offer a good master" (621). Presenting d'Artagnan with a commission as a lieutenant in the musketeers, Richelieu changes an adversary into a supporter.

The duke of Buckingham is a galant lover, both of danger and a beautiful queen. Dumas's description of the duke highlights the character that his conversation with the queen will confirm: "Sure of himself, convinced of his own power, certain that the laws which rule other men could not reach him" (122), the duke is brought down only through a complicated intrigue. Ready to cause the deaths of many men in a war so that he has a reason to return to France, he dies happy, knowing that the queen still loves him and regretting nothing. Dumas uses the historical facts as the starting point for his creation of a believable aristocrat for whom love and glory are intertwined.

With deft descriptions and rapid dialogue, Dumas gives life also to such characters as Monsieur Bonacieux, Monsieur de Tréville, and John Felton. Madame Bonacieux says her husband is miserly and greedy, which the latter's actions confirm. The reader can see this ordinary tradesman as he passes from fear at his arrest by anonymous guards to obsequiousness when facing the cardinal. The reader feels little sympathy for this man whose fear and greed overcome any concern for his wife. Monsieur de Tréville, on the other hand, is a surrogate father to his musketeers, advising them and defending them to king and cardinal alike. His concern for his men is illustrated when he urges d'Artagnan to leave immediately on his undisclosed mission but to take his three friends to provide more strength through numbers. De Tréville even offers the young man money for the journey. John Felton, the young English officer, is portrayed in all his naivety as Milady works on his susceptibilities and convinces him to attack Buckingham. His reactions to Milady's assumed piety and tale of alleged violence committed against her are portrayed through description of his expressive reactions and remarks. " 'God has so willed it,' he said with a fanatic's resignation" (562). These characters, like the major actors in the drama of this adventure story, live both on the pages and in the reader's memory.

## THEMES

In a novel such as *The Three Musketeers*, the themes are related more to adventures than to philosophical insights. Reflecting a common human desire for ideals, glory, worlds to conquer, causes to defend, friendship, and love, the tale traces these themes through the coming of age of a young man as he learns about the ways of the world. The conflicts that d'Artagnan and the others must confront take on "the dimensions of struggles between right and wrong, good and evil" (Stowe 74). And yet these conflicts are often begun simply because of human tendencies toward jealousy and revenge.

D'Artagnan rides into Meung with a heart full of dreams of future adventure, glory, and love, yet he is a comic figure at the beginning with his too long sword and his peculiar-looking yellow horse. His father has given him his first ideals: he can make his way in the world because he has a noble family and a lineage that has instilled courage in their worthy descendant. D'Artagnan's father emphasizes this point: "Understand that it is by his courage and by his courage alone that a gentleman can make his way nowadays" (3).

It takes a few adventures for d'Artagnan to focus his courage. Rashly attacking the man who laughs at him and challenging Athos, Porthos, and Aramis one by one to duels, d'Artagnan goes on to find solidarity and friendship with the three musketeers and uses his courage to fight for the common cause. This cause includes first and foremost helping Madame Bonacieux protect the queen. An idealistic adventurer will be convinced that the cause of a beautiful woman is true and just; d'Artagnan is immediately ready to rush off to London on the queen's mission after hearing of her need for a champion. The older and wiser Monsieur de Tréville convinces d'Artagnan to involve his three friends in the journey, and the impetuous d'Artagnan learns the value of friendship. "All for one, and one for all" is their ruling motto and serves them well throughout all their adventures.

War is another adventure, and the siege at La Rochelle involves d'Artagnan and the three musketeers. However, in this novel war remains an adventure. The starving residents of La Rochelle and the dead bodies in the Saint-Gervais bastion never seem quite real. Gallantry under fire and clever use of what a situation provides are the aspects of this war that Dumas emphasizes. He appears to consider its causes more personal than political, presenting as probable reasons for the English–French conflict at La Rochelle the love of Buckingham for Queen Anne and the cardinal's jealousy at Anne's refusal of his attentions.

Love as a theme has several aspects. D'Artagnan is romantically in love with Madame Bonacieux and puts her requests ahead of a summons from Richelieu. Others are more cynical concerning both the lady and women's feelings in general. Aramis warns his friend: "Woman was created for our destruction, and all our miseries come from her" (90). And d'Artagnan himself is quite content to share Kitty's bed, although he remains devoted to Madame Bonacieux. His relationship with Milady is more complex.

Attracted to her beauty and repelled by her intrigues, he admits that he has deceived her about the Count de Wardes. It is not completely clear if he confesses because he wants to be loved on his own merits or if his honor requires complete honesty. In addition, loving one's mistress does not stop one from asking for and receiving money from her. Aramis and Porthos both equip themselves for the siege with monetary gifts from their mistresses. Dumas, as narrator, notes that in the seventeenth century such gifts were perfectly acceptable.

D'Artagnan comes of age through his adventures. He attains glory through his exploits. He finds causes to defend and women to love. His friendship with Athos, Porthos, and Aramis is built on trust and confidence, and those qualities never fail. He achieves his heart's desire when the cardinal gives him a commission in the musketeers after Milady's execution. Yet, worthy of the position as he is, d'Artagnan seems to realize that it might not be as wonderful as he had thought: "Then I will have no more friends" (624), he says to Athos, after learning that his three friends have new plans. He has learned that conquering new worlds and foiling evil don't necessarily provide complete happiness. Athos reminds him that time will give him the opportunity to change bitter memories to sweet ones. Athos seems to imply that d'Artagnan will eventually understand that his essential values of defending noble causes, love, and friendship are worthwhile and can be pursued even as a new lieutenant in the musketeers.

## NARRATIVE STYLE

Narration primarily through dialogue characterizes Dumas's style. The writer has his characters talk to each other in order to advance the action, or even explain background. Direct author intervention is rare, and it is evident that Dumas started out as a dramatist. Chapters conclude at a point when the curtain could go down, or, since the novel was initially published in a newspaper, when a pause in the action leaves the reader in suspense and eager for the next installment. Description is usually limited to setting the scene or providing atmosphere. It may be true that Dumas's dialogues owe their length to his being paid by the line, but the rapid verbal exchanges heighten the sense of surprise or terror that their pace maintains.

Eavesdropping is another technique Dumas uses to provide background and knowledge, for the characters and for the reader. D'Artagnan avails himself of this procedure first in his lodgings. He discovers a way to listen through his floor to what is transpiring below and thereby is able to rescue Madame Bonacieux. Later she joins him in listening to her husband's conversation with the man from Meung. Athos is also able to learn information helpful to the musketeers' cause when he discovers that the stovepipe in the inn carries the conversation between Milady and the cardinal in the room above to the listening ears below. The technique adds to the sense of adventure characters and readers feel.

Dumas is interested most of all in telling his story in an entertaining way and does not concern himself with images and symbolism in *The Three Musketeers*, yet he uses the contrast between night and day to highlight different events. The story starts in broad daylight as d'Artagnan rides into Meung. He enters Monsieur de Tréville's home in the morning and schedules his duels for daylight. However, d'Artagnan's nighttime adventures are even more dramatic. He follows Madame Bonacieux at night, spends one night outside the inn where he is supposed to meet her, and has most of his direct encounters with Milady at night. His last individual encounter with Milady ends in the morning light as d'Artagnan rushes from her house wearing Kitty's clothes. Comedy occurs during the daylight hours.

The dramatic climax of the novel takes place at night as the musketeers, d'Artagnan, the executioner, Lord de Winter, and the servants surround the house where Milady has sought refuge. Thunder, lightning, storm clouds, and then the rising moon create a dramatic scene with the contrasts between light and darkness. The majority of the actors in this scene become spectators observing the play of moonlight on the executioner's sword. Night may be a time for pleasure for lovers, but it is also a time for punishment of despicable crimes.

History forms the essential of Dumas's plot with real events providing the basis for much of the action and historical personages furnishing many of the characters. Even many of the secondary actions can be factually documented, including the story of the queen's diamonds. However, Dumas's use of people, events, and places expresses his imagination; he creates a new historical reality in the world of his novel. D'Artagnan's actual historical existence vanishes behind his words and actions. Dumas biographer André Maurois says that Dumas loved history but did not necessarily respect it: " 'What is history?' he said. 'It is the nail on which I can hang my novels' " (Maurois 172). Dumas uses contemporary historical sources as a starting point and is consistent with the facts, but simplifies and dramatizes them more than he changes them. Little touches reflecting seventeenth-century manners and dress or incidents and names add to the feel of the novel and a sense of historical authenticity. Inventiveness and imagination, the essentials of Dumas's style, are used so effectively that even over 160 years after the novel's publication readers are entertained by the exploits and adventures of d'Artagnan and his friends, and all the other characters involved in Dumas's imaginative world of reality.

## HISTORICAL CONTEXT

France enjoyed a period of stability and relative prosperity during the 1840s after the turmoil that had started in 1789 with the French Revolution. The country had gone through several changes of regime after the Revolution, including a republic, an empire, and the restoration of the Bourbon monarchy. As a result of the July 1830 Revolution, Louis-Philippe, from the Orléans branch of the French royal family, became king and governed as a parliamentary monarch, complete with a legislative assembly. By 1840 France was experiencing a period of political calm, economic prosperity, and peace. François Guizot, a historian who became a politician, served as prime minister throughout the 1840s until the Orleanist monarchy fell in 1848. He believed sincerely in the idea of a government by all the elites, that is, those men of wealth, family background, and education, and also believed in the principle of equal opportunity. Guizot felt that every man was free to get rich. If a man did not achieve wealth, he could only blame his own limitations, not an unjust society (Wright 122). Although highly unpopular as a politician, Guizot had the support of Louis-Philippe and was also adept at political maneuvering. For example, he offered hostile deputies salaried positions in the government. Guizot also encouraged business expansion, sometimes with government aid but most often through a hands-off policy (Wright 123).

The only major legislative act connected with Guizot's name occurred when he was minister of public instruction in 1833. The act established primary education schools in every one of France's 38,000 communes (municipal entities). The schools were neither free nor compulsory, but they were a step forward toward education for all children. Teachers received more training and also acquired more status and better working conditions. The expanded opportunities for at least an elementary education created a wider reading public, one that Dumas's novels would attract.

Louis-Philippe's government supported the business community through protective tariffs against imported products, a low level of taxation for businesses plus a policy of noninterference, government concessions, and financial guarantees. The regime also supported public works projects such as canals, roads, and railroads. However, both railroads and business enterprises developed more slowly in France than in other European countries, such as England and German states. The introduction of machines also progressed more slowly in France, as labor was cheap. Workers also objected, often violently, to being replaced by machines. The banking system was conservative and did not often risk capital on unknown men or projects. Banking and most industrial development remained in the hands of families well established financially before the Revolution.

Opportunities for political power were also based on birth and wealth. Louis-Philippe did reduce the entrance fee for eligible voters, and the number increased from 90,000 to about 170,000 in the early years of his reign (Wright 169). Owning land was still an important form of wealth, and those men considered part of the middle bourgeoisie could achieve higher social status, with an increase in wealth and lands. Some of the richest members of the upper bourgeoisie also acquired titles, becoming barons and counts.

Citizens such as shopkeepers and clerks were considered part of the lower bourgeoisie. While they couldn't gain enough wealth to rise to voting status, they did find a source of pride through service in the National Guard. Citizens who paid a direct tax became part of the guard and had to furnish their own weapons and uniforms. Although Charles X dissolved the guard in 1827, Louis-Philippe reconstituted it in 1831. However, the guard's discipline and influence diminished during the 1840s, and it did not support the monarchy in the Revolution of February 1848.

While the life of industrial workers and peasants employed on farms was not particularly favorable during the 1840s, the legal status of women rendered them the largest disadvantaged group. According to law the family was organized in an authoritarian and hierarchical fashion. The law designated the father as the sole manager of all family property, including that brought to the marriage by his wife. Divorce was illegal from 1816 to 1884, and penalties for adultery were much more severe for women than for men. Educational opportunities for girls were confined chiefly to the Catholic Church, and the first state secondary schools for girls were not established until the late 1860s. Fathers arranged their daughters' marriages as they pleased.

Rumbles of discontent were evident in France, especially among the middle class, as the 1840s continued. The poet Lamartine, who would play an important role in the Revolution of 1848, said as early as 1839 that France was bored (Wright 129). Prosperity and stability began to be equated with stagnation and cowardice. While Dumas was more concerned with writing entertaining novels and enjoying the results of his earnings, some of his contemporaries, such as Victor Hugo, were interested in doctrines of democracy or socialism as well as what they saw as the essential nobility of the common man. With the relative amount of freedom of expression in the 1840s, caricaturists such as Honoré Daumier used their cartoons to satirize the governing group, suggesting that those in authority were neither as respectable nor as dignified as they portrayed themselves.

Literature during the nineteenth century also reflected freedom of expression. By the time Dumas began seriously writing novels in the 1840s, the literary movement known as Romanticism had influenced all literary genres. The search for universal and abstract truth that had characterized seventeenth- and eighteenth-century literature in France gave way to the description of a concrete and specific experience. Poets were expressing more personal and visionary feelings in their poems and experimenting with rhythm by varying the number of syllables in a line of verse or changing the place of the accented syllable. Playwrights were no longer concerned with observing the unities of time, place, and action or with separating comic and tragic elements. Novelists, often inspired by the historical novels of the English writer Walter Scott, sought inspiration from past ages or in stories of adventure that kept the reader in suspense until the last moment.

In *The Three Musketeers*, Dumas reflected his era's interest in previous ages as well as his society. He saw himself as a writer whose chief purpose was to entertain the widest possible audience, not as a being apart from the common herd of humanity. The reading public was increasing in the nineteenth century with the increased opportunities for education and the achievement of a higher standard of living. Dumas and his public also profited from the new role of newspapers in publishing fiction by installments. Emile de Girardin started the custom in 1836 with his daily paper *La Presse*. Other newspapers followed *La Presse*'s lead, and those who could write stories that kept readers excited to read the next segment benefited from this means of publication (Hemmings 116). Not all nineteenth-century French novelists would follow Dumas's example. Gustave Flaubert deplored the century's increasing emphasis on mass production and viewed the writer more as a solitary artist, striving for perfection in his literary works. Dumas, seeing the writer as an entertainer, found nothing wrong in using collaborators or in profiting as much as possible from his efforts. His novels provided pleasure, and his readers appreciated his abilities as a storyteller. Considering the historical context within which Dumas wrote helps explain his wide audience in his own time. However, as a prime storyteller whose tales and characters reflect universal human emotions, he has transcended his time period to remain popular with a public who, more than 160 years later, also enjoys the entertainment to be found in a novel full of interesting people, places, and events, set in a different era.

# 4

## Alexandre Dumas
## *The Count of Monte Cristo*
### 1845

### BIOGRAPHICAL CONTEXT

The beginnings of *The Count of Monte Cristo* can be traced to a trip Dumas made in 1842 when he was living in Florence. He took Louis-Napoléon Bonaparte, nephew of the emperor, to visit the island of Elba, an excursion requested by the young prince's father, Jerome Bonaparte. They decided to go hunting on a nearby island, but the peasant accompanying them said that hunting would be even better on another island, also close by, the island of Monte Cristo. However, since the island was deserted, anyone who landed there was subject to quarantine for five or six days. Dumas and the prince discussed taking such a risk but followed instead Dumas's suggestion of sailing around the island. He wanted to fix the geographical location in his memory so that he could later give the island's name to a novel he would write in memory of the trip taken with the prince (Stowe 116).

Dumas did not start writing the novel immediately, but by 1844, the same year as the complete publication of *The Three Musketeers*, *The Count of Monte Cristo* began appearing in serial form in the *Journal des Débats*. The last episode concluded in the January 15, 1846 issue, and the novel was published in its entirety (18 volumes) that same month.

Dumas's inspiration for the plot of this novel came from an anecdote he discovered in police files. A poor shoemaker named François Picaud had been falsely denounced and imprisoned for seven years. During his time in prison Picaud had served an Italian cleric, a political prisoner, and had inherited the

Italian's fortune at the latter's death. Picaud then took revenge on those who had wronged him. Dumas's first version started with his hero, the Count of Monte Cristo, in Rome, befriending a young Frenchman. The Frenchman would be Monte Cristo's guide in Paris as the count sought to punish those who had caused his own false imprisonment. Maquet, Dumas's collaborator, suggested that this part of the story should follow an account of the count's early life. In one of his collections of memoirs, written many years later, Dumas tells of discussing the idea with Maquet and deciding that his collaborator was right. The next day the two roughed out the novel's general outline; they worked together over the next year and a half, refining and elaborating characters, motivations, and details of action (Stowe 117–18).

During the same period, 1844–1846, Dumas was working on other novels and plays, both with Maquet and alone, planning his own Château de Monte Cristo to be built at Port-Marly near Paris, and finalizing his separation from Ida Ferrier. He and his son were sharing a country residence in Saint-Germain-en-Laye and getting along as well as they ever had. Dumas *fils* did not have a good relationship with his stepmother and was relieved at her departure for Italy after the separation. Dumas *père* enjoyed guests' visits in the country, but left a party or a dinner to return to his writing when copy came from Maquet (Schopp 330). The theatre continued to be part of Dumas's life, and a play titled *Les Mousquetaires* was performed at the Théâtre de l'Ambigu in October 1845. The play was based on events from *Vingt Ans après*, a novel chronicling the musketeers 20 years after their first adventures. The following year saw the completion of *The Count of Monte Cristo*, the publication of at least four other novels, and a trip to Spain and Algeria for father and son. Dumas's life would continue to follow a similar pattern until his death in 1870. Making money in large amounts, he spent even more. Writing, traveling, and forming new relationships with various women, Dumas never ceased being an imaginative storyteller whose works enjoyed popular acclaim during his lifetime and whose popularity continues to the present day.

On November 30, 2002, to recognize the bicentennial of his birth, Dumas received the ultimate accolade from the French government. His remains were transported to the Panthéon in Paris where they joined the tombs of other important French political figures and writers, including Victor Hugo.

## PLOT DEVELOPMENT

The plot of *The Count of Monte Cristo* is organized into three sections, each section featuring a city as the central point for its action: Marseilles, Rome, and Paris. The first 30 chapters center on Marseilles, the following 8 involve Rome and its surrounding countryside, and the rest of the novel, chapters 39 through 117, takes place in Paris and nearby locations. The highly intricate story is quite easy to follow as it centers on Edmond Dantès, a young, promising, and relatively innocent seaman, who suffers an extreme fall from happiness yet is able to rise again to a position of wealth and power. His use of that power to orchestrate vengeance on those who caused the fall leads to a final disappearance but one that indicates the probability of happiness.

Dantès's story opens when he returns with the ship *Pharaon* to Marseilles on February 24, 1815. Dantès, the first mate, has taken charge of the ship when the captain dies at sea. During the voyage the ship stops at the island of Elba, where the deposed emperor Napoléon is in exile, on orders of the dying captain. Dantès receives a letter on Elba that he is to deliver to Bonapartist supporters in Paris. He is welcomed back to Marseilles by Monsieur Morrel, the ship's owner, and promised a permanent captaincy before the ship sails again. Dantès has two goals before leaving for Paris: settle his father's debts with their neighbor, Caderousse, and marry his fiancée Mercédès. However, unbeknownst to him, Dantès has two adversaries: the envious ship's accountant, Danglars, and a jealous fisherman, Fernand, who also loves Mercédès. Fernand and Danglars, as Caderousse watches, compose a letter to the king's prosecutor that accuses Dantès of being a Bonapartist conspirator. Fernand, encouraged subtly by Danglars, sends the letter to the prosecutor. During the party celebrating his forthcoming wedding, Dantès is hauled off to appear before the prosecutor, Monsieur Noirtier de Villefort. Villefort, at first sympathetic to Dantès, is an ambitious man who is supporting the royalists in power after Napoléon's fall and trying to ignore the fact that his own father still supports the exiled Napoléon. Therefore, he decides to destroy the letter accusing Dantès, swears Dantès, who doesn't understanding what is happening, to secrecy, and sends him to prison so that he can never reveal what Villefort has done. The prison is the Château d'If, an island fortress just outside the Marseilles harbor.

Several chapters recount the efforts of Mercédès and Morrel to learn what is happening to Dantès while Villefort is working to cover his political bases. Villefort goes to Paris and is there when Napoléon lands on the French mainland. Villefort meets with his father, who is convinced Napoléon will succeed. The reader learns that Mercédès, unaware of the plot, is grateful for Fernand's support, that Fernand and Caderousse both serve in the army, and that Danglars goes to work in Spain.

The next chapters chronicle Dantès's imprisonment and how his loneliness and ignorance of why he is imprisoned torture him. After six years all hope of release is gone, and Dantès decides to commit suicide by refusing to eat. One day, growing weaker, he hears noises—another prisoner trying to escape. When the other man breaks through and finds himself in Dantès's cell, the latter begins to know Abbé Faria, the prisoner all the guards call mad. The Abbé has been promising for years to share an immense fortune, whose location only he knows, with anyone who will help or allow him to escape. The story is too fantastic for anyone to believe him, even Dantès. However, in Abbé Faria, Dantès has found a second father, a resourceful, intelligent, and compassionate man. Through their years of meeting in secrecy, Faria is able to give Dantès the academic education the young man has lacked as well as lead him to understand who was responsible for his imprisonment. Their bond grows close, and when Faria grows too ill to escape, Dantès refuses to leave him.

Dantès escapes after Faria's death by taking the place of Faria's body in the sack the guards will take out to bury. His feat of freeing himself from the heavy canvas bag as it sinks toward the bottom of the sea is an extraordinary but believable act from a man desperate for freedom after 14 years in prison. He is able to swim to a nearby island through the stormy seas and joins a group of smugglers. Eventually he reaches the island of Monte Cristo and finds the treasure Faria insisted he had buried there. The treasure is real and overwhelmingly immense. After selling four diamonds from the treasure, Dantès gives money to one of the smugglers who has befriended him. The man is to purchase a small ship and sail to Marseilles in order to learn what has happened to Dantès's father and Mercédès. He returns with the news that the father is dead and Mercédès has vanished. Dantès himself, in the yacht he has purchased, then goes to Marseilles. In his disguise as an Englishman, Lord Wilmore, he buys the building where his father had lived and rewards the people he questions in the village where Mercédès lived with a new fishing boat.

Dantès takes on a new disguise when he visits Caderousse—that of a priest, Abbé Busoni. He finds Caderousse and his shrewish wife running an inn that attracts very few clients. Abbé Busoni reports that Dantès is dead but has entrusted the Abbé with rewarding those who had helped his loved ones. Caderousse tells the Abbé that Dantès's father died of starvation, refusing help. He also recounts how he observed while in a drunken state the plot of Danglars and Fernand to denounce Dantès. Ship-owner Morrel, says Caderousse, tried hard to intercede for Dantès but is now ruined because of lost ships and others' bankruptcies. Danglars is now a wealthy baron, and Fernand, also with a fortune and a high position in society, married Mercédès. Caderousse doesn't know what has happened to Villefort, the prosecutor, other than he married and left Marseilles. The Abbé gives Caderousse a diamond as a reward.

Disguised as an English clerk, Dantès visits the mayor in Marseilles. He learns more about the role of Villefort in Dantès's imprisonment. The mayor also reports that Morrel is a man of honor, undeserving of the financial misfortunes he is enduring. The disguised Dantès meets with Morrel and also his son Maximilien and his daughter Julie. Dantès intervenes in Morrel's affairs and saves the family from financial ruin. He even supplies a new ship so that Morrel can start over. Watching the arrival of this ship and the family's happiness, a man in the crowd is taken out to his own ship, remarking, "farewell, goodness, humanity, gratitude. Farewell all those feelings that nourish and illuminate the heart! I have taken the place of Providence to reward the good; now let the avenging God make way for me to punish the wrongdoer!" (260). The reader feels certain that the unidentified man is Edmond Dantès.

The second section of the novel prepares the way for Dantès, now transformed into the wealthy and mysterious Count of Monte Cristo, to set in motion the vengeance he seeks. As an opening scene, a young Frenchman, the Baron Franz d'Epinay, stops at the island of Monte Cristo to shoot goats. There he has a strange experience with a man who calls himself Sinbad the sailor. The two visit a cave filled with unimaginable riches, and Franz accepts a teaspoonful of hashish from Sinbad and experiences some strange and wonderful dreams. Continuing his trip, Franz goes to Rome where he joins Albert de Morcerf, the son of Fernand and Mercédès (Fernand now has the title of Count of Morcerf).

The Roman adventures of Albert and Franz take place in 1838, during the Carnival before Lent. They meet the mysterious Count of Monte Cristo in their hotel. Franz recognizes the count as Sinbad. The count comes to the rescue when Albert is captured by bandits. He secures Albert's release without paying any ransom. In his gratitude Albert invites the count to visit him in Paris in exactly three months, on May 21 at 10:30 A.M. The discerning reader can see the hand of the count behind the experiences the two young men have during the Carnival season and is aware that the count has achieved his goal of an entrée into Paris society by his rescue of Albert.

The third and final section of the novel involves the count with all those who had been instrumental in his arrest and imprisonment, including their children. Although all the count's adventures from the time he obtains his fortune to his arrival in Paris are never completely revealed, Dumas does use chapters where other characters talk about the count to give the reader information necessary to follow the story's development.

The count begins his Parisian stay by breakfasting with Albert and his friends, who include Maximilien Morrel. These young men are very impressed by the mysterious person of the count. During this breakfast references are made to Maximilien's sister's happy marriage, a proposed marriage of Albert to Danglars's daughter Eugénie, and the count's beautiful slave Haydée.

Before leaving Albert, the count is introduced to the young man's parents, who express their gratitude for their son's rescue. The father, Fernand, has no idea that the count is Dantès, but both the count and Mercédès turn pale at the sight of one another, evidently an indication that Mercédès may realize who the count really is.

In the next few chapters Bertuccio, the count's steward, reveals his connection with the history of the house just purchased by the count in the Paris suburb of Auteuil. This tale from the past involves Villefort and a child he had with his mistress, a child born in that very house and buried alive by its father in the garden but saved by Bertuccio. The reader learns in a later chapter that the mistress is Madame Danglars. The baby grows up to become a criminal and is manipulated by the count to present himself in Paris as an Italian aristocrat. He too will play a role in his parents' downfall. The reader also learns of Bertuccio's involvement with Caderousse, as well as how he became the count's steward.

Chapter by chapter Dumas unfolds the story of the count's vengeance. Relentlessly, this enigmatic man exposes his enemies' past crimes or initiates their exposure by someone else. He also puts actions into motion that make each object of his vengeance obligated to him. The count has already saved Albert de Morcerf from the Italian bandits. Now in Paris, his servant Ali is able to stop the horses running away with Madame de Villefort and her son, thus earning the gratitude of Monsieur de Villefort. The count is able to make Danglars his banker by suggesting that other banks might be more obliging, thus setting up this man, motivated solely by money, for eventual bankruptcy when the count demands cash for the millions he has on deposit. He has established new connections with Fernand, Villefort, Danglars, and even Caderousse, and will poke and prod until all four have lost what they most value.

The 79 chapters in this third section move smoothly from the revealing of past information to the telling of events involving the various characters in the novel's present time. Because Dumas relies on narration by the characters to impart knowledge of the past or move the present along, the reader keeps up with what is happening. Dumas also is able to move the action from one set of characters to another without losing the reader or the momentum of the story. In addition, because these people are members of the same segment of Parisian society, they cross paths at various points and are believably involved in each other's lives.

The Count of Monte Cristo obtains his vengeance as both Caderousse and Fernand are dead, Villefort is mad, and Danglars is financially ruined by the novel's end. The children fare somewhat better as the count begins to realize that not all the sins of the fathers must be visited on their children. When Albert de Morcerf learns the truth of his father's ignoble actions against Edmond Dantès and in Haydée's homeland, he vows to make his own way in the world and takes up a military career. Eugénie Danglars avoids two unwanted marriages: her father refuses the proposed marriage with Albert for what he considers a better one with Benedetto, the pseudo-Italian aristocrat; the marriage contract with Benedetto is about to be signed when the groom is arrested for the murder of Caderousse. Eugénie, with some help from the count, is able to leave for Rome with her friend Louise where she plans to earn her own living. And the count actively helps Maximilien Morrel marry Valentine de Villefort when he realizes the depth and sincerity of the young couple's love.

As the novel closes, the count realizes that he has done that which he set out to do: his enemies have suffered nearly as much as he did during the 14 years in the Château d'If. Although he has achieved his purpose, the count expresses some doubt about some of the unforeseen consequences of his vengeance. He is about to leave the reunited Maximilien and Valentine, asking them to take Haydée into their care. Haydée, however, refuses to be parted from the count, whom she loves. Perhaps the Count of Monte Cristo can start a new life through this woman who attaches him to life: "God, I can see, does not wish my victory to end with that regret. I wished to punish myself, but God wants to pardon me. So, love me, Haydée! Who knows? Perhaps your love will make me forget what I have to forget" (1076).

## CHARACTER DEVELOPMENT

Events develop the characters in *The Count of Monte Cristo*, and the pace of these events is too rapid for Dumas to dwell on his characters' psychological depths. The reader comes to know them through their actions, what they say to themselves and to others, and what others say about them.

Edmond Dantès, the young sailor of the novel's opening section, is the most complex of all the characters. Because of what happens to him at the moment of his youthful happiness, he undergoes a transformation during his imprisonment and returns to the world a different person, one so obsessed with being the agent of Providence that he loses sight of human emotions, including his own.

From the moment of his return to Marseilles in the ship *Pharaon*, Dantès is open and frank in his actions and reactions. After informing the ship's owner about the voyage, his next thought is to see his father and then his fiancée. While he realizes that he and Danglars do not like each other personally, Dantès is willing to say that the purser carries out his duties faithfully and competently. He does not recognize Danglars's envy of his position nor is he aware of Fernand's jealousy of Mercédès's love for him. Innocent and naïve, Dantès cannot fathom the reasons behind his arrest or his subsequent imprisonment. During the early years of his incarceration, Dantès goes through every range of human emotion, from pride in his innocence to hope of justice to despair and finally to thoughts of suicide by starvation. His interactions with others are limited to prison personnel, but the reader sympathizes with this unjustly imprisoned man and relates to the thoughts he expresses in the silence of his cell.

Dantès's life changes when he meets the Abbé Faria, another prisoner innocent of the charges against him. His time with the Abbé is one of learning and testing. At the age of 19 Dantès has learned much about sailing and the art of leadership, but his education has not progressed beyond these things. From the Abbé he learns more languages, history, the sciences, and even basic human psychology. He observes the ways in which the Abbé thinks and analyzes information; for example, Faria determines by questioning Dantès who was responsible for the original denunciation and the role of the magistrate in Dantès's continued imprisonment. Dantès's character is also tested in this relationship when the Abbé's repeated seizures prevent the two from escaping together. The young man refuses to leave without his beloved friend and thereby proves his nobility of heart, his loyalty, and his worthiness to know the Abbé's secret, the location of the hidden treasure.

Edmond Dantès is a different person when he escapes from the Château d'If. Physically, intellectually, and emotionally changed by 14 years in prison, he is now set to discover what has happened to his loved ones and his enemies. With the buried treasure uncovered and available to finance his new life, Dantès is now the Count of Monte Cristo, enigmatic, impassive, and skilled at creating the image he wants to project. His character and personality are often described by others—he is a vampire according to the Countess G. in Rome—or by himself as when he tells Villefort that he is a superior being, impenetrable and capable of achieving the goals he has set. He goes implacably on his chosen way, seeking vengeance against those who have wronged him without being concerned about how others may be hurt in the process. The count exposes past crimes or forces their exposure, works behind the scenes to set up the catastrophes designed to ruin the lives of his enemies, and appears to have walled off his human feelings. He is an intelligent instrument of an implacable Providence, and readers may now feel an aversion to this count who seems to have lost his humanity. However, he begins to wonder if he has gone too far when he sees Maximilien Morrel's love for Valentine de Villefort. From that point on, humanity returns to the count's nature and can be seen in his actions; he protects Valentine and even mourns the death of Madame Villefort and her son Edouard, although Madame has poisoned Valentine's grandparents and attempted to kill Valentine. The count refuses to accept Mercédès's self-reproach for her marriage to Fernand and finally, with Haydée, sails away, leaving with Maximilien and Valentine a letter concluding with the lessons that he has learned: he is not God's equal, he feels remorse in his heart, life is good with the person one loves, and wisdom is summarized in the two words "wait" and "hope" (1077).

The young Edmond Dantès is more three-dimensional than when he becomes the Count of Monte Cristo. His emotions and his development are more evident; he is recognizable as a human being. The count is seen through his actions and the images others form of him; he is unknowable as a person. He becomes human again as he begins to reach his ultimate goal and realizes what he has lost in this quest. This character in all his aspects provides the impetus for the intriguing and dramatic story. He is more than the symbol for themes that the author wishes to illustrate, and he is believable even at his most enigmatic.

The four characters responsible for Dantès's downfall—Caderousse, Fernand, Danglars, and Villefort—are portrayed through their ongoing evil deeds. Caderousse shows his greed from the novel's beginning: he takes the money Edmond left for his father's care as payment for a debt that the son had already paid. He dooms himself further when he relates what he knows about the past 14 years to the count, disguised as the Abbé Busoni; for example, Caderousse made no effort to help Dantès's father, who starved to death. Caderousse's actions after receiving the valuable diamond from Abbé Busoni are consistent with his character as a man of greed who is never content with what he has. His criminal deeds are revealed by other characters who tell how his life has intersected with theirs. In the novel's final section, he extorts money from Benedetto when the latter is playing the role of the rich Italian aristocrat and robbing the count's house. His stabbing as he leaves the house after the count has stopped the robbery confirms for the count that Caderousse has brought on his punishment by his own actions. The assassin is Benedetto, a criminal friend whom Caderousse also betrayed. Monte Cristo tells the dying man of the many opportunities to become an honest man he wasted. When Monte Cristo reveals himself as Edmond Dantès, one of the friends Caderousse betrayed, Caderousse repents, seeing in the count the reflection of divine justice. The reader may question why it's the revelation of the count's true identity that elicits repentance, but the scene is effective as an illustration of the theme of vengeance.

Fernand, the fisherman and sometimes smuggler at the novel's beginning, lets himself be overcome by jealousy and sends the fatal note denouncing Dantès. When he reappears in the story line, the reader learns through what other characters discover and relate that Fernand has risen to his title of Count de Morcerf by his betrayal of others. Fernand never loses his love for Mercédès, however, and also loves his son Albert. He is immensely relieved to see Albert returning after the duel he was to fight with the count. Going to the count for an explanation and an offer to fight the duel himself, Fernand is crushed to learn the count's true identity. Once he learns that Mercédès and Albert have left the family mansion and rejected him, suicide is the only answer for Fernand. His love for wife and son is the redeeming characteristic of this man who otherwise hides behind the arrogance of the social and financial position he has achieved through betrayal of others.

Danglars's jealousy and hatred of Edmond Dantès are evident from his first words to Monsieur Morrel when the ship *Pharaon* returns to Marseilles in the novel's first chapter. Skirting outright accusations, Danglars intimates that Dantès's visit to the island of Elba was not innocent. His manipulative traits are visible as he works on Fernand and Caderousse to denounce Dantès. The cold and calculating aspects of his character are also seen in his negotiations for his daughter's marriage. Danglars will drop Albert de Morcerf as a potential son-in-law when Andrea Cavalcanti, also known as Benedetto, appears to be a more prestigious candidate. Family means nothing to Danglars compared to his money, and the Count of Monte Cristo realizes this, manipulating this enemy so that his fortune is lost. Danglars is a psychologically believable character whose path to ruin is both consistent and predictable.

Villefort's character is defined by his overwhelming political ambition. Yet Dumas is able to nuance the magistrate's personality by indicating hints of human feelings. The betrothal party prior to his first marriage shows Villefort with more regard for his fiancée than for her social position. In spite of his feelings about his father's Bonapartist convictions, Villefort does see that the elderly man is cared for after his stroke. Villefort is another father who ignores his daughter's feelings about her proposed marriage, but he grieves when he believes Valentine has succumbed to the poison administered by her stepmother. Once he realizes that the son he fathered in his adulterous affair with Madame de Danglars is the criminal he is persecuting, he is sure that his actions precipitated Madame de Villefort's own crimes. Too late to save her and their son, Villefort expresses repentance as he shows the count their bodies and then goes mad. Of the four initial enemies of Edmond Dantès, Villefort is perhaps the most interesting as Dumas depicts his character through his actions and the reactions he expresses. As despicable as the others, Villefort seems to be the only one who fully understands what he did; this knowledge precipitates his madness.

Another group of characters are a positive force in Edmond Dantès's life before he becomes the count: Mercédès, Monsieur Morrel, and the Abbé Faria. Mercédès, Edmond's fiancée, does all she can to work for his release. The reader learns more about Mercédès's life when Caderousse tells about her efforts to help Dantès's father, her marriage with Fernand because she had no other source of support, and how she has educated herself to alleviate her unhappiness. Her character becomes more evident when she reappears in the novel during the Paris section. Her somewhat melancholy appearance, the concern her son expresses for her health, and her attempt to welcome the count to her home, all reveal a woman whose love is directed toward her son but whose life is not happy. When she sees that her son's life is threatened by a duel with the count, personal honor becomes more important than the family name which she knows Fernand purchased with tarnished coin: Mercédès tells Albert the truth about his father's acts. In the farewell meeting with the count, Mercédès berates herself for her lack of courage when Edmond disappeared and also blames herself for Fernand's death. Seen chiefly through others' eyes until she relates what she is thinking and feeling in the final farewell scene with the count, Mercédès is a sympathetic and poignant character.

Monsieur Morrel is a man of honor who lives up to his commitments to the best of his ability. He plays his role during the first section of the novel, supporting Edmond and never losing faith in the young man's innocence. When business misfortunes threaten to overwhelm him, his main concern is for his family and his employees. This character is revealed through his actions and his conversations with his family, especially with his son.

The Abbé Faria becomes Edmond Dantès's surrogate father when the two meet in prison. The older man is seen by his jailers as crazy because of his tale of buried treasure. Even Edmond is not completely convinced of the treasure's existence, but he sincerely appreciates the Abbé's friendship, knowledge, and ability to reason and teach. The interactions between the two prisoners reveal the Abbé's character as resolute, humane, and resourceful.

The younger generation is not a concern to the count at the beginning of his quest, except for perhaps Maximilien Morrel. However, they are interesting characters in their own right. Maximilien, seen briefly as his father faces bankruptcy, is introduced again at the beginning of the Paris section as someone who has saved the life of one of Albert de Morcerf's friends. He reveals his faithfulness and sense of honor through his relationship to Valentine de

Villefort, believing there is no happiness for him if he cannot marry Valentine. As is true for Dumas-created characters in general, Maximilien is portrayed through his actions and conversations, with little introspection. His behavior is predictable and believable.

Valentine herself is a traditional daughter in a wealthy nineteenth-century family. She sees no other recourse than the marriage her father arranges, although she loves Maximilien. When the proposed marriage falls through, Valentine gains courage and vows to marry only Maximilien. A sweet and loving young woman devoted to her paralyzed grandfather, Valentine represents pure young womanhood. She is conventional but sympathetic, and the reader can be pleased that she will not have to pay for her father's sins.

Eugénie Danglars is less conventional. Again the reader learns of Eugénie's character through the reactions of others to her. The young men of her social set find her handsome but cold; Albert feels that she might make a satisfactory mistress but not a wife. Eugénie herself expresses her opinions about marriage and life in conversations with friends and finally with her father. These comments and interactions make Eugénie's secret departure for Rome with her friend Louise an inevitable and believable outcome for this young woman whose yearning for independence highlights her character.

Albert de Morcerf, son of Fernand and Mercédès, is the count's instrument for entrance into Parisian society. On his first appearance in the novel Albert is a somewhat frivolous young man whose conversations with his traveling companion, Franz d'Epinay, reveal his interests to fall along the lines of wine and women rather than art and music. His casual air is also seen in his encounter with the bandits who abduct him, but he is truly grateful to the count for obtaining his release. Albert's sense of honor, however, brings him to challenge the count to a duel in order to uphold the family name. This same sense of honor leads him to renounce the family fortune, treacherously obtained, in order to make his own way. Albert explains his own actions in conversations with his friends, with the count, and finally with his mother. His character is not so much transformed as it is revealed as he is tested by events and decides to act according to what he believes is right.

Benedetto, alias Andrea Cavalcanti, is the offspring of an adulterous relationship between Villefort and Madame Danglars. He is as evil as his parents are despicable. A criminal almost from birth, Benedetto is perfectly willing to play any role that will be financially profitable. Other characters recount his early history, but he condemns himself with his own words and actions. He is also part of the count's revenge against Villefort and is last seen in the courtroom on trial for murder, telling how the presiding magistrate, Villefort, had attempted to murder his own infant son, that is, Benedetto himself.

Benedetto's own fate is left in the courtroom as Villefort, overwhelmed by the realization of his own acts, removes himself from the case.

Madame Danglars and the second Madame de Villefort are also characters who reveal themselves through their actions. Dumas does not explain Madame Danglars's motivations for her affairs, her financial manipulations, or her lack of warmth toward her daughter. It is sufficient to show her punishment: her shame is brought out in court, her daughter has left, and her lover drops her. Although she still has money because of financial speculations with her lover, she is left with no reputation and no role in society. Madame de Villefort is depicted as a woman with one reigning passion, her young son Edouard. In order that he might inherit an immense fortune, she poisons four people that she feels stand between her child and this fortune. Only her stepdaughter Valentine survives. Her actions are prepared for the reader through a conversation she has with the count on the subject of poisons. When her husband denounces her crimes, she kills herself and their son. Again, Dumas uses what others say to and about a character, plus the character's own words and deeds, to create a believable female character. She serves as one of the instruments of the count's vengeance but makes her own choices and lets her maternal love become tainted by obsessive jealousy.

Monsieur Noirtier, Villefort's father and Valentine's grandfather, is paralyzed by a stroke and cannot speak by the time he appears in person. His political activities during the Bonapart era are revealed through others' accounts, but his love for Valentine and his efforts on her behalf are communicated effectively through facial signs that she and others can understand.

Franz d'Epinay, Lucien Debray, and the journalist Beauchamp are secondary characters involved chiefly in the Paris section of the story. All three serve to enlighten the reader about the main characters' motives and actions but are not particularly memorable as individuals.

Numerous minor characters have roles in the working out of the story lines in this novel and are interesting more in terms of the plot than in their own right. However, Haydée, the count's slave, deserves special mention. The count purchased Haydée after her father, the Ali Pasha of Janina, was betrayed by Fernand and killed. Haydée is the object of much speculation by Parisian society. She is completely devoted to the count, yet acts of her own volition in appearing to testify before the House of Peers whose members are judging the accusations against Fernand, who is a member of this body by virtue of his position as the Baron de Morcerf. Haydée relates the story of Fernand's treachery with a calm dignity that shows an inner strength. Her own words and actions reveal her character. As the novel ends, she is finally able to convince the count of her love by refusing his attempt to leave her in the care of Maximilien and Valentine.

## THEMES

The themes of revenge, betrayal, wrongful imprisonment, redemption, and honor that play out in *The Count of Monte Cristo* can be most clearly seen against the background of the fall, living death, and resurrection of the main character, Edmond Dantès. Innocent at the novel's beginning, this young man is unaware of the dangers surrounding him but is also wary of the happiness that appears to be his. At his engagement dinner he notes, "Happiness is like one of those palaces on an enchanted island, its gates guarded by dragons. One must fight to gain it" (34).

Dantès falls into a living death when he is put into solitary confinement in the lowest dungeon of the Château d'If. The education he gains from Abbé Faria transforms him as much as his sufferings do. He is able to leave his imprisonment as a transformed being, but one whose sole reason for existing is to gain revenge on those who injured him—with a short pause to reward those who tried to help him. Revenge will be the recompense for his suffering, and it is to be as slow and painful as possible for its targets, as slow and painful as Dantès's 14 years in prison were for him.

Once he has escaped from the Château d'If, found the treasure buried on the island of Monte Cristo, and become the Count of Monte Cristo, this transformed person begins his quest. As he explains to Villefort, he has his pride, but a pride that he lays before God. However, the count also relates that he has asked God to take him into Providence, the symbol of the count's ultimate ambition, and that indeed, God has made him one of the agents of Providence (477). As such the count will resort to manipulation and work quietly behind the scenes, so to speak, to allow his targets to bring about their own destruction, since revenge through merely killing the target is not sufficient for this agent of Providence. During the Rome episode the count expresses his feelings on slow and deliberate revenge in a discussion with Albert de Morcerf and Franz d'Epinay, asking if a few seconds of pain are sufficient punishment for one who has caused years of suffering: "in return for a slow, deep, infinite, eternal pain, I should return as nearly as possible a pain equivalent to the one inflicted on me" (333).

Throughout most of his quest, the count remains convinced that he is the agent of Providence and that his targets are bringing about their own destruction because of past and present sins. He feels no concern when his enemies' children suffer also, murmuring when he sees Albert de Morcerf's distress while reading his mother's letter about his father's actions, "It is written that the sins of the fathers shall be visited on the sons, even to the third and fourth generation" (820). In his meeting with Mercédès before the scheduled duel with Albert, the count insists that he is not the cause of Fernand's downfall: "These are not misfortunes, they are a punishment. I am not the one who has struck Monsieur de Morcerf; Providence is punishing him" (849). When the count tells Mercédès that he will not kill Albert but will let himself be killed, for her sake, he is still concerned with appearing before the world as the agent of Providence. His pride in the role he is playing drives the count to add a codicil to his will to explain his act. He calls his decision "rightful pride, nothing more" but wants the world to know that his decision not to kill Albert is made by his own free will (856).

However, the count's conviction that he has acted as he should because his quest is righteous is severely shaken when he cannot save young Edouard, Villefort's son. The count has set up the boy's mother in a way, giving her the drug that is benign or poisonous depending on the dose. Madame de Villefort kills herself and Edouard when her husband reveals that he knows the truth of her use of the drug to poison four people. The count realizes that the death of this child means he has gone beyond the limits of vengeance. When Maximilien asks if the count has anything more to do in Paris, the latter replies, "Pray God that I have not already done too much" (1025). During his farewell to Mercédès the count expresses a similar remorse, noting that from a trusting and forgiving individual he had become "vengeful, secretive and cruel—or, rather, impassive like fate itself, which is deaf and blind.... Woe betide whomsoever I met on my path!" (1034).

The Count of Monte Cristo, having avenged himself on his enemies, looks into "the abyss of doubt" (1036). A visit to the Château d'If brings back the bitter memories of his living death in that place, and these memories awaken again the thirst for vengeance. The sight of the Abbé Faria's bed and then the recovery of the book written by Faria on strips of cloth remove his doubts about the essential justice of this revenge: the first words he reads in the book are his vindication—"You will pull the dragon's teeth and trample the lions underfoot, said the Lord" (1043). However, the Count of Monte Cristo wants to accomplish a final good deed. He has tested the depth of Maximilien's love and grief for Valentine and can restore the young lovers to each other. The count's own redemption remains somewhat ambiguous—he has no remorse for encouraging his enemies on the path of their own destruction. However, he does renounce visiting the sins of the fathers on their children by helping Albert de Morcerf, Eugénie Danglars, and Valentine de Villefort and by regretting that he was unable to save Edouard de Villefort. Dumas, at least, believes that the count has another chance for happiness, for the count and Haydée sail off together. Redemption in this novel is summed up in the final phrase: wait and hope.

The count's wrongful imprisonment is, of course, the reason for his desire for revenge, the theme that plays out through the novel, and an important aspect of this theme. Abbé Faria's imprisonment is also unjust; he says it is because he wanted a united Italy, a plan unacceptable to the ruling princes and the Vatican. Both men were also betrayed, the count by Fernand and Danglars with Caderousse's knowledge and Villefort's compliance (Villefort promised Dantès his help but sacrificed the young man to his own political ambitions); the Abbé accuses the "royal simpleton" in whom he had put his trust but is not specific concerning this person's identity (131). While death keeps the Abbé from exacting revenge, his instruction and guidance enable Dantès to become the Count of Monte Cristo and achieve his goal. Dumas appears to suggest that only the superior man, morally and intellectually, can counteract injustice.

Honor is also a subsidiary theme to revenge. It is most clearly evident in Albert de Morcerf when he believes himself obligated to challenge the count to a duel in order to uphold his own family's honor. Albert believes the count is responsible for making public his father Fernand's dishonorable acts in betraying the Ali Pasha of Janina, Haydée's father. When Albert learns the extent of his own father's betrayals, his honor impels him to call off the duel and reject his father and especially the family fortune in order to make his own way in the world. The count's honor, in turn, leads him to the decision to let Albert kill him once he has promised Mercédès that he will not kill her son. Mercédès's honor causes her to tell Albert the truth she has learned about Fernand's role in the count's imprisonment and like her son, she refuses to profit from the fortune Fernand gained through his many dishonorable actions. And when Fernand is being judged by his peers, Haydée comes to the House of Peers to relate the truth of what happened in Janina. She emphasizes that the count does not know of her decision to tell her story, but that she has long looked for an opportunity to avenge her father's betrayal. Being a woman, Haydée's honor and revenge are fulfilled through words, not deeds. Fernand has no defense for her accusations.

Through the long and complex development and resolution of the revenge theme, with its related themes of wrongful imprisonment, betrayal, and honor, Dumas the novelist achieves his goal: his hero is avenged, and good ultimately triumphs over evil, with direct help from his hero. The count, while no longer the innocent Edmond Dantès who loves his Mercédès, believes that his cause was just, that in spite of the suffering of some innocents, God has given him a second chance at happiness with Haydée. The count has reached the point where he too can wait and hope.

## NARRATIVE STYLE

A dramatist before he was a novelist, Dumas uses techniques from his theatrical writing in *The Count of Monte Cristo:* he relies on dialogue to present both characters and actions; he ends chapters at a point where the curtain could come down and leave the audience waiting for the next scene. Dumas avoids, for the most part, interjecting his personal comments about ideas and characters. He does rely on long narratives at various moments in the novel to provide the reader information necessary for understanding how what transpired in the past is affecting present actions. For example, in chapters 42 through 45, Bertuccio, the count's steward, relates how his life had intersected with both Villefort's and Caderousse's and who Bertuccio really is. The count knows most, if not all, of these events, but the reader must hear them in order to follow the story's unfolding.

Dumas's style in *The Count of Monte Cristo* shows both romantic and realistic elements. French writers, and readers, in the first half of the nineteenth century were intrigued and attracted by the exotic and the fantastic. Dumas's imagination created a fabulous treasure, hidden in an underground grotto, that seems to be unbelievable until Dantès actually finds it, exactly as the Abbé Faria had described. And Dantès discovers the treasure after an astonishing escape from prison. Franz d'Epinay's experience on the island in the grotto is equally fantastic, and Franz himself finds the adventure unreal. His dreams in the grotto are colored by the drug the count (aka Sinbad the sailor in this scene) gives him, and the use of a drug such as hashish represented escape and heightened perceptions in the 1840s. When the reader first meets Haydée, she is dressed in her native attire and reclining against cushions, a picture resembling a faraway world. The count himself is a Romantic hero, adventuresome, solitary, mysterious, and powerful.

The novel begins and ends on the Mediterranean coast, where European cultures encounter directly those from the Orient, a region that nineteenth-century French writers and readers found exotic and intriguing. Beyond the setting, Dumas incorporates this interest by references to the Greek struggle for independence from the Turkish empire in the 1820s (the story of Haydée) and to the French conquest of Algeria in the 1830s (Albert de Morcerf joins the military detachment sailing to Algiers).

Dumas, however, anchors his fantastic and exotic elements in a realistic environment. The settings are identifiable, described briefly but concretely:

Marseilles, Rome, and Paris are real cities depicted in the novel as they were in the 1840s, complete with street names and references to real places. Even the hotel in the Rome section was one known to Dumas, and the other Roman landmarks would have been recognized by both traveler and resident. But Dumas is not presenting a travel guide to Rome, or to any of the other places mentioned in the novel. He is creating an atmosphere that his readers can both feel and accept through a judicious use of references to real people such as artists and political figures, to real events such as Napoléon's return from Elba to France in 1815, and to real operas and plays that were being presented in Paris during the 1840s. Yet *The Count of Monte Cristo* is not a historical novel but more a novel of manners, with its emphasis on human behavior in action. It is an adventure story that goes beyond the factual event that inspired its author. This story takes place in a time and world that his first readers would recognize and that readers in the years to come would find both interesting and believable. In fact, as Dumas noted in the introduction to a later work, the people and places were so believable that someone in Marseilles was selling fish-bone pens made by the Abbé Faria himself (cf. Stowe 126).

Dumas's intention was to write a story that was entertaining and involved the reader. His style reflects this intent, with its combination of the realistic, the romantic, and the fantastic. A careful translation, such as the most recent one by Robin Buss in 1996, creates a readable novel that entertains its readers as its author intended.

## HISTORICAL CONTEXT

During the 1840s France enjoyed a period of stability and relative prosperity after the turmoil that had started in 1789 with the French Revolution and had continued through several different regimes. From 1789 to the July 1830 Revolution, the French government was a republic, then an empire, and finally a restoration of the Bourbon monarchy. Louis-Philippe, from the Orléans branch of the French royal family, became king in 1830 and governed as a parliamentary monarch, complete with a legislative assembly. By 1840, France was experiencing a period of economic prosperity, political calm, and peace. François Guizot, a historian who became a politician, served as prime minister throughout the 1840s until the Orléanist monarchy fell in 1848. He believed sincerely in the idea of a government by all the elites, that is, men of wealth and/or distinguished by family background and education, and also believed in the principle of equal opportunity. Guizot felt that every man was free to get rich, and if he did not, he could only blame his own limitations, not an unjust society (Wright 122). Although highly unpopular as a politician, Guizot had the support of Louis-Philippe and was also adept at political maneuvering. For example, he offered hostile deputies salaried positions in the government. Guizot also encouraged business expansion, sometimes with government aid but most often through a hands-off policy (Wright 123).

The only major legislative act connected with Guizot's name occurred when he was minister of public instruction in 1833. The act established primary education schools in every one of France's 38,000 communes (municipal entities). The schools were neither free nor compulsory, but they marked a step forward in the area of education. Teacher training was also increased, and teachers acquired more status and better working conditions. The expanded opportunities for at least an elementary education created a wider reading public, one that Dumas's novels would attract.

Louis-Philippe's government favored the business community through protective tariffs against imported products, a low level of taxation for businesses plus a policy of noninterference, government concessions, and financial guarantees. The regime also supported public works projects such as canals, roads, and railroads. However, both railroads and business enterprises developed more slowly in France than in other European countries, such as England and the German states. The introduction of machines also progressed more slowly in France, as labor was cheap; also, the laborers objected often violently to being replaced by machines. The banking system was conservative and not inclined to risk capital on unknown men or projects. Banking and most industrial development remained in the hands of families financially well established before the Revolution.

Opportunities for political power were also based on birth and wealth. Louis-Philippe did reduce the entrance fee for eligible voters, and the number increased from 90,000 to about 170,000 as his regime progressed (Wright 169). Owning land was still an important form of wealth, and those men considered part of the middle bourgeoisie could rise to the upper bourgeoisie as their wealth and lands increased. Some of the richest members of the upper bourgeoisie also acquired titles as Danglars does in *The Count of Monte Cristo*. The appeal of more established titles can also be seen in this character as Danglars proposes a marriage for his daughter with the man he thinks is an Italian prince rather than with Albert de Morcerf whose father's title is of recent origin.

The lower bourgeoisie, such as shopkeepers and clerks, couldn't gain enough wealth to rise to voting status but did find a source of pride through service in the National Guard. Citizens who paid a direct tax became part of the guard and furnished their own weapons and uniforms. Although Charles X dissolved the guard in 1827, Louis-Philippe reconstituted it in 1831. However, the guard's discipline and influence diminished during the 1840s, and it did not support the monarchy in the Revolution of February 1848.

While the life of industrial workers and peasants employed on farms was not particularly favorable during the 1840s, the legal status of women rendered them the largest disadvantaged group. According to law the family was organized in an authoritarian and hierarchical fashion. The father was designated by law as the sole manager of all family property, including that brought to the marriage by his wife. Divorce was illegal from 1816 to 1884, and penalties for adultery were much more severe for women than for men. Educational opportunities for girls were confined chiefly to the Catholic Church, and the first state secondary schools for girls were not established until the late 1860s. Fathers arranged their daughters' marriages as they pleased. Both Valentine de Villefort and Eugénie Danglars were faced with marriages they did not want but could not refuse. The story line created by Dumas freed both young women to follow their own hearts.

As the 1840s continued, there were rumbles of discontent in France, especially among the middle class. The poet Lamartine, who would play an important role in the Revolution of 1848, said as early as 1839 that France was bored (Wright 129). Prosperity and stability began to be equated with stagnation and cowardice. While Dumas was more concerned with writing entertaining novels and enjoying the results of his earnings, some of his contemporaries, such as Victor Hugo, were interested in doctrines of democracy or socialism as well as what they saw as the essential nobility of the common man. With the relative amount of freedom of expression, caricaturists such as Honoré Daumier satirized the governing group with sarcastic cartoons suggesting that those in authority were neither as dignified nor as respectable as they portrayed themselves.

Freedom of expression was also reflected in literature during the nineteenth century. By the time Dumas began seriously writing novels in the 1840s, the literary movement known as Romanticism had influenced all literary genres. The search for universal and abstract truth that had characterized seventeenth- and eighteenth-century literature in France gave way to the depiction more specific and individual experiences. Playwrights were no longer concerned with observing the unities of time, place, and action or with separating comic and tragic elements. Poets were expressing more personal and visionary feelings in their poems and experimenting with rhythm by varying the number of syllables in a line of verse or changing the place of the accented syllable. Novelists, often inspired by the historical novels of the

English writer Walter Scott, sought inspiration from past ages or in stories of adventure that kept the reader in suspense until the last moment. Dumas reflected many of these literary trends in his works, but he also reflected his society. He did not see himself as a being apart from the common herd of humanity but as a writer whose chief purpose was to entertain the widest possible audience. The reading public was increasing in the nineteenth century because of the increased opportunities for education and the achievement of a higher standard of living.

Dumas and his public profited from the new role of newspapers in publishing fiction by installments. Emile de Girardin started the custom in 1836 with his daily paper *La Presse*. Other newspapers followed *La Presse*'s lead, and those who could write stories that kept readers excited to read the next segment profited from this means of publication (Hemmings 116). Not all nineteenth-century French novelists would follow Dumas's example. Gustave Flaubert deplored the century's increasing emphasis on mass production and saw the writer more as a solitary artist, striving for perfection in his literary works. Dumas, representing the writer as an entertainer, saw nothing wrong in using collaborators or profiting as much as possible from his own efforts. His novels provided pleasure, and his readers, perhaps bored with life as Lamartine had implied or perhaps not, appreciated his abilities as a storyteller. It is interesting to consider the historical context within which Dumas wrote, for it helps explain his wide audience in his own time. However, as a prime storyteller whose tales and characters reflect universal human emotions, he has transcended his own time period to remain popular with a public who, more than 150 years later, still enjoys the entertainment to be found in a novel full of interesting events, people, and places.

# 5

## Gustave Flaubert
## *Madame Bovary*
### 1857

### BIOGRAPHICAL CONTEXT

Many experiences during Gustave Flaubert's childhood and early adulthood influenced the development of his important novel, *Madame Bovary*. He was born in Rouen, a city in the Normandy region of France, on December 12, 1821, and kept a home there or in nearby Croisset until his death on May 8, 1880.

Flaubert's father was a doctor, in charge of the hospital Hôtel Dieu, and as a child Gustave and his younger sister Caroline liked to climb up on walls overlooking the operating room and watch the procedures there. Father and son had different temperaments and were often in disagreement, although the son admired his father greatly and wanted to please him (Bart 6–8). Imaginative and meditative, Gustave read widely and, even at an early age, felt that most of humanity was stupid and boring.

During Flaubert's youth the literary movement known as Romanticism was sweeping France, and the young man read many works in which "heroes felt violently; heroines loved passionately" (Bart 20). The romantic heroes and heroines sought their true love unceasingly, and fate usually intervened to keep the lovers apart. As an adolescent, Flaubert found this type of dream fascinating; as a man, he would explore attempts to live out such passionate aspirations.

Flaubert's parents were concerned that he study for a recognized profession, although the family fortune would permit him to live without the need for earning a living. Gustave registered for law courses in Paris but soon returned home to study for his exams; instead of reading law, he continued in literature, wrote, and dreamed. He went to Paris every few months to keep his school registration current—and to visit dance halls and brothels with his friend Ernest Chevalier. Never quite at home in Paris, Flaubert alternated between periods of somewhat frantic study and other times when he would neglect his studies completely. He failed in his first attempt to pass the law exams and joined his family at the Normandy resort town of Trouville. He was developing the writer's observant eye at this time, looking at people he met with the possibility of using them as the starting point for fictional characters.

In August 1843, Flaubert again failed his law exams, but this year in Paris he met Maxime du Camp, who was to be an important friend and a traveling companion during the next decade. Du Camp was also passionately interested in literature and had permission from his guardian to pursue a career as a writer.

However, before any trips, Flaubert experienced what would change his life: an attack during which he lost consciousness after "feeling that he was being carried off in a torrent of flames" (Bart 90). At first the attacks occurred almost every day, then became more infrequent, but similar attacks would affect Gustave the rest of his life. Diagnosis was uncertain in the nineteenth century, but it is probable that Flaubert suffered from a type of epilepsy (Bart 94–95). His life would be changed as he attempted to devote the majority of his remaining energy to his writing. Social activity would be restricted to certain people and limited time periods. And he would no longer have to study law.

Flaubert started work on a novel after the onset of his illness. This novel would become the first version of *Sentimental Education*. He also read widely among both French and Latin authors with the aim of strengthening his own prose style. In June of 1844 the Flaubert family moved to Croisset, the house approximately four miles from Rouen and located on the banks of the Seine River. Gustave became more and more sure that he should and would live only for his art (Bart 103).

In 1845 his sister Caroline was married, and the entire family accompanied the newlyweds on their honeymoon trip down the Rhône to Marseilles and then on to Italy. When he returned to Croisset, Flaubert had accumulated impressions and memories that would influence his later writings.

The next year Flaubert's life was marked by the death of his father, and two months later his sister Caroline died of childbed fever. Gustave and his mother were left alone at Croisset, with his mother taking on the major responsibility of Caroline's baby daughter, also named Caroline. Flaubert became almost a recluse, spending long hours reading widely and writing. Only a few friends visited, but Flaubert's growing friendship with Louis Bouilhet, whom he had known slightly during their school days in Rouen, became a welcome part of his life. Bouilhet was a writer but also gave lessons in Latin and French composition in order to live. He and Flaubert read their writings to each other during their regular meetings until Bouilhet died in 1869.

During a trip to Paris in July 1846, Flaubert met Louise Colet during a gathering at the home of the sculptor Pradier. Louise was known for her beauty as well as for her poetry. Flaubert fell in love, but the affair progressed relatively slowly, due to Flaubert's timidity. He would use this experience as a model for explaining the "slow psychological elaboration of a love affair" in his novels (Bart 142). The relationship was stormy, as Louise wanted Gustave's complete devotion and attention while Gustave tried to convince Louise that art should be supreme over love. Voluminous correspondence and infrequent meetings characterized their liaison until they ended their relationship in 1854.

More travel marked the next formative phase for Flaubert, the writer. He and Maxime Du Camp carried out an extensive hiking journey in Brittany in 1847, with Flaubert developing his capacity for observation of people and places. The next two years Flaubert devoted himself chiefly to writing. These were difficult years personally as his family situation caused stress: his mother's sadness over the death of her husband and daughter did not lessen, little Caroline's father was losing his sanity, and the child herself was affected by the melancholy household. Flaubert went to Paris on occasion for a change of scenery and was there in June 1848 when demonstrations brought down the Orléans monarchy. His health grew worse during this time period, and he was urged to seek warmer climates. After finishing *The Temptation of Saint Anthony* in 1849, Flaubert set out for the eastern Mediterranean with Maxime du Camp. First, however, he read *The Temptation* to Du Camp and Louis Bouilhet. His two friends found well-written passages but felt the work as a whole was a failure.

The lengthy trip, on the other hand, convinced Flaubert that he did know how to write and that he wanted to write "of the nature of love, to anatomize it for a postromantic world made foolish or fatalistic by its misconception of it" (Bart 184). He would have the outline for *Madame Bovary* ready within 60 days of his return to Croisset.

The itinerary for this voyage was extensive. Flaubert and Du Camp visited most of the Near East over 22 months. They saw Egypt, Syria, Palestine, the island of Rhodes, part of Turkey, Greece, and Italy. Parting from his mother was extremely difficult for both Flaubert and Madame Flaubert. The latter agreed to the trip only because it was to help improve her son's health. She

would join him in Italy for the final part of the journey. This anguish at parting would give Flaubert a model for Emma Bovary's feelings after Rodolphe
Boulanger leaves her.

Other experiences during the 22 months of travel would appear both in
*Madame Bovary* and future works; for example, Flaubert and Du Camp set a
crew member's broken leg during the trip on the Nile River, much as Charles
Bovary would do for Emma's father. While traveling, Flaubert thought seri-
ously about what to write. Several themes interested him, including that of
Don Juan, the eternal, unsatisfied lover.

Flaubert returned to France toward the end of June 1851. His health was
improved; he established relations with more than one woman, and even saw
Louise Colet again. However, most of his time was spent at Croisset, reading,
reflecting, and writing. He decided to write the story of Madame Delamare's
daughter-in-law, who committed suicide after numerous lovers and overwhelming debts. Madame Delamare was an acquaintance of Flaubert's mother
and had related her daughter-in-law's escapades to the Flauberts during a 1845
visit to Croisset (Bart 131). This story was the Don Juan theme, changed as to
the time, place, and sex of the protagonist. Flaubert decided to call his heroine
Emma Bovary; *Madame Bovary* was born September 19, 1851 (Bart 242).

Flaubert spent five years writing, and rewriting, his novel. Most of the time
he was at Croisset but went to Paris from time to time for short periods. At
Croisset, quiet was in order until Gustave rang his bell at about 10 A.M. to
announce that he was awake. After lunch and a walk with his mother and
niece, Flaubert would give Caroline her lesson and then work steadily until
dinner at 7 P.M. He returned to his writing around 9 P.M. and worked well into
the night. Weekly visits from Louis Bouilhet were the only break from routine for months at a time, other than the visits to Paris three or four times a
year (Bart 251–52).

In 1852 Maxime Du Camp, now editor of the *Revue de Paris*, advised
Flaubert to move to Paris in order to take his place among the literary leaders
of the era. Flaubert wanted no part of what he considered a chase for fame,
and the two friends were estranged for several years.

Louis Bouilhet moved to Paris in 1853, since he needed to live in the capital in order to pursue his own literary career. Although the weekly visits had
to cease, the two friends wrote each other regularly, often discussing their
problems with their writing. By 1854 Flaubert decided to spend the winter in
Paris, enabling him to discuss literary concerns directly with Bouilhet and
other friends as well as have more varied activities in his life.

In April 1856 Flaubert finished *Madame Bovary*. A copy was made and sent
to the printer. Du Camp purchased the novel for his *Revue*, and Flaubert

looked forward to seeing his creation appear as a serial, as books often did in the nineteenth century, before being published in book form. However, Du Camp and his editors criticized aspects of the novel, which infuriated Flaubert. After heated exchanges and some changes, the first installment of *Madame Bovary* appeared in the *Revue* of October 1, 1856. The second installment, however, had scenes that Du Camp was sure would cause difficulties with the government and would probably lead to suppression of the *Revue*. The offending scenes were eliminated in the December installment, but Flaubert insisted that a disclaimer from him be included in the issue. He could not understand the fears of the *Revue*'s editorial staff but found they had reason for concern when he and the magazine were accused in December 1856 on charges of corrupting public morals (Bart 357–58).

Flaubert immediately started lobbying, calling on friends of the Flaubert family in Rouen as well as influential persons he knew in Paris. It was never clear which Ministry was involved in the case against the novel. By mid-January 1857, it was evident that he would need to defend himself and his work in court. During the trial the prosecutor attacked four scenes in particular: Rodolphe's seduction of Emma, her interest in religion between her two affairs, the affair with Léon, and the death scene. The tone of the book was considered immoral. Flaubert's attorney read passages before and after the criticized scenes in order to establish their context and also argued that Emma's fate would not attract anyone to imitate her conduct (Bart 360–61). The judges found that the book failed "to attain the objective of good literature, which they stated to be adorning and refreshing the spirit by elevating the mind and purifying manners" (Bart 361). But in conclusion they noted that Flaubert's aim had been elevated and that the novel was not pornographic. Flaubert, the publisher, and the printer were acquitted.

The complete novel was published by the firm of Michel Lévy, with copies coming off the presses in April 1857. The public, attracted by the notoriety of the trial, assured the commercial success of the novel, although Flaubert had sold the rights to Lévy for a period of five years and for the amount of 800 francs. He was sorry he had not negotiated a higher figure (Bart 362). Many critics were at a loss when confronted with a novel so different than what had gone before. Sainte-Beuve, the most influential critic of the mid-nineteenth century, did appreciate Flaubert's style and his impersonal handling of irony (Bart 364). However, the novel was not successful solely on the basis of the trial; discerning readers discovered that their original impression was correct, and *Madame Bovary* continued to rise in public esteem. Flaubert's book and his thoughts were now public property, so to speak; he could no longer express his ideas on art in private (Bart 366).

## PLOT DEVELOPMENT

Flaubert divided his novel into three sections, with each section containing a number of relatively short chapters. This structure enables the reader to follow the stages in Emma Bovary's life and trace the development of both the characters and the themes the author presents in this story, a story of unrealistic expectations that are never fully understood by the woman who holds them.

Charles Bovary is introduced in the first chapter, for Flaubert felt it important for the reader to know Charles before meeting Emma. In this introduction the reader sees Charles entering school as a gawky adolescent. From his absurd hat, described in minute detail, to his inability to even articulate his name, Charles is a laughable figure. His parents are presented next: the father, a former assistant army surgeon, squanders his wife's dowry and never manages to work hard enough to achieve economic success; the mother, in love with her dashing husband at the beginning of the marriage, becomes disillusioned and bitter about his escapades, devoting herself to her son and to efforts to increase the family fortunes. When he is finally sent to school, Charles is only able to achieve mediocre results through his hard work but is pushed to study medicine by his mother. Starting off as a diligent student, Charles forgets his good resolutions and eventually stops attending class. He completely fails the examinations for becoming a Public Health Officer. With hard work he learns all the questions by heart and succeeds in passing on his second try. His mother locates a practice for Charles and also a wife, a somewhat older widow who appears to have some money. Charles, thinking that now he is an independent adult, discovers that his new wife is a demanding master, dictating his conduct and requiring numerous services from her husband.

Charles's life takes a new turn when he is called out one night to Monsieur Rouault's farm, Les Bertaux, to set the owner's broken leg. The farmer has one daughter, Emma, and Charles notices many details of the young woman's appearance, from the whiteness of her nails to the candor of her glance. Charles succeeds in setting the broken leg, and Emma's father makes a good recovery. Charles pays numerous visits to the farm, enjoying his time there. When his wife becomes jealously suspicious, Charles agrees to stop his visits but decides that such a prohibition actually gives him the right to love Emma. Not long afterwards, the notary managing his wife's money absconds with all her money. Her property is discovered to be heavily mortgaged. A week later his wife has a seizure and dies the following day.

In chapter three Charles is consoled by Monsieur Rouault, also a widower, who has come to pay his bill. Encouraged to visit the farm and Emma, Charles comes often. Father Rouault decides that Charles would be an acceptable son-in-law and basically puts words in the young man's mouth when Charles has difficulty in coming to the point. The father does admit that it would be well to consult his daughter and tells Charles he will open the shutter if Emma agrees to the marriage. Some 49 minutes later, the shutter bangs against the wall, and the engaged couple spends the winter planning the wedding. The 43 guests at the spring wedding will spend 16 hours feasting, and the celebration will carry over to the next day.

The wedding procession, the guests, the banquet, all are presented with Flaubert's usual meticulous attention. The following morning the guests are amazed at Charles's evident happiness and Emma's inscrutability.

Emma spends the first days of her marriage deciding on alterations to the house in Tostes. Charles, happy with his new situation, is overjoyed by Emma's every gesture or act. Emma, on the other hand, wonders why she had thought herself to be in love. The happiness that she had expected from this love is lacking, and she wonders what exactly words such as felicity, passion, and rapture, which had seemed so wonderful in novels, mean in real life.

In the following chapter Flaubert presents Emma's early life. At the age of 13, she had become a boarder at the convent school in the nearby town. Emma found a "mystic languor" (27) in the smell of incense, the coolness of the holy water, and the glow of the candles. Her tumultuous nature is at first enthralled with the readings in the schoolroom and then by the very romantic novels loaned to the girls by the woman who comes to the convent monthly to do the mending. When her mother dies, Emma cries a great deal but inwardly feels she has achieved a more ideal grief than the ordinary person. The nuns realize that Emma's faith has slipped through their hands and are not sorry to see her leave when her father decides she should return home. But being in charge of the household is not fulfilling after awhile, and when she meets Charles, "she considered herself utterly disillusioned, with nothing more to learn, nothing more to feel" (30).

Emma decides that traveling to far away places would be the means to find the happiness, undefined, that she seeks. She hopes, wishes, and desires that Charles would understand instinctively her unease, her secret longings. Charles, content beyond his imaginings, cannot live up to Emma's expectations: "But this man knew nothing, taught nothing, desired nothing" (32). However, one extraordinary event will disrupt the tranquil melancholy of her existence: Monsieur and Madame Bovary are invited to a ball at La Vaubyessard, the home of the Marquis d'Andervilliers.

The following chapter features the ball, the high point of Emma's existence. Her perceptions of the chateau, its inhabitants and guests, the dancing, and all the activities of this glorious period are colored by her expectations of what such an event must offer. For example, she admires the old duc de Laverdière for what he allegedly was during the eighteenth century and ignores the reality of the drooling old man he has become. To insure that Charles does not impinge on her enjoyment, she won't let him try the dances and relegates him to the position of uncomprehending observer. The details of the event are portrayed as they affect the senses, and "in the great dazzlement of this hour" (40), Emma reaches the pinnacle of this experience during her first waltz, with a man familiarly called a Viscount. She does not want to sleep after the ball concludes, wishing above all to "prolong the illusion of this world of luxury" (42) that has thrilled her so much. On the way home, Charles needs to make a repair on their vehicle and finds a cigar case in the road. This case becomes a symbol for Emma of the world she desires to inhabit, and the contrast between this world and home irritates her so much that she fires the maid when dinner isn't ready on their arrival home.

The final chapter in part one presents Emma's increasing boredom after the excitement of the ball. She begins a fantasy life through imagination, buying a map of Paris and planning shopping trips, reading novels, and visualizing a life of passion and pleasure. Charles's lack of ambition enrages her, and she is sure nothing interesting will ever happen to her in the boring town of Tostes, among all its boring residents. Her depression makes her physically ill, and in an effort to help Emma, Charles finds a place in a market town, Yonville-l'Abbaye. Preparing for the move, Emma finds her wedding bouquet and throws it into the fire: "the paper petals, withering away, hovering in the fire-place like black butterflies, finally vanished up the chimney" (53). When the move is made, Emma is pregnant.

Part two opens with the description of Yonville, located near Rouen, the principal city of the Normandy region. Flaubert presents the town and its inhabitants with meticulous care. Those who will play a role in the life of Emma and Charles are introduced as they converse in the Golden Lion Inn, run by Madame Lefrançois, while waiting for the arrival of the Hirondelle, "a yellow box stuck on two large wheels" (62).

Continuing the introduction of people and places in the following chapter, Flaubert uses the technique of simultaneous conversations, and the reader meets Léon Dupuis, a lawyer's clerk, as he and Emma exchange views on landscapes, music, and literature. Meanwhile Homais, the pharmacist, is monopolizing his talk with Charles, telling him all about how his practice will be. Dinner lasts over two hours, and Emma is hopeful as she prepares for bed in this new home that things will be better.

Money worries are mentioned for the first time in the next chapter. Because the Bovarys can't afford the type of layette Emma would like, she dismisses the idea of preparation for the new baby. When her daughter is born, she faints on hearing that the baby is a girl. She had wanted a son since a "man, at least, is free…" (70). The baby's name is subject to much discussion, and Emma chooses finally to name the baby Berthe because she remembered hearing a young woman called by that name during the ball at La Vaubyessard. The baby is cared for by a wet nurse, and Emma decides one day to visit her child, asking Léon to accompany her.

Their growing attraction develops in the next chapter through proximity and Sunday evenings spent at the Homais home. Public opinion believes that something is going on between Emma and Léon, but at this point their alliance is based on similar tastes in books and music. Léon realizes he is falling in love while such a thought hasn't yet occurred to Emma.

By the time Léon accompanies Homais and the Bovarys on a Sunday excursion to a flax mill, Emma decides that Léon is in love with her and wonders why she couldn't have met him first. Soon after, Monsieur Lheureux, a local merchant, visits Emma and persuades her to purchase a few small items on credit. Emma, feeling she has been sensible in the matter of these purchases, redoubles her efforts to be a model wife and mother. Léon finds her virtuous and inaccessible in this role, but Emma is repressing signs of her rage, hatred, and exasperation that Charles doesn't sense her torment.

In chapter six Emma tries to talk with the priest about her unhappiness, but he misunderstands her message and recommends a cup of tea. Léon decides to move to Rouen and then to Paris, "tired of loving for nothing" (94) and urged by his mother to continue his studies in order to further his career. He and Emma say good-bye in a restrained fashion; his kisses are for little Berthe.

With Léon's departure, Emma believes that "her only hope of happiness" (99) is gone. She flits from activity to activity, finishing nothing she starts. Charles's mother feels that all his wife needs is some hard work. What she meets, however, is a new man: Rodolphe Boulanger de la Huchette brings his servant to Charles to be bled, a standard treatment in the nineteenth century. Rodolphe, bored with his current life, is attracted to Emma, senses her boredom, and decides to seduce her: "Poor little thing! Gasping for love, just like a carp on the kitchen table wants to be in water" (104). He does wonder how he will get rid of her once his attraction has run its course.

The agricultural fair is the principal topic of chapter eight, but this fair serves as the background for the presentation of characters, themes, and the next phase of Emma's story. Everyone is there: Homais is orating on his knowledge of agronomy to innkeeper Madame Lefrançois, who is paying more attention to business at her rival's café; Emma is strolling with Rodolphe, who is making fun of the mediocrity of the people and the place. Later, Rodolphe and

Emma watch the speeches and prize-giving from the council chambers. The counterpoint of the official discourse, the prize-giving and Rodolphe's verbal seduction, creates a masterful scene, as the reader is able to listen to all participants with a certain sardonic detachment. The festivities conclude with damp fireworks, but Homais doesn't let this mishap stop him from writing a very laudatory account of the event that appears in the Rouen paper.

During the next two chapters Emma and Rodolphe carry on their passionate affair. After their first horseback ride together when they become lovers, Emma is overjoyed at having this new relationship. She feels that she is beginning something wonderful "where everything would be passion, ecstasy, delirium" (130). Enjoying midnight trysts, letters, and visits to Rodolphe's chateau in the early morning, Emma refuses discretion to the point where Rodolphe's feelings change to indifference.

Emma, wondering why she detests Charles so much, tries again in chapter eleven to push her husband into glorious action. Spurred on by an article that Homais reads on a new operation to cure a club foot, Emma and the pharmacist convince Hippolyte, the stable boy at the Golden Lion, to undergo this operation that Charles will perform. When disaster results and Hippolyte's leg is amputated, Charles seeks consolation for a result that he doesn't understand. Emma pushes him away with disgust and detests him even more.

In the following chapter Emma proposes that she and Rodolphe leave Yonville and live together in some exotic place. She continues to buy items from Lheureux, even applying a patient's payment to her debts without telling Charles. Rodolphe agrees implicitly to take Emma away, but after a tender scene in the moonlight, he writes her a farewell letter that is delivered by his servant the following morning.

Emma rushes to the attic to read this letter. Overcome, she thinks of throwing herself from the attic window. Swooning when she sees Rodolphe pass by the window in his tilbury, Emma becomes seriously ill. Charles, frantic about her condition, also has serious worries about money, having also become indebted to Lheureux.

During her illness Emma becomes more affected by religious feelings, even having a vision of God. The priest recognizes her fervor and sends for religious books. Next Homais suggests that Charles take Emma to Rouen to the opera. Convinced that the excursion will do his wife good, Charles persuades Emma to go.

Part two concludes with the Bovarys attending the opera and finding Léon there. Emma pays no more attention to the stage, and the three leave before the opera's end. Charles suggests that Emma stay in Rouen to attend the performance again in order to see all of it.

Part three opens with Léon's decision to make Emma his mistress; his experiences in Paris have overcome his timidity. A comic scene in the cathedral—the verger tries to play tour guide to first Léon and then Emma—ends in an all-day ride around Rouen in a closed carriage. Emma's second adulterous affair is underway.

The next three chapters detail Emma's growing involvement with both Léon and Lheureux. When she arrives in Yonville after this first stay in Rouen, she learns of the death of her father-in-law from Homais. The latter is so incensed at the carelessness of his clerk, Justin, who has opened the locked cabinet where Homais keeps poisonous substances including arsenic, that he blurts out the news. Lheureux persuades Emma that she should hold Charles's power of attorney, and she goes off to Rouen to allegedly consult Léon because of his legal knowledge. They enjoy their time together as if these days were a honeymoon. As Léon neglects his work for Emma, she becomes more and more embroiled with Lheureux. She also manipulates Charles into suggesting weekly piano lessons in Rouen so she can continue to see Léon.

During her journeys in the Hirondelle, Emma often sees a blind tramp who sings about young girls seeking love. Lheureux spots her with Léon and manipulates Emma into signing more notes. Charles too is increasingly in debt and appeals to his mother. The elder Madame Bovary is scandalized and insists that Emma give up the power of attorney. Charles takes Emma's side, and heedless in her escapades, she becomes more and more "irritable, greedy, and voluptuous" (224).

Both the financial problems and Emma's disillusion with the love affair increase. Léon also feels that it is time to end their affair; he is about to be made senior clerk. Emma now blames Léon for her disappointment with love and life. At the time of the mid-Lent carnival, Emma attends a masked ball that lasts the entire night. Feeling feverish, she returns home to find that legal proceedings for debt have begun against her. Rushing to Lheureux, Emma learns that it's too late for more notes to be signed. Lheureux wants money.

Soon a bailiff and his crew arrive to make an inventory for the forced sale of the house and contents. Charles, out visiting patients, is unaware of the situation. The next day Emma goes to Rouen to ask Léon for help, encouraging him to steal from his office for her. Unsuccessful in attempts to obtain money from the lawyer and the tax collector in Yonville, she hides at the home of the wet nurse and sends her to find out if Léon has arrived with money. No one has come.

Emma seeks out Rodolphe as a last resort. He feels attracted once again—until she mentions money. Completely beside herself and hallucinating,

Emma staggers across the fields, arriving at the pharmacy. Forcing Justin to give her the key to the locked cupboard, Emma grabs a handful of arsenic and swallows it. Charles is frantic, but Emma refuses to explain anything. She lies on her bed, and the death agony begins. Other doctors are called, and Homais is there to participate with comments and advice. The priest comes to give Emma the last rites. She gives the cross he holds out to her "the greatest loving kiss" of her life (265).

The watch by the body, a customary ritual in the nineteenth century, is punctuated by more disagreement between the priest and Homais. Emma's body is now dressed in her wedding gown. Charles says his farewell, asking for locks of Emma's hair.

Emma's father comes to Yonville, overcome by this event. During the funeral service Charles tries to think of Emma in heaven but is filled with rage and despair at her death and the thought of the casket being buried in the ground. When all is completed, that evening Justin is seen weeping over the grave.

Emma's story is finished, but Flaubert in a final chapter recounts what happens to Charles. The money problems are so severe that Charles is forced to sell, one by one, nearly all his possessions. There is no money to clothe Berthe, and the Homais children no longer play with her. Charles discovers Emma's love letters finally, and when he sees Rodolphe at the horse market, he merely says that fate is to blame. Soon after, when Berthe comes to call him to dinner, she finds that Charles has quietly died. Berthe must earn her living in a factory, and Homais, successful in all his activities, receives his *Légion d'Honneur* medal.

## CHARACTER DEVELOPMENT

The reader sees Emma for the first time as Charles sees her, in physical detail, her dress, her nails, her hands, her eyes. As the courtship develops, Emma continues to be presented as she appears to Charles, pricking her finger and sucking it as she sews, savoring the last drops of liquid from her glass, and wanting a midnight wedding by torchlight yet sitting through a hearty feast marked by loud voices and sweating bodies. What Emma is like as a person only comes out little by little.

Flaubert establishes her in this marriage she grows to detest before describing her life before Charles meets her. Her activities and thoughts during her convent education, her enthrallment with the sensual aspects of Catholicism and the romantic novels the girls read in secret reveal her essential desire for a life that will fulfill her vaguely defined longings. Emma's efforts at the beginning of her marriage to reach what she seeks emphasize the aspirations that characterize her and foreshadow her eventual downfall. The boredom of nineteenth-century provincial life in France contrasts with her desires for exotic passion, and her reflections as her life unfolds reveal her ever-increasing dissatisfaction with her lot.

Even her adulterous affair with Rodolphe proves to be commonplace after the first euphoria. Again, Flaubert develops Emma's ongoing disillusion and unhappiness through her thoughts and actions, letting the reader into her inner reflections and outer actions as she pushes Rodolphe into agreeing to run away with her. Rodolphe lets her down, and the reader can feel pity at Emma's unhappiness. The affair with Léon is not the answer to her innermost longings either, and Emma's disintegration into debt and despair results in suicide. Even the suicide reflects her frenzy as she coerces Justin, Homais's apprentice, into unlocking the cabinet where the arsenic is kept, and then stuffs the white powder into her mouth. As she receives the last rites of the church, Flaubert puts the final touches on the portrait of the unfulfilled woman: Emma kisses the crucifix with the same sensual fervor that she had kissed her lovers, but at the actual moment of death she hears the blind man from Rouen singing his song about seduction outside her window and dies in hysterical laughter.

The reader is not sure whether to pity or condemn Emma. Flaubert has created a woman who defies a cut and dried analysis, but that is the strength of the development of this character, seen through her actions, presented through her reflections. She is sensual, focused on herself and her emotions, extreme in her aspirations, and mundane in her attempts to realize them. In another age or setting she might have succeeded; in her own time and place she was doomed.

Charles Bovary frames Emma's story with his entry into a new schoolroom beginning the novel and his death ending it. The entry presents his character in a visual way: the reader sees this gawky country boy, wearing a completely absurd cap, stumble into a school room, not knowing what is expected of him or what to do. The other boys and the teacher find him ridiculous, which he is in his lack of comprehension concerning schoolroom behavior. Through telling the story of Charles's early life and his misadventures in medical school, Flaubert emphasizes his character's essential mediocrity in action. Well-meaning but timid, happy once Emma consents to marry him but completely uncomprehending of his wife's longings and her utter boredom with his love, Charles blunders through his life with Emma and his work with the sick and injured. The reader sees Charles through Emma's eyes and is well aware of her growing disgust for her husband and her life as a small-town wife and mother. Emma's ongoing manipulation of Charles and his gratitude for what he thinks is her help in financial matters emphasize his inherent stupidity and his wish to please her no matter what. In the midst of his grief over Emma's death, Charles is forced to accept the truth of her adultery and his and Berthe's financial destitution; he blames fate and dies quietly, unable from beginning to end to cope with what he doesn't understand. Once Charles has married Emma, Flaubert switches the focus to Emma's thoughts and what she sees, presenting only rarely what Charles thinks and sees: for example, Charles's dreams for his daughter's future, although a counterpoint to Emma's dreams of escape with Rodolphe, reveal both his care and concern for Emma and Berthe and his lack of awareness. Berthe would grow up to look just like her mother, talented and charming. They would find her a good husband: "he would make her happy; it would last for ever" (158). Flaubert never wavers in presenting Charles as a wistful, yearning mediocrity, but a hint of sympathy is evident for this man who loves wholeheartedly and dies of his grief.

Rodolphe Boulanger de la Huchette, with his aristocratic name (based on the name of his property), is, on the surface, the epitome of the romantic hero in the novels Emma devoured during her convent education. But, from the beginning of Rodolphe's interest, it is evident through his words and thoughts that he sees Emma as a conquest to enjoy and then discard. His character is revealed first by his thoughts as he begins his campaign of seduction, then by his willingness to conduct the affair with meetings in the dead of night, and finally by his letter of rejection. It is a masterpiece of cynicism cloaked in the language of renunciation for Emma's sake. The fact that he pieces the letter together from others he has received only emphasizes his view of women as objects of physical pleasure. Even Rodolphe's initial embarrassment when he meets Charles by chance after Emma's death disappears before Charles's willingness to blame fate: "Rodolphe, who had controlled this particular fate, thought the man rather soft-hearted for someone in his position, comical even, and slightly despicable" (285–86). Detached from compassion for others, Rodolphe is developed as a character concerned with his own gratification above all.

Léon Dupuis, Emma's second lover, is introduced as he sees Emma enter the inn at Yonville. Their initial conversation reveals that both are dreamers with similar longings for something other than their own mundane existence. As they develop a friendship against the background of Sunday evenings at the Homais home and walks in the country, the townspeople comment on the relationship. Léon's growing love for Emma remains unspoken, expressed in his thoughts alone as he watches her play the role of model wife and mother. He decides to counteract his attraction to Emma by going to Paris for further study. Once they meet again, Léon's character is less timid, and he vows to begin an affair with Emma. Paris has had its effect: Emma is persuaded to go for a ride in the cab because it is done in Paris. Yet, once the affair is consummated and the honeymoon days are over, Léon again is portrayed as somewhat timid as he reacts to Emma's aggressive and possessive behavior and feels "the lowliness of his position" (219). He is unable to break off the affair although bored with it and afraid for his position, as Flaubert indicates by recounting Léon's thoughts as a counterpoint to Emma's frenzies. When she demands money as the financial disaster looms closer, he is unable either to lie to her or to do as she asks. After Emma's death, Charles receives a letter from Léon's mother announcing her son's marriage. The fact that the marriage is announced by his mother is Flaubert's final nuance in the portrait of a man, mediocre in his own timid way, who chooses the conventional path of a middle-class employee after a tempestuous affair that leads only to unhappiness.

Homais, the pharmacist, serves as the model bourgeois and a focus for Flaubert's satirical view of what he sees as the bourgeois mentality. Homais reveals his character through his own words, many of them, in fact. The reader first sees him at the inn at Yonville, with an expression of self-satisfaction on his face. Homais has well-chosen words to say on every subject. He tells Madame Lefrançois, the innkeeper, that she must move with the times. His faith is to be found in science and in the printed word. He writes articles for the newspaper that give his own interpretation of an event and not necessarily the facts. An opportunist of the first order, Homais reads about an operation on a club foot, encourages Charles, with Emma's support, to perform the operation, and disclaims any responsibility for the event or its outcome after the operation fails miserably. Oblivious to the feelings of others, he never hears what they say because he is too busy talking. His wish for the *Légion d'Honneur*, that award established under Napoléon for meritorious public service, is the one thought he does not verbalize. He merely guards this wish as a secret aspiration and works toward his goals in such ways as helping the local prefect in elections and petitioning the king. Homais is so certain that he is right in all his pronouncements that his public defers to his wisdom, and after Charles's death, three doctors fail to succeed in Yonville. Homais "is doing infernally well" (286). He receives the *Légion d'Honneur*.

Flaubert adds many secondary characters to the novel, showing their most striking characteristics as they relate to each other or to Emma. Madame Bovary, the mother of Charles, is portrayed in the early chapters that describe Charles. Disappointed in her marriage, she devotes her love to her son and later competes with her daughter-in-law for Charles's affection, criticizing Emma's extravagances and telling her son directly that all Emma needs is some hard manual labor (100). Monsieur Bovary, Charles's father, is shown as an unfaithful, lazy husband and a relatively indifferent father. Yet when he visits Charles and Emma, the latter finds him a romantic figure because of his adventures in Napoléon's army.

Several of the secondary characters are introduced in the opening chapter of part two, before the Bovarys arrive in Yonville. Flaubert shows them at the inn, waiting for dinner and the arrival of the coach. Madame Lefrançois and Homais give their descriptions of Monsieur Binet the tax collector, punctual and predictable, and Monsieur Bournisien the priest, known for his strength at harvest time. With the arrival of the coach, Monsieur Lheureux (whose name in French means the happy one) comes on the scene. He has been one of the travelers and has tried to console Emma about the loss of her dog, who had run away during a coach stop.

The priest and the merchant will play a significant role in Emma's eventual downfall. Flaubert portrays the priest's lack of understanding in a well-crafted scene that takes place in the church when Emma goes for spiritual counseling. She is trying to find an answer, a solution to her unhappiness. Monsieur Bournisien, distracted by the rowdy behavior of the boys in his catechism class, thinks she is suffering chiefly from the hot weather, advises a cup of tea, and offers some Biblical verses as consolation. Their conversation brings out the priest's limitations; the description of his appearance—greasy cassock, fleshy face and neck—only emphasizes M. Bournisien's interest in food and drink and his inability to provide either spiritual guidance or comfort. The limitations of his faith are reiterated in his discussion with Homais as they watch by Emma's dead body. Both men are shown as narrow in thought as they talk and are easily distracted from their argument by the wine and cheese left for their enjoyment.

Lheureux is developed as an insinuating, clever tempter. He is shown observing Emma's behavior, figuring out her relationship with Rodolphe, and using his knowledge to enmesh her ever deeper in debt. His explanations of why she doesn't need to pay him immediately and his ability to persuade her that payments can be used to acquire more possessions sound logical to Emma's ears. It is only when he obtains the legal judgment against her that she realizes what this smooth talker has done. Completely unsympathetic, Lheureux is indifferent to Emma's predicament but conniving enough to come to her funeral and express his pity: "The poor little lady! What an awful thing for her husband" (277).

Other townspeople appear from time to time in Emma's story. Flaubert will introduce them with descriptions of their appearance as they are seen by another character or paint their brief portrait through their words and actions. Catherine Leroux, the farm worker who receives an award at the fair, is described with meticulous detail as she appears to those at the ceremony. Her appearance shows she has spent her life in hard manual labor; her incomprehension of what is happening reveals her lack of experience with people. This crowd may be indifferent and the officials impatient with Catherine's initial lack of response, but the reader can feel sympathy for her timidity, due to Flaubert's talent at creating a memorable portrait.

Flaubert's characters are created to illustrate his themes, yet because of his ability to describe them physically as others see them and to reveal their personality through their own thoughts and words, they come alive in distinctive ways and stay in the reader's memory after the book has been closed.

## THEMES

Flaubert illustrates several themes through his story of provincial lives, *Madame Bovary*'s subtitle. The search for the unattainable, alienation, disintegration, constriction of a narrow world, inadequacy and failure, reduction of all values to the importance of money, the role of fate in life—these themes are universal but presented as they apply to individual lives in a specific environment.

Emma's entire story reflects her search for what she never attains, romantic love. Her definition is colored by the novels she read during her time at the convent school: "They were about love, lovers, loving, martyred maidens swooning in secluded lodges,... aching hearts, promising, sobbing, kisses and tears, little boats by moonlight, nightingales in the grove, *gentlemen* brave as lions, tender as lambs, virtuous as a dream..." (28). Since this definition is not based on anything real, Emma is doomed to be disillusioned as everyone and everything she grasps tenaciously fail her. The real in her world is narrow, boring, disappointing, and leads to disintegration.

Lack of understanding, loneliness, and alienation are an integral part of the search for the unattainable. Charles does not understand the why of his alienation and loneliness in school. Nor does he realize the depth of his wife's alienation until he finds her letters from Rodolphe and Léon. Emma finds no true understanding from any of the men in her life, nor does she understand them. When she thinks of confiding her longings, she has no words to express them: "But how could she give voice to an elusive malaise, that melts like a cloud, that swirls like the wind?" (31). Emma's failure to understand herself and others and her failure to be understood lead to her final disaster.

Emma's ultimate disintegration in a painful death causes the disintegration of Charles's life. He is left to try to pay an avalanche of debts, even those he doesn't really owe. His child has ragged clothes and no playmates. When Charles finds Léon's letters to Emma, his disintegration is nearly complete. After seeing Rodolphe, Charles has only to die.

The narrow, constricted world of the provinces is present from the beginning of the novel, when Charles enters the schoolroom with its rules and routines. Tostes, where he sets up his first practice, is a small town in all its aspects. The move to Yonville, however, merely accentuates the narrowness of provincial life. After the description of the town in all its details, including the contents of Monsieur Homais's display window, the reader learns that there is nothing further to see, other than the cemetery which was enlarged after the last cholera epidemic.

The theme of inadequacy, along with its attendant aspect of failure, reveals itself through all the main characters. Although Emma's physical appearance attracts men, her efforts to achieve the type of love she thinks she wants are futile, given the inadequacies of the men she meets. Charles may love her unconditionally, but he is mediocre in intellect and deficient in understanding. Rodolphe knows all the words and moves to seduce Emma, but he wants her only for finite moments of physical pleasure. Léon and Emma think they share the same tastes in music and literature and the same view of the boring world they inhabit. However, Léon's temperament and character are inadequate to meet Emma's passion or her expectations, and their affair ends in both wishing to escape. Monsieur Bournisien is a sincere but inadequate priest who fails utterly to understand his own faith beyond reciting learned platitudes. Homais, although the most self-assured resident of Yonville and one who does not fail to achieve his aspirations, comes across to the reader as a pompous, self-righteous, inadequate human being. He never accepts responsibility for failures to which he contributes and, once Emma is dead, keeps his children from playing often with Berthe, because he is rising in society as Charles sinks.

Homais and Lheureux exemplify the bourgeois reduction of all values to money that Flaubert also portrays as an overarching theme of provincial life. The epilogue to Emma's story outlines the ongoing prosperity and financial dealings of both men. And Emma's downfall is due less to her adulteries than her debts. She could hide the former from Charles, but the latter become only too evident when the bailiff and his men arrive to take possession of the household furnishings.

Fate is a theme that is touched on but never fully treated. Rodolphe tells Emma during the agriculture fair that their meeting and love are due to fate. Charles, crushed by the failure of his operation on Hippolyte's foot and Emma's anger at this new evidence of her husband's inadequacy, calls the disaster the fault of fate. Rodolphe writes to Emma that she must accuse fate for separating them. And Charles repeats the same word when he tells Rodolphe that what has happened is fate's fault, not Rodolphe's. It is interesting that the references to fate are shared by the two men, so different in character and action. And it is difficult to tell if Flaubert is using the word fatality as a cliché or as a term for the human condition. Like many of the words and ideas in Madame Bovary, its interpretation is left to each reader.

## NARRATIVE STYLE

An author's style is characterized by the choices made among the various ways of expressing actions, ideas, setting, and characters. Flaubert labored over his choices, rewriting, discarding, and showing rather than telling his characters' thoughts and actions. A major choice was the use of free indirect discourse, the closest translation English can provide of the French term, *le style indirect libre*. With this technique characters are not quoted directly but their comments are mixed in with the narrator's voice: "She gave up the piano. What was the point? Who would be listening?" (49). Emma is obviously thinking these questions, but there are no direct or indirect connections such as "Emma thought that…" An attentive reader does not miss the shift in voice between narrator and character, but the author presents smoothly different points of view and succeeds in internalizing the narrative for the reader.

Dialogue does not play a large role in the novel. No one talks at great length with anyone else; the characters' thoughts and words are conveyed impersonally by a narrator who remains evidently detached from what is being told. Yet this sparing use of dialogue makes it all the more effective when it happens. The conversation between Emma and the priest when she is seeking spiritual consolation is one of the rare examples. It brings out vividly the lack of communication between people, who so often talk at cross purposes and fail to understand each other's meaning.

Flaubert's use of descriptive images is the most striking example of his stylistic choices. He was preoccupied—one could even say obsessed—with the right word, *le mot juste*, and his care at choosing words and their juxtaposition leave the reader with memorable pictures.

The scene at the ball that the Bovarys attended while living in Tostes shows the reality that Emma thinks should be hers: luxury, icy champagne, handsome men, and a swirling waltz. Her enchantment masks for her the reality of the old aristocrat at the dinner; she sees only the man who is said to have slept in a queen's bed, not the drooling old man with a bib tied around his neck.

One of the most memorable pictures is Rodolphe's verbal seduction of Emma at the agricultural fair. Played out against the background of official speeches and the distribution of prizes to farmers and their animals, the scene focuses on reality, but what a reality. The speakers on the platform are pompous, speaking in clichés and mixed metaphors. Rodolphe, upstairs in the city hall with Emma, also speaks in clichés, but he is using the vocabulary of romantic love that Emma has longed to hear. And the animals provide background remarks as they bellow or bleat. The reader can appreciate the irony of this juxtaposition and Flaubert's choice of words that present the intertwining of Emma's longings with the prize awarded for the finest pig or manure.

Emma's death scene also shows Flaubert's ability to create atmosphere with a choice of words that reveal Emma's physical suffering, Charles's bewildered agony, and Homais's delight in scientific explanations. The scene concludes with the contrast between Emma's passionate kiss of the crucifix as the priest administers the last rites and her "atrocious, frantic, desperate laugh" (267) as she hears the raucous voice of the blind man singing his risqué words under her window. Again Flaubert has emphasized the contrast between the mystical raptures Emma sought and the physical degradation she found.

Flaubert's word choices lead to interesting uses of physical objects as symbols. Windows may at times represent Emma's longings for an elsewhere that would fulfill them. She is often looking out from a window opening. After the ball, she leans out of the window of her room at the chateau, ignoring the cool, damp air to relive those wonderful moments of luxury she has just experienced. But the morning following the arrival in Yonville she sees Léon from her bedroom window, nods, and closes the window, ready to see if this move to the new town will fulfill her dream. Emma is seated by an open window in the town hall when Rodolphe begins his seduction plan. She reads Rodolphe's farewell letter near the attic window from which the open country can be seen and thinks of jumping out. Emma falls seriously ill after Rodolphe's departure, and the windows looking out over the garden remain shut. When she is able to sit up again, her armchair is placed by the street-side window, but all she sees is the unvarying routine of a Yonville day. Open or shut, windows reflect Emma's state of mind.

Two objects become symbols of the disintegration of Charles and Emma's relationship. When she arrives in Tostes, the wedding bouquet of Charles's first wife is still in the bedroom. Charles immediately takes it to the attic.

When Emma is sorting things in preparation for leaving Tostes, she pricks her finger on the wire from her own wedding bouquet. She tosses it into the fire, and it bursts into flame like straw. Emma's unrealistic expectations about marriage have vanished equally quickly. The plaster statue of a priest located in the garden begins to crumble, damaged by the weather. On the way to Yonville, it falls from the coach and breaks into pieces, just like the Bovarys' life will eventually shatter.

Horses become a symbol for sensuality. At the fair their spirited appearance is contrasted with the placidness of cows. Emma begins her physical affair with Rodolphe as they pause during their first horseback ride—a ride Charles has urged for the sake of Emma's health, another example of the irony Flaubert subtlty inserts into the story. The affair with Léon is consummated during a ride in a cab through Rouen. Again, the picture is subtle; the reader remains outside the cab, seeing only the reactions of the passersby and the driver as the cab lurches along and the horse's speed varies, depending on shouted directions from the cab's interior.

The blind man is a symbolic comment on Emma's downfall. This figure suffers from a disfiguring disease and empty eye sockets. He appears during the affair with Léon and seems to represent Emma's increasing disintegration. He sings an innocent love song, a contrast with his disgusting appearance. The blind man appears again when Emma is returning from her attempt to get money from Léon for the debts. In the coach with her is Homais, who feels such repulsive figures should be locked away. This time the man throws his head back and howls while rubbing his belly. Emma throws him her last five-franc piece. When the beggar is heard singing a vulgar song under Emma's window as she is dying, Emma's tragedy is complete. Her life has descended to a grotesque parody of the romantic dreams she sought. In the epilogue Homais, who has failed to cure the blind man of his skin disease as he had promised, sees that he is condemned to an asylum.

In addition to his use of the right word and free indirect discourse, Flaubert made the stylistic choice to keep the author's voice impersonal. Although Flaubert stays away from imposing himself directly into his work, the reader is able to assume certain attitudes on his part because of the choice of images, for example, Rodolphe compares Emma's ripeness for seduction to a fish gasping on a table (104). Yet, Flaubert is quoted as saying, "Madame Bovary, c'est moi" ("I am Madame Bovary," Steegmuller 281). He most probably felt an underlying sympathy for Emma and for Charles. And with his emphasis on the inane pronouncements Homais makes, Flaubert reveals his distaste for pretentious mediocrity and perhaps his despair at the triumph of such a person: the book concludes with Homais's receiving the Legion of Honor.

An author who concentrates so totally on the use of language in his novel will challenge any translator. His readers who know English only will wonder if the translator has found the right word. In addition to that difficulty, the translator must also deal with Flaubert's use of the imperfect tense. As Beryl Schlossman, professor at Emory University, notes: "Flaubert's imperfect absorbs characters' momentary perceptions into a time frame of rhythmic continuity" (Schlossman, in *Approaches*, 73). The same sense of continuity cannot be achieved with the various past tenses in English. Another difficulty involves Flaubert's search for the right word, which reflects the precision of his native language. Certain phrases lose their edge when translated into their less precise English equivalent. However, there are good translations of *Madame Bovary* that do not equal the original but offer English readers a ready entrance into the world of banality, boredom, and mediocrity that Flaubert depicts so acutely.

## HISTORICAL CONTEXT

Gustave Flaubert started work on *Madame Bovary* as the short-lived Second Republic was drawing to a close. An observer of the political scene, Flaubert, unlike Victor Hugo, did not participate in the Revolution of 1848. He had attended a reform banquet held in Rouen in 1847 but was disgusted rather than impressed by his fellow citizens' enthusiasm for politics. These dinners were organized by opponents of King Louis-Philippe's regime in an effort to overcome the government prohibition against political meetings. Flaubert went to Paris in February 1848 to observe what was going on but remained detached from the events taking place. In a letter to his mistress, Louise Colet, he commented only that a new government could not be "more bourgeois or ineffectual than the old, and I wonder whether they can be more stupid" (Steegmuller 121). He continued to regard all parts of the political spectrum as inept and incapable of improving life in France (Steegmuller 125).

A provisional government attempted to establish order and address the economic problems that were plaguing France. In June 1848 a violent civil insurrection took place in Paris over a three-day period, provoked in large part by the failure of the government to solve the unemployment problem. A temporary military dictatorship under General Cavignac took over governing the country, and the Constituent Assembly completed a constitution by the end of 1848. During the first presidential election for the new republic, held in December 1848, Louis-Napoléon Bonaparte, nephew of the late emperor, was elected president. The new president appeared to side with conservative elements in the legislative body but was also interested in social issues. By the summer of 1851, when Flaubert returned to France after his 22-month trip to the eastern Mediterranean regions, the relationship between president and legislature was at a stalemate. The legislature refused to grant the president a constitutional amendment to permit a second term, and it also would not vote for funds to enable him to pay personal debts (Wright 141). The president began planning a coup d'état, working closely with elements of the army, especially with those who wanted a return to the glory of the first Napoléon's empire.

The coup took place December 2, 1851, with the leading legislators being awakened in the early morning and arrested. The president also announced a drastic revision of the constitution of 1848. The revisions called for an extension of the president's term to 10 years and for a reduction of the powers of the legislature. The nation was asked to accept these changes, which it did through a plebiscite. The changes were approved by 92 percent of the voters. Repression of the protests that occurred caused the death of several hundred protesters and the arrest of 26,000; 10,000 were deported to Algeria (Wright 144). Opposition leaders such as Hugo chose exile before they could be arrested. A year later, on December 2, 1852, Louis-Napoléon proclaimed himself emperor Napoléon III (Napoléon I's son had died in 1832). There was no open resistance, and the transformation from republic to empire was ratified by 97 percent of the voters.

Flaubert happened to be on one of his trips to Paris at the time of the coup d'état in December 1851 and, again, he regarded the entire event as revealing the utter stupidity of the bourgeoisie (Bart 250). The proclamation of another empire reinforced his opinions. The early years of the Second Empire were marked by tight control of the press and public meetings. Hugo chose exile, and Flaubert withdrew to his home at Croisset and his work on *Madame Bovary*. However, he admired Hugo's political and moral stance concerning the Second Empire. Believing that censorship was completely wrong, "a monstrosity, a thing worse than homicide, treason against the soul" (quoted in Steegmuller 268), Flaubert served as an intermediary for Hugo's correspondence with friends in France. Letters were sent to friends of Louise Colet in London and from there to Flaubert (Steegmuller 268–70). Return correspondence followed a similar route.

While France settled into a sort of complacent prosperity in the 1850s, albeit a prosperity that did not include all its citizens, Flaubert continued writing *Madame Bovary*, observing yet disdaining his fellow men and women. The novel presents a realism that goes beyond the relating of exact physical details to a social portrait of the bourgeoisie in particular, with equal scorn for mediocre religious expression (the priest) and misunderstood scientific principles (the pharmacist). Realism, with its emphasis on the concrete and the everyday or ordinary aspects of life, was making itself felt in both literature and art during the 1850s, but the government position was to attack any work that was considered an affront to public morality. Journal or newspaper articles that the government considered a criticism of France or of any part of society favored or supported by the government was brought to court. Often the publication was suppressed and its writers and editors fined. It was in this context that Flaubert and the *Revue de Paris*, the journal in which *Madame Bovary* was first published, were called into court. The *Revue* had already been suspected of liberalism, and the themes and characters of Flaubert's novel provoked scandalized reactions. Although the court noted a preference for works that dealt with life more as it should be than as it is, Flaubert and the *Revue* were acquitted of the charges of immorality and being antireligious.

Definitely part of the historical context in which Flaubert wrote *Madame Bovary* is the role of women in the France of the 1850s. Women were still subject to laws denying them equal roles in marriage. A double standard existed concerning adultery, with penalties being more severe for women than men, and divorce would remain illegal until 1884. Education for girls was minimal. Like Emma Bovary, most young girls were educated in convents. Flaubert is scathing about the novels Emma read in secret during her time at the convent, while Emma's mother-in-law is certain that Emma's discontent is caused by her membership in the reading library. However, Flaubert sees Emma as representative of the unhappiness of many women living in the provinces, and in Paris too, with limited choices of how they are to live their lives: "My poor Bovary, without a doubt, is suffering and weeping at this very instant in twenty villages of France" (quoted in Steegmuller 282).

Flaubert presents his chosen provincial towns and their inhabitants with a careful eye for detail but with impersonal observation underlying description. Living in a time and place that comes alive in *Madame Bovary*, Flaubert reflects yet remains separate from his historical context by striving for and reaching a dispassionate tone. The result is a novel that depicts its historical context yet presents a universality of character and theme, and continues to attract and intrigue readers today.

# 6

## Victor Hugo
## *The Hunchback of Notre-Dame*
### 1831

### BIOGRAPHICAL CONTEXT

Victor Hugo was a well-established writer in 1831 when he published his novel set in fifteenth-century Paris, *The Hunchback of Notre-Dame*. Born in 1802, Hugo began to write seriously at the age of 14 while attending the lycée Louis-le-Grand in Paris. According to a Hugo biographer, Samuel Edwards, Hugo's literary output by age 16 included translations of the Roman poet Virgil, a tragic play, more than 100 poems, and a comic opera (Edwards 32).

It is helpful in understanding Victor Hugo to note his somewhat tumultuous childhood. His father, Leopold Hugo, an officer who rose to the rank of general under Napoléon Bonaparte, and his mother, Sophie Trebuchet Hugo, did not get along. They were often separated and also disagreed concerning the upbringing of their three sons. In 1811 Madame Hugo and the boys journeyed to Spain to join General Hugo, evidently uninvited. However, experiences during this voyage and stay in another culture influenced later Hugo works. For example, seeing the Gothic cathedral in Burgos, Spain, awakened an interest in architecture, expressed most graphically in *The Hunchback of Notre-Dame*.

Sophie and her sons returned to Paris the next year and resumed life in Paris where they lived in a house with a wonderful garden and its own chapel. General Hugo and his wife were legally separated in 1813, and the general was granted legal control of his three sons. Victor preferred his mother at this point, feeling that his father was completely at fault in the breakup of his parents' marriage, but had to accept that his father controlled where he would live and attend school. However, in 1818 his formal schooling ended, and Victor returned to live with his mother.

Continuing to write after finishing his studies at Louis-le-Grand, a well-known Paris secondary school, Hugo entered several poems in a contest sponsored by the Academy of Toulouse. His poems won first and second prize and earned him 150 francs. He then entered a contest for poets held by the French Academy and came in fifth in a field of several hundred. Before his eighteenth birthday, Hugo had gained some recognition as a writer and, with his older brother Abel, who worked in the publishing business, came up with the idea of publishing a literary magazine. *Le Conservateur littéraire* would feature poetry, fiction, articles, and literary criticism. The first issue appeared in 1819, with Victor providing most of the content (Edwards 35, 38). Abel served as business manager, and the journal lasted until 1821, when the brothers' mother died, leaving many debts. Any funds the sons had were needed to pay their mother's debts.

Victor knew poverty over the next year, living alone in a tiny attic room and earning only small sums by selling a poem or an article now and then. He also spent time with Adèle Foucher, the neighbor's daughter whom he had first met when the Hugo family was living near the Fouchers in 1809. It was now 1819, and Adèle's parents were not at all happy that their daughter loved an impoverished poet. They agreed, however, that the two could correspond, and many letters were exchanged over the next months. Victor was gloriously in love and idealized Adèle—who indicated in many letters that she did not and could not understand her beloved's poetry. Victor refused to believe her statements, and it was only several years after they married on October 12, 1822 and became parents that he realized Adèle meant what she wrote.

Victor's brother Abel had collected his recent poems and published them in June 1822 in a volume titled, in French, *Odes et poésies diverses*. The 1,500 copies sold rapidly, enhancing Victor's reputation and earning him 750 francs in royalties, not a small amount for the time. In addition to his love poems, the volume included many poems with a religious theme. At this time in his life Victor was still estranged from his father, a bonapartist, and quite royalist in his sympathies. Louis XVIII, brother of King Louis XVI who had been guillotined during the French Revolution, became king after the defeat of Napoléon at Waterloo in June 1815. The king read this book of poetry, was quite pleased with it, invited Hugo to tea, and presented him with 1,200 francs. These financial windfalls enabled the marriage with Adèle to take place.

The young couple soon became parents; Léopold was born in July 1823 but died two months later. Daughter Léopoldine was born in August 1824, followed by her two brothers, Charles in November 1826 and François-Victor in 1828, and her sister Adèle in 1830.

With his marriage Victor became closer to his father, and in talking with the older man about his experiences under Napoléon, Victor began to modify his royalist views somewhat. He did learn that in spite of his support of the regime, he could obtain no favors for his father, who wanted to be restored to active military duty (Edwards 54). However, Victor received the cross of the *Légion d'honneur* for himself and wrote an ode in honor of the coronation of Charles X, Louis XVIII's successor, in 1825.

During the remaining years of the 1820s Hugo published works of poetry and entered the world of the theatre, writing plays. He also became a more influential figure in the literary world in Paris and well established financially because of his book sales. *Nouvelles Odes*, appearing in 1824, was sold out in two weeks, and Hugo received an advance royalty for a second printing. His poem in honor of Charles X also earned him 1,500 francs. During the next five years almost everything he wrote made money, and his father, who had disapproved of the son's decision to earn a living through literature, apologized.

Hugo noted that his success was due in large part to unrelenting hard work. Typically, he began his workday at 8 A.M. and wrote until 2 P.M. After dinner with his wife and spending time with his children, he returned to his writing table and wrote until 8 P.M. He normally spent the next few hours reading for research purposes. By 11 P.M. Hugo was ready for some social life, either entertaining friends or visiting other writers until around 2 A.M. After a few hours of sleep he was ready to begin again (Edwards 60–62).

This schedule led to regular publications during the remaining years of the 1820s. In 1827 Hugo published the play *Cromwell*, with its preface outlining Hugo's ideas for a new type of theatre. An augmented version of the 1826 *Odes et Ballades* appeared in 1828 and another volume of poetry, *Les Orientales*, came out in 1829 along with a short novel, *Le Dernier jour d'un condamné*. The year 1830 was marked by the "Battle of *Hernani*," Hugo's play that is considered the landmark of Romanticism in the theatre (cf. the historical context section of this chapter). In 1831, along with *The Hunchback of Notre-Dame*, Hugo published another play, *Marion de Lorme*, and *Les Feuilles d'automne*, a collection of poems.

During the last years of the 1820s Hugo was reading widely and thoroughly for *The Hunchback of Notre-Dame*, consulting histories of fifteenth-century Paris, works of archaeology, and dictionaries of demonology. The outline was prepared by 1828, and he had promised the manuscript to the publisher Gosselin by April 15, 1829 (Barrère 66). However, because of his other projects, Hugo obtained a delay until September 1, 1830. The mini-revolution of July

1830 slowed his progress, and the publisher granted him an extension to December 1 and then to February 1, 1831. He was finished by January 15, and the novel appeared in mid-March. The novel received wide acclaim, and the original edition soon sold out. Hugo's book started a new interest in the Middle Ages and gothic architecture, and the writer himself had assured his dominant position in French literature before he turned 30 years old.

## PLOT DEVELOPMENT

*The Hunchback of Notre-Dame* is an intricately composed novel divided into 11 books with each book having a varying number of shorter chapters. To introduce his characters, his themes, and his atmosphere, Hugo devotes nearly one-fifth of the novel to one day, January 6, 1482: the day of the kings and the feast of the fools. This introduction gives him the opportunity to present fifteenth-century Paris, its appearance, its inhabitants, and its habits. All the threads of the story are visible; the reader has only to follow their intertwining and then their unraveling over a six-month time span.

In book one the reader sees much of what is happening from the viewpoint of Pierre Gringoire, a poet and would-be dramatist. His play is scheduled to be performed before the Cardinal de Bourbon and ambassadors from Flanders, in Paris to complete negotiations for a royal marriage, plus representatives of the university, the city, and the town. While waiting for the arrival of the important personages, the crowd becomes restive. Gringoire's efforts to get the play underway are in vain. Instead the crowd, incited by one of the Flemish businessmen, calls for the election of the pope of fools, that is, the person who can make the most grotesque faces before the audience. Quasimodo, the bell ringer of Notre-Dame cathedral whose "whole person was a grimace" (*Hunchback* 52), is elected. When the majority of the spectators leave to follow the papal procession, Gringoire perseveres with the play but loses the remaining spectators when they run to the windows to see La Esmeralda, a beautiful gypsy girl, who is dancing with her goat in the square before the Palace of Justice.

Gringoire's misadventures continue in book two. Financially destitute because he has not been paid for his play, he seeks a quiet corner to sleep and goes to the Place de Grève where there will at least be a bonfire. In a short digression Hugo describes the appearance and function of this square, site of executions in the fifteenth-century city, and comments on the replacement of these sites by the guillotine. The next chapter returns to Gringoire, who discovers that the food has run out, but a young girl's dancing enthralls him, and her goat's answers to questions entertain him. The girl is a gypsy, and a voice in the crowd calls out that her tricks with the goat are witchcraft. When the parade of fools enters the square, it is evident that Quasimodo is proud of the attention. However, his badge of office is ripped from him by a man who turns out to be the Archdeacon Claude Frollo from the cathedral. Gringoire, then following the gypsy through the streets, tries to help when she is grabbed by Quasimodo and another. However, the girl is rescued by a captain of archers on horseback. She asks his name—it's Phoebus—and then flees. Gringoire, later seized and taken to the Court of Miracles to be tried by Clopin, king of the crooks, is about to be hanged. The gypsy girl, who is La Esmeralda, agrees to marry Gringoire according to the gypsy rite in order to save him. The marriage does not mean that she will live with him as his wife. Gringoire, consoled by some supper, offers to be her friend. He answers Esmeralda's question about the meaning of the word Phoebus—it refers to a handsome god who was an archer.

Book three, one of the shortest of the novel, offers a portrait of the cathedral of Notre-Dame, its architectural history, and the changes caused by time, revolution, and restoration. This description leads to another that presents what can be seen of Paris from Notre-Dame's towers. Hugo also details the growth and development of Paris, its various parts, and their characteristics.

Book four features Quasimodo and Claude Frollo. First, the reader learns how the four-year-old Quasimodo was adopted by Frollo, in spite of the opinion of several old women of the area who felt such a deformed child should be burned as spawn from the devil. Frollo's background is then presented. Always with a thirst for learning, Claude takes over the raising of his baby brother Jehan when their parents die. He adopts Quasimodo both through a sense of compassion and of earning credit with heaven. Quasimodo grows up in the cathedral, identifying with the building, its sculptures, and especially its bells. He is also devoted, body and soul, to Claude Frollo. As time passes, Claude, disappointed in the development of his brother, a "genuine devil" (157), becomes more and more engrossed in the illicit aspects of human knowledge, at least according to those who observe his visits to certain houses in the city. He is also known for his hatred of gypsies and women, especially gypsy women.

Claude's interest in the illicit is illustrated in the first chapter of book five. One evening he is visited in his small room in the cathedral by the king's doctor and a stranger who is really King Louis XI. In their discussion Claude denigrates medicine and astrology, saying that alchemy is the only thing that is true and certain. He is sure also that "the book will kill the edifice" (173), referring to the invention of printing. This statement is explained in the following chapter, where Hugo engages in his tendency to present his own ideas.

He relates the predominance of architecture up to the fifteenth century, discusses Gutenberg's invention of the printing press, and concludes by reiterating that printed books have killed such architectural models as cathedrals because they are less durable and more costly than books.

In book six another thread of the plot comes into focus, and Hugo also comments on the fifteenth-century judicial system when Quasimodo is brought before the provost and auditor of Paris. Quasimodo is sentenced to be flogged. Claude Frollo's brother, Jehan, also present, mocks the proceedings.

The following chapter introduces a small, walled-up cell, located at the corner of the Place de la Grève. Called the rat hole, this cell has served as a refuge to a succession of recluses who occupy it, praying, for the rest of their lives. Two Parisian women, along with their visitor from Rheims, arrive with a cake for the current occupant. The visitor is relating the story of a certain Paquette la Chantefleurie, her promiscuous life, her adorable child who had a pair of pink satin shoes, and the disappearance of this child who was exchanged for a deformed four year old. The recluse has a tiny, pink satin shoe in the corner of the cell.

Meanwhile, Quasimodo is being flogged at the pillory in the Place de la Grève. Claude Frollo flees from the sight of his ward's suffering, but La Esmeralda brings him water. She recoils, however, when Quasimodo tries to kiss her hand in gratitude.

Phoebus returns to the story in book seven as he visits his fiancée, Fleur-de-Lys. She and her friends see Esmeralda dancing in the square below their windows and ask Phoebus to invite the dancer to their chamber. Jealous of La Esmeralda's talent and beauty, the girls criticize her clothes and investigate a sack that contains some wooden letters. When Djali the goat spells out Phoebus with these letters, Fleur-de-Lys sobs and faints.

Claude Frollo is also watching the dancing gypsy from his tower in Notre-Dame. He sees a man next to Esmeralda and runs down to the square to discover Pierre Gringoire. Quizzing Gringoire, Claude learns the story of the dramatist's gypsy marriage and wants to be sure that this marriage is platonic.

Hugo continues his depiction of Esmeralda's effect on the men who see her, describing Quasimodo's seemingly changed relationship with his bells after his flogging. He rings them less often. As time passes, however, the bells appear to regain their role in his life until Quasimodo sees Esmeralda dancing in the square in front of Notre-Dame on Annunciation Day, March 25. The sound of the bells dies away.

A few days later Jehan Frollo goes to his brother's tower to ask for money. He observes, unseen, Claude lamenting his failure to make gold and mentioning women's names, including that of Esmeralda. Jehan understands he shouldn't have overheard these muttered comments and pretends he has just arrived. Claude gives Jehan some money when Master Jacques is heard coming.

Master Jacques, the king's attorney, has come to ask when he should arrest Esmeralda for witchcraft. He also wants Claude's help in making gold. Claude, seeing a fly blunder into a spider's web, compares this entrapment to his own search for knowledge; he is trapped without being able to break through.

In the following chapter Jehan and Phoebus are followed by Claude as they head to a tavern. Claude shudders when he hears the two young men mention Esmeralda's name. The threads of the plot lead in the next chapter to Phoebus's making his way to a rendezvous with Esmeralda. A figure hidden in an all-enveloping cloak gives him money for the room where he is to meet the dancer with the stipulation that this unknown figure may hide there in order to view for himself the girl involved.

Esmeralda arrives, so much in love with Phoebus that she is willing to give herself to him. As Phoebus begins his seduction, the unknown man, Claude Frollo in person, bursts from his hiding place and stabs Phoebus. When Esmeralda recovers from her faint, she finds herself surrounded by soldiers and no Claude in sight.

Book eight tells the story of Esmeralda's trial and aborted execution. Pierre Gringoire observes as both Esmeralda and Djali are accused of witchcraft. When she pleads innocent, she is sent to the torture chamber. Hugo gives the reader all the details of the torture procedures in 1482 Paris. Esmeralda cannot withstand the pain and confesses to all the accusations against her. Her sentence is first penance, then a fine, and finally execution.

Claude comes to the dancer's cell, finally driven to confess his tormented love for her, saying that all his feelings and actions are because of fate. Esmeralda spurns him and asks about Phoebus. Claude insists that Phoebus is dead.

As the time for the execution draws closer, the recluse in the cell at the corner of the Place de la Grève laments about her lost child. She is ecstatic when she learns that the prisoner to be killed is a gypsy. Meanwhile Phoebus, very much alive, again visits Fleur-de-Lys and assures her he has never loved anyone else. However, when the two go to the balcony and see that Esmeralda is the prisoner, Phoebus turns white and Fleur-de-Lys is again jealous. Claude is included in the scene as part of the procession of priests and tries yet again to give Esmeralda his love. The execution is interrupted when Quasimodo swings down to the gallows on a rope, snatches Esmeralda, bounds into the cathedral shouting "sanctuary," and carries the girl up to the bell tower.

As book nine opens, Claude has fled the scene before Quasimodo's rescue and has spent the day in a half-mad state, walking outside the city. His return as night falls is presented against the background of a detailed description of the Ile de la Cité and the almost hallucinating impression Claude has of his surroundings. He climbs to the cathedral tower and sees Esmeralda and her goat Djali as two white, specter-like figures.

Hugo gives his readers an explanation of sanctuary, which he illustrates through relating Quasimodo's care of Esmeralda and the latter's grief about her situation. She finally begins to feel some compassion for the hunchback when he explains his understanding of her fright and the reasons for his action. However, when Esmeralda sees Phoebus in the square before Notre-Dame, she sends Quasimodo after this man she thinks she loves. Quasimodo fails to persuade Phoebus to come to Esmeralda. Unhappy at Quasimodo's report, Esmeralda blames him for her unhappiness.

Knowing that Esmeralda lives, Claude is tortured by his sexual desires. Leaving his cell where he has cloistered himself since execution day, Claude tries by force to persuade Esmeralda to love him. She blows the whistle Quasimodo had left for her. When Quasimodo realizes he has stopped the attack but has seized his master, he drops him and flees. Claude leaves, now jealous of Quasimodo also.

Misunderstandings accumulate throughout book 10. Claude finds Gringoire and persuades him Esmeralda is going to be taken from sanctuary and executed. Gringoire comes up with a plan to involve the gypsies and other underworld figures in the rescue attempt. Jehan again appears, participating in the distribution of weapons at the criminals' tavern. When the attack comes, Quasimodo doesn't understand that rescue is the goal so fights back with all his might. Jehan reaches the gallery by ladder, which is thrown back by Quasimodo. The attackers are furious as Jehan dies and attack with renewed efforts.

The scene returns to King Louis XI, alone in his room in the Bastille going over lists of expenses. When the king is informed of the attack, he is overjoyed to think it is against the Paris bailiff. Gringoire, arrested, manages to plead successfully for his life. When the king is finally informed that the revolt is against Notre-Dame and the monarchy, he decides to send the cavalry. The attackers are killed or driven away. When Quasimodo goes to Esmeralda's cell, he finds it empty.

Book 11 unwinds the entrapment of Claude Frollo, Quasimodo, and Esmeralda. Esmeralda has been taken from the cathedral during the fighting by Gringoire and a man in black. Gringoire takes Djali, and Esmeralda resists no longer, believing it's futile to resist fate. After Claude fails to persuade Esmeralda not to hate him at least, he gives her to the recluse in the cell. After railing at the girl, Paquette shows her the tiny pink shoe. When Esmeralda brings out the shoe's mate, Paquette realizes she has found her long-lost daughter. The reunion lasts only moments, for soldiers come and carry away Esmeralda. The mother is pushed away so violently that she hits her head and dies. The hangman starts up the ladder with Esmeralda.

Quasimodo has been seeking Esmeralda everywhere in the cathedral. He finally realizes it was Claude who freed his love. From one of the cathedral's towers the two watch the tiny figure of Esmeralda dying on the gallows. Quasimodo throws Claude from the balustrade. All that the hunchback has loved is now dead.

The end has come: Claude has died and is not buried in consecrated ground, Quasimodo disappears, Gringoire does save Djali and has some success with his plays, and Phoebus has his own tragedy, according to Hugo, with a bit of humor; he gets married. Some time after these events, Hugo says, two skeletons are found entwined in the cemetery of Montfaucon, where all the hanged of Paris are buried. The deformed skeleton is clasping the woman's skeleton. When they are separated, both crumble.

## CHARACTER DEVELOPMENT

Hugo is more interested in his characters' dramas and how they relate to the novel's themes than in the individual characters themselves. Yet, he creates memorable actors for these dramas: Claude Frollo, the priest doomed by his various lusts; Quasimodo, the deformed man overwhelmed by his love for the dancing gypsy girl; the gypsy girl herself, Esmeralda; Pierre Gringoire, the writer, observer, and even participant in the main dramas. The supporting cast too is memorable: Phoebus, the handsome but unworthy recipient of Esmeralda's love; King Louis XI, illustrating the historical changes marking the end of the Middle Ages; Jehan Frollo, the madcap student who believes in nothing but his own pleasures; the recluse in her cell, mourning her lost child; and all the inhabitants of the Parisian underworld, representing the people and their potential power to overwhelm events.

Claude Frollo, the archdeacon of Notre-Dame, is nearly, but not completely, the caricature of the sexually repressed scholar. Even while readers deplore Claude's actions toward Esmeralda, they can feel pity for his tortured soul. From the beginning Claude's parents destined him for the priesthood. Since he is scholarly by nature, Claude takes advantage of the opportunity to study provided by his connection to the Church. He moves rapidly through the various fields studied in the fifteenth century, mastering theology, science, and languages, but not interested in people until his parents die and he takes his baby brother under his care. His compassion for the infant is extended to the little monster he finds at the doorway to Notre-Dame on Quasimodo Sunday, the Sunday following Easter. Hugo indicates that Claude's compassion is affected by his thought of earning credit through his good works for his brother, "a sort of putting out of good works at interest, which he transacted in his brother's name" (147). As Jehan grows up, he reveals a frivolous approach to life that saddens Claude and drives him more deeply into his studies. Those around him are sure that he has moved from legitimate study to being concerned with those areas considered illicit, for example, alchemy, or the creating of gold. When Claude tells the king's physician that he is still groping for answers to his questions, his choice of words indicates a torturing dissatisfaction with study: "I am still bloodying my face and knees on the stones of the subterranean passage. I can see, but not clearly" (171). Hugo develops this image of mental torture through Claude's actions and reactions as the story unfolds. As the archdeacon watches Esmeralda dance on the square far below his room in Notre-Dame's tower, his posture reveals that his intensity now includes a woman, and a gypsy at that, a creature whom he detests and yet who obsesses him. Throughout the remainder of the novel Claude's character is brought out through his actions and reactions regarding Esmeralda. Mental torture becomes physical when Claude realizes that Esmeralda has been brought to the church, and Hugo emphasizes the dramatic aspect of his sufferings in describing Claude's torment and despair at Esmeralda's repulsing his advances. The reader is left with the image of a spiritually empty priest who pursues his longings for the infinite to a death that symbolizes his downfall: he is pushed from the tower of Notre-Dame by the one whom he had helped. Claude lands on one of the gargoyles, but when his hands can no longer hold him, he falls spinning to the pavement below.

Quasimodo is presented first through how the world around him views this unfortunate. He is chosen the pope of the fools with full approval of the crowd—no one could be uglier than this being whose "whole person was a grimace" (52). The reader is told Quasimodo's history, how he is found one morning after mass at an entrance to Notre-Dame: a human monster probably about four years old. Claude Frollo, then a young priest, adopts him. Through the years Quasimodo identifies completely with the church and especially with the bells he learns to ring—even though those same bells have deafened him, severing his connection with the world and people other than Notre-Dame and Claude. Hatred becomes his response to the hatred shown to him, yet he feels an undying gratitude to Claude and experiences a complete identification with the church, his sanctuary. Hugo emphasizes Quasimodo's deformed physical appearance and creates a link between body and soul in describing the hunchback's often malicious actions. However, the beast becomes less bestial once he has encountered beauty. His devotion focuses on Esmeralda once the dancer has given him water, and when she is in danger, he tries his best to give her the sanctuary he has found in Notre-Dame. Hugo focuses on revealing the soul that is confined in the deformed body through Quasimodo's attentiveness to Esmeralda's wants and needs, without ever a chance of being loved in return. The beast reappears with the attack by the Truands, and Quasimodo shows no compunction in his efforts to repulse the attack or when he pushes Claude off the church roof. However, when both are dead, Quasimodo can only sob, "Oh, all that I ever loved" (498). In his portrait of this deformed being, Hugo leaves the reader feeling pity for the bell ringer whose life has been so limited by his deformity.

Hugo chooses to present Esmeralda chiefly as she appears to those who love her, lust after her, or simply notice her dancing. For Claude Frollo she becomes an obsession, a temptation in the form of beauty that diverts him from his obsession of creating gold. She obsesses Quasimodo, but he also wants to protect this fragile girl from those who persecute her. Phoebus lusts after Esmeralda, but also fears her alleged link to the world of magic. Gringoire is interested in the beautiful, graceful dancer but, like Quasimodo, is willing to help her if he can. The dancer herself is revealed through her love for Phoebus and her gestures of compassion toward Gringoire and Quasimodo. She has fallen in love with Phoebus's appearance and never quite realizes that he does not return this love. Esmeralda accepts a gypsy marriage with Gringoire to save him from being hanged when he is condemned by the criminals' court. She also brings water to a suffering Quasimodo when he is being flogged by judicial order, and this compassion is repaid by his undying devotion. An innocent, loyal, infatuated girl, Esmeralda is doomed by her unrequited love for Phoebus, her refusal to give in to Claude's demands, and a judicial system that fears the differences of her gypsy upbringing.

Pierre Gringoire, the would-be famous playwright, is perhaps representative of Hugo himself as he goes from exaltation to despair during the attempted performance of the play that was to bring him fame and fortune. Although Hugo was already famous when *The Hunchback of Notre-Dame* was published, he expresses Gringoire's feelings with an understanding of one who knows how it feels to have one's words take life on a stage. The reader views the events of the first part of the book from Gringoire's point of view until the novel's themes emerge fully. His actions and reactions show him as a resilient man, capable of keeping on after the turmoil of his play's performance. He comes to the brink of disaster when the underworld court condemns him and Esmeralda saves him by a gypsy marriage. Even when Esmeralda brings out her dagger as Pierre attempts to embrace her, he accepts the realities of this marriage and offers to be her friend. Yet, Pierre never quite understands others' motivations and bumbles his way through events. Reappearing on the scene after Esmeralda finds refuge in the cathedral and not realizing Claude's feelings or Quasimodo's, Pierre suggests to Claude Frollo that the underworld mount an attack to rescue Esmeralda. Pierre's intent is to help; the result is the death of Esmeralda and Claude, among others. Yet, he saves Djali and finds some success as a dramatist after all these tumultuous events. The reader sees a basically good-hearted soul who rarely foresees the consequences of a decision but does what he can—and is perhaps the only character who comes to a happy end.

Among the memorable secondary characters is Jehan Frollo, Claude's rebellious brother. Jehan appears in all the crowd scenes as one who appears to live to incite riots. Although Claude, after the death of their parents, has done his best to bring up Jehan, the latter lives only for excitement, refuses to study seriously, and comes to visit Claude to ask for money. He meets his death at the hands of Quasimodo during the attack on Notre-Dame as he has met life, with derisive laughter.

King Louis XI is another vividly drawn, albeit minor, character, and his reign symbolizes for Hugo the transition out of the Middle Ages. Two scenes are especially important: the king's visit, in disguise, to Frollo's cell and the king at work in his study in the Bastille as the members of the underworld, the Truands, are attacking Notre-Dame. In the first scene, the king has come to sound out Claude about science and medicine and hears the archdeacon relate that only alchemy counts among the sciences. The second scene shows the king berating his councilors about the high cost of operating the government. Yet, he doesn't begrudge the cost of the iron cage for important prisoners. Obsessed with security issues and power, the king isn't worried about the attack on Notre-Dame until he is told that the revolt isn't against the bailiff of Paris but against himself. Furious, Louis XI orders the revolt crushed. The king's interactions with others and his commands to officials and servants reveal his character, and the reaction of two Flemish envoys puts the finishing touch on the portrait of the monarch whom they call a man sick in body and evil in mind (454).

Phoebus, the handsome archer in the king's guards, is the catalyst for Esmeralda's downfall. Her love for him brings her to a rendezvous with a superficial man who is interested merely in a sexual encounter. She is arrested for stabbing her would-be lover, but Phoebus's only thought after this event is to distance himself as far as possible from Esmeralda. His moral cowardice is revealed when the troops trace the gypsy to the recluse's cell, and Phoebus refuses any part in the hanging of witches. He remains deaf to Esmeralda's cry of his name. His character is portrayed through his actions, and the reader can only wish that Esmeralda would see beyond the surface beauty that enthralls her.

Hugo is skilled in developing a large supporting cast who play their roles vividly only to vanish when their scene is concluded. The recluse in the cell has more than one scene, and her story is first told by two women who want to amaze their visitor. She is given a chance to speak in her own words when Esmeralda is left before her cell. It is a fierce maternal love that the recluse expresses, and she regains her daughter only to lose her again. Fleur de Lys and her friends flit and flirt upon the stage and provide an audience for the final act, but the underworld figures, the Truands, are perhaps the most memorable figures in the supporting cast. Hugo describes in detail their physical and moral wounds, both real and imaginary. They are a group alienated from the other levels of society and as such, destined in 1482 to be trampled by the forces of order. Their passionate attack on Notre-Dame, theoretically to rescue Esmeralda, becomes an effort to plunder the cathedral's riches when there is a counterattack from above. These violent characters are depicted in dramatic night scenes, with light coming from flickering firelight that makes the surroundings appear darker. With his minor as well as his major characters, Hugo illustrates a world seemingly governed by fate and change.

## THEMES

A wealth of themes characterizes *The Hunchback of Notre-Dame*: there is the emphasis on fate, the contrast between beauty and the beast, the link between knowledge and power, the representation of change and development from monolithic opinion to individual ideas through the contrast between the cathedral and the printed word, and the types of repression that affect humankind and hint at future upheaval. Hugo weaves together this multitude of ideas into a rousing tale, but one that ends in many deaths rather than in resolution and reconciliation.

Hugo's inspiration for his overarching theme of fate came from seeing the Greek word for fate carved on a pillar inside Notre-Dame. In the novel, Claude Frollo himself carves the word, in Greek, on the wall in his cell high up in the cathedral. The tormented priest sees fate governing all things, even the death of a fly in a spider's web. He tells his visitor to lift no hand to save the trapped fly and compares himself to the fly, blithely seeking the light but doomed to fail, to be caught: "You did not see the subtle spider's web, spread by destiny between the light and you; you flew into it, wretched fool, and now you struggle, with crushed head and torn wings, between the iron antennae of

Fate!" (277). He even blames fate for his lustful love for Esmeralda, telling her that the hand of fate had touched him when he first saw her dance. Although Claude is the one who denounced Esmeralda to the authorities as a witch, he still accuses fate: "It is fate that seized you and delivered you to the terrible operations of the machine which I had secretly set in motion!" (326). And, as he rushes from the cathedral before Esmeralda's aborted execution, he again laments the role of fate: "he scanned the double twisted path along which Fate had driven their two destinies, to the point of intersection, where she had pitilessly effected a collision" (352). In the priest's mind, fate, rather than his own actions, is the cause of his downfall. Although he struggles to reach his goals, he is doomed to fall from the heights, broken on the pavement in front of this cathedral where he has labored.

Esmeralda, who is far from sharing Claude's thirst for knowledge or even his torments, also accepts the futility of struggling against fate. After Gringoire and Frollo take her from Notre-Dame during the Truands' attack, she is left with the priest: "Just then she realized the futility of trying to resist fate" (466). Fate appears to be inexorable and inevitable in the world Hugo depicts in this novel.

This world also contrasts beauty and the beast. The most obvious representatives are Esmeralda and Quasimodo. Hugo describes Quasimodo's physical being in great detail, starting at the novel's beginning, when this deformed creature is elected pope of the fools. Looked at as the devil's child by the old women who saw the four year old left by a door at Notre-Dame, Quasimodo carries this association with the devil throughout his life. Treated with fear and loathing by all who see him, except Claude Frollo, Quasimodo responds maliciously and bitterly to most human contact. The cathedral becomes his haven, the bells his faithful friends. He is not completely beast, but not recognizably human. Hugo equates the bell ringer's love and gratitude for Claude Frollo to the submissiveness of a slave and the vigilance of a most faithful dog. Quasimodo responds to Esmeralda's compassionate act—giving him water after his flogging—by developing an adoring love for this beauty.

Esmeralda exemplifies beauty. Crowds run to watch her dance; men are attracted by her beauty. Even the thugs and cutthroats of the Court of Miracles soften when she appears, and the spectators at her hanging are moved when they see her being transported to the gallows, still beautiful in spite of her sufferings in prison. The dancer herself is chiefly concerned with beauty, not her own but that of Phoebus, the handsome archer who rescues her from her first abduction by Quasimodo and Frollo. Esmeralda does not realize the shallowness of character masked by a handsome face. The glimmerings of compassion she feels for Quasimodo as he cares for her in sanctuary are erased once she learns Phoebus still lives. Esmeralda blames the hunchback for Phoebus's failure to respond to her plea, and she spurns Claude Frollo one last time by emphasizing the archer's beauty compared to the priest's ugliness. And she gives up completely after she hears Phoebus's voice refusing to help the men trying to extract the witch from the recluse's cell. Esmeralda huddles in the corner of the cell, repeating brokenly the name of her beloved.

Beauty does not always equal goodness nor beast wickedness. Esmeralda shows compassion toward Gringoire and Quasimodo yet loves one whose beauty is only physical. Quasimodo is capable of extreme violence and also tender compassion. The grotesque inhabitants of the Parisian underworld mix violent cruelty with care of their own. Fleur-de-Lys, Phoebus's fiancée, and her pretty, pampered friends treat Esmeralda's hanging as a spectator sport, and Fleur-de-Lys is jealous of the gypsy dancer's beauty, realizing its effect on Phoebus. With all these contrasts Hugo indicates that beauty is not completely pure nor beast completely tainted. Quasimodo has a certain beauty of soul that underlies his grotesque appearance. Esmeralda remains beautiful to the end but never learns to look beyond the surface. Beauty and beast crumble to dust together.

The themes of the printed word replacing architecture as the book of the human race and the search for knowledge equaling a will for power are linked. Both play an important role in the unfolding of the story and especially in developing the character of Claude Frollo. Claude is the character fixated on learning, on wanting to unlock the secrets of the universe. He chooses to focus on alchemy after studying all the subjects available for his perusal in fifteenth-century France. If he could discover how to create gold, Claude believes he could go farther than the throne of France; he could recreate the empire of the east (171). Ultimate knowledge will equal overwhelming power. King Louis XI is also attracted by this idea. Yet, the king is old (Claude insists that he is too old to gain this ultimate knowledge), and he is also ill. Claude fails to create gold before his fall from the heights of the cathedral, and King Louis XI dies in 1483. Neither ultimate knowledge nor ongoing power is attainable.

Claude is also the character who states unequivocally, "the book will kill the edifice" (173), the phrase that summarizes the theme of the power of the printed word. Hugo expands on this theme in the following chapter (book 5:2). He traces the history of architecture, expressing his point of view that, through its buildings, humanity reveals the various stages of its development: "Not only every religious symbol, but every human thought has its page in that vast book" (177). Yet, the invention of the printing press in the 1440s, only a few decades before the year of the novel's action, has changed the role of architecture and diminished its importance as a recorder of ideas and beliefs. With the spread of ideas through the printed word, new possibilities for human progress are available. Hugo likens this situation to a new tower of Babel, but for him, the tower is a positive image, one that emphasizes man's potential rather than man's conflicts.

Hugo illustrates these conflicts by contrasting the theme of revolution and revolt with repression. Because of Hugo's technique of interspersing references and explanations of historical events after 1483 into his narrative, the reader receives the impression that the time is not yet ripe for revolution. In Hugo's mind, the replacement of the feudal system by monarchical power as the Middle Ages draw to a close is a foretaste of the Revolution of 1789 in France: ordinary people would revolt against privileges and prerogatives that were out of their reach. The Truands attacking Notre-Dame are precursors of the Parisians storming the Bastille (and in 1483 the king resides in the Bastille, whose destruction will come to epitomize the French Revolution). Hugo's attitude toward the people seems ambivalent in this novel. The Truands are violent, hideous in appearance, marching through the dark night toward the cathedral, an angry mob with torches highlighting their pitchforks and pikes. In this attack they will be routed and killed by the king's troops, and Quasimodo, says Hugo, does not recognize that the Truands are his natural allies. However, Hugo has the Flemish envoy warn the king of the future success of the underclass: "the people's hour has not yet come" (450).

As another aspect of this theme of repression and revolution, Hugo brings in medieval justice. In book two, chapter two, the reader learns about the various ways criminals are executed in the Middle Ages, and Hugo does not neglect the opportunity to give his opinion of the "miserable guillotine" of his day which at least vanishes after performing its duty, rather than remaining as a permanent part of the Parisian landscape (62). Justice in the Paris of 1483 is also literally deaf to human rights: when Quasimodo is brought before Master Florian, after an attempt to abduct Esmeralda (at Frollo's instigation), neither the judge nor the accused, both deaf, hears what the other is saying, or understands the questions and answers. The judge arbitrarily assigns punishment without understanding either the criminal or his crime. The accused never comprehends the accusation or the judgment.

Esmeralda's trial for the alleged killing of Phoebus gives the novelist another opportunity to criticize the judicial system. Gringoire attends the trial without knowing that Esmeralda is the accused because he finds trials a form of entertainment, "the judges being usually so delightfully stupid" (300). Torture is routinely used to extract confessions, and Hugo describes the torture chamber in detail. Once Esmeralda has confessed to all her supposed crimes, the attorney tells her that her confession has enlightened justice and notes that she can testify to the leniency with which she has been treated (313). Both detail and dialogue reveal Hugo's opinion of the system in which innocent girls are accused, tortured, thrown into dark and dank cells, and finally hanged in a public spectacle. Her body is thrown into a common vault at Montfaucon, the building that receives the remains of all those put to death in the name of justice: the guilty and the innocent, the bad and the good.

## NARRATIVE STYLE

In *The Hunchback of Notre-Dame* Victor Hugo gives life to both inanimate and animate objects. Visual description highlights the novel's setting. The author devotes paragraphs and pages to describing in picturesque detail various sites important in the narrative, from the Great Hall of the very first chapter to the vault of Montfaucon in the last chapter. He devotes an entire chapter to the city of Paris itself (book 3:2). His presentation of Paris as viewed from the towers of Notre-Dame leads to a discussion of the growth and development of the city, its three parts—the city, the university, the town—and the characteristics of each part in the fifteenth century. At times the wealth of description may seem a digression away from the story. However, although Hugo is never shy about presenting his personal point of view, this point of view helps the reader feel a vivid sense of place and understand more fully the author's intent and the themes being revealed.

The cathedral of Notre-Dame de Paris becomes almost a living, breathing character in Hugo's panorama of fifteenth-century Paris. Even before describing the city, the novelist presents Notre-Dame, describing the building and all its symbols with special attention to both appearance and meaning. The first chapter of book three reveals both the architectural history of the cathedral and all the changes caused by time, revolution, and restoration. Hugo has definite opinions concerning these changes and throughout the novel never hesitates to express them, hoping to convince the reader of the truth of the author's convictions.

Hugo's descriptions create pictures in the reader's mind, and the image of the spider web and the fly in book 7:6 becomes an especially striking metaphor for the theme of fate in the novel. As Claude Frollo and Master Jacques pause in their discussion, a fly in search of sun blunders into a large spiderweb covering the window of Frollo's cell. Master Jacques starts to free the fly when he is stopped by the archdeacon, who says the fly should be left to fate, that is, death caused by the spider. He continues by comparing his own search for knowledge, for the eternal truth, to the fly's search for the sun. Fate, in the form of a spider, traps the fly. Frollo is caught like the fly in his own search, and there will be no escape.

Contrasts between light and dark, between the vertical aspirations toward the heavens of the cathedral towers and its underground foundation weighting it to the earth, between the glorious sounds of the bells and the roar of the attacking mob, and between the sublime and the grotesque—such contrasts characterize Hugo's narrative and descriptive style. A writing style rich in vocabulary, in phrases that create pictures that are nearly tactile as well as visual, it pulls the reader into Hugo's fifteenth-century world.

The author himself is very much present in this world. He chooses to be the narrator, to explain and to emphasize exactly those aspects of people, place, and time that he wants readers to notice and ponder. And he uses his digressions from the story line to amplify connections between that medieval world and his own of the early nineteenth century, including references to the centuries in between. A historical novel by its context, *The Hunchback of Notre-Dame* becomes a novel of ideas through its themes and a dramatic novel through its author's use of descriptive language to present themes and characters, setting and period.

## HISTORICAL CONTEXT

Victor Hugo was writing *The Hunchback of Notre-Dame* during the very moment France was undergoing a mini-revolution. The Bourbon king, Charles X, abdicated on August 2, 1830, after several days of rioting in Paris, and was succeeded by Louis-Philippe d'Orléans from another branch of the royal family. The Bourbon monarchy had been restored in France following the 1814 defeat of Napoléon and again after Napoléon's 100 days reign, begun after his escape from the island of Elba, ended at Waterloo in 1815. Louis XVIII, brother of Louis XVI, the king guillotined during the French Revolution, was the first restoration king. On his death another brother became King Charles X.

The 15-year restoration was a time of literary, intellectual, economic, and political change. France was trying to find stability in government that would incorporate both ideals of the Revolution and principles from the old regime. The country had been transformed by the Revolution, and a theoretical equality of status had been established, at least for men. Even members of the new nobility formed by Napoléon were equal before the law to all other citizens. However, women were legally treated as children with no property

rights separate from their husbands. Napoléon had let stand the legal possibility of divorce, but divorce would be made illegal in 1816 during Louis
XVIII's reign. Napoléon had also created a centralized and relatively efficient
administrative structure to run the country plus the Bank of France, which
gave France a sounder system of public finance. Historians disagree on how
much Louis XVIII accepted the changes or believed in them; he evidently
understood that an attempt to restore the old regime in all aspects would
result in chaos, not to mention opposition from other European nations.
However, a faction of extremists, or ultra-royalists, were not inclined toward
compromise. In legislative elections following Louis's return to the throne, a
majority of ultras became members of the Chamber of Deputies. Louis, in an
effort to find a balance, appointed moderate ministers to many posts. However, in later elections more deputies of liberal tendencies were elected, and
moderates appeared to control the government. However, after the assassination of the king's nephew, the Duc de Berry, by a fanatical bonapartist in
1820, the ultras brought down the moderate ministers. At the death of Louis
XVIII in 1824, Charles X became king. His coronation at the cathedral in
Rheims seemed to indicate a possible return to the past—Victor Hugo, in his
anti-Napoléon phase, wrote an ode celebrating the coronation and earned a
royal pension.

The Chamber of Deputies enacted certain measures that also indicated a
possible return to the past, including one to indemnify those who had lost
property because of the Revolution. This measure did insure that those who
held current title to the properties were allowed to keep them. Disagreements
between ministers also played a role in the downfall of the ultra government
in 1828. The new ministers did not hold the king's confidence and were dis-
missed in 1829. Charles's choice of replacement ministers was so unpopular
that the legislative opposition began a campaign for a change of constitution
and dynasty. Charles X dissolved the Chamber of Deputies early in 1830 and
ordered new elections for July. The opposition gained a majority in the new
Chamber, and the king and his unpopular ministers prepared decrees that dissolved the new Chamber, changed the electoral system, and abolished liberty
of the press. Once the decrees were known, the "three glorious days" followed: some demonstrations on July 27, violent street clashes on July 28, and
barricades throughout Paris on July 29. The royal garrison basically abandoned the capital to the rebels. A group of liberal politicians and journalists
had been meeting from the start of the crisis but had difficulty agreeing on
what to do. By July 30, posters calling for Louis-Philippe d'Orléans to be king
were plastered on walls throughout Paris. The duke hesitated because Charles
X had not officially abdicated. The king did so on August 2, in favor of his

grandson, but Louis-Philippe announced that no conditions had been set, and he accepted the throne as an expression of the will of the French people. Charles X, not wishing more violence, accepted what had happened and left France for another exile. Victor Hugo finished his novel as a new attempt at a constitutional monarchy got underway.

During this same 1814–1830 period, change and transformation also affected literature and the arts in general. The Revolution and the ongoing wars had marked the period from 1789 to 1814. Aristocratic patrons were no longer supporting writers, and the upheavals and stress of the time undermined the certainty and rationalism that had characterized the Enlightenment of eighteenth-century France. The new generation of writers, artists, and musicians searched for new ways of expressing the doubts and anxieties they were feeling. By 1830 the term Romanticism was being used to describe the intellectual and artistic spirit, a spirit concerned with revolt against the accepted order of things and for self-expression. Since individual uniqueness was a given for these writers, a precise definition of Romanticism is difficult. However, it is fair to say that those called Romantics looked at the world as not static but ever evolving. Often they were concerned with leaving what they considered the dullness of their era for a more exotic place or historical era. Yet, they also wanted to participate in the life of their own time. For example, in *René* and *Atala,* set in the new world of the United States, François-René de Chateaubriand expressed through his characters the *mal du siècle,* this unease of those seeking direction during a time of perceived upheaval. The author, who felt that the monarchy and the church were the pillars on which society should rest, participated in the government during the Restoration as ambassador to Berlin and London, then as minister of foreign affairs. Many writers interested in going beyond the rules of literature as professed by their predecessors of the seventeenth and eighteenth centuries met together in salons in Paris or published in the journals, such as the one founded by the Hugo brothers. Charles Nodier, librarian of the Bibliothèque de l'Arsenal in Paris, became the focal point of one literary salon, which met in his living room Sunday evenings. Nodier himself wrote poetry, short stories with fantastic plots and themes, and even a dictionary of maxims. Writers, critics, and artists came to talk about their work and exchange their ideas. Hugo participated in the far-ranging discussions of the group and learned from Nodier how to take advantage of the commercial potential of his works.

Later, by 1827, many writers were gathering at the Hugo apartment to talk more intentionally about their goals for their writing. Alexandre Dumas was among those who came, along with writers such as Alfred de Vigny, Alfred de Musset, Prosper de Mérimée, and Honoré de Balzac. After the triumph of

Hugo's play *Hernani* in 1830, the gatherings became less frequent as the writers pursued their own directions. Romanticism can be called a direction but not a literary school.

The theater was one literary arena that served as a rallying point for these new trends in literature. Hugo published the preface to his play *Cromwell* in 1827, writing that playwrights should forget the three unities of time (24 hours), place (one setting), and action (one plot line) that had characterized French theater for nearly two centuries. He also stated that comic elements could and should be inserted into so-called tragedies, that the setting should give the impression of life rather than a static location, and that dramatists should give full sway to their individual talent. All these ideas came to life for the public in the Hugo play *Hernani*, which was first performed at the Comédie Française on February 25, 1830. The performance was marked by a near riot as supporters of the new ideas clashed with those who upheld the long-time rules, but cheers drowned out the boos—and quite a few of the actors' lines (Robb 149–50).

The context in which Hugo wrote *The Hunchback of Notre-Dame* was one of change—in the political realm and in the literary realm. By 1831 a constitutional monarchy had replaced a king who believed he held the office by divine right. Writers felt called to express their imagination and individual feelings rather than strive for a universal ideal of reason and beauty. Wealth and birth still counted in both realms, education remained chiefly the province of the Catholic Church, but the reading public was increasing. Writers like Hugo were able to earn money from publishers as well as obtain stipends from the king. During the years of Louis-Philippe's regime there would be additional changes to all aspects of French life, thus enlarging the context in which novelists such as Alexandre Dumas, Gustave Flaubert, and Victor Hugo would write and publish.

# 7

## Victor Hugo
## *Les Misérables*

### 1862

#### BIOGRAPHICAL CONTEXT

Victor Hugo began work on the novel that was to become *Les Misérables* in November 1845 after being named a peer of France in April 1845 by King Louis-Philippe. As a peer of France, Hugo was a member of the upper chamber of the National Assembly and could call himself Viscount Hugo. However, during the 18 years until the publication of *Les Misérables*, Hugo's political ideas would undergo fundamental changes, and his novel would also change. The first working title for this novel was *Jean Tréjean*, soon changed to *Les Misères*.

In addition to working in a sporadic fashion on his novel, Hugo continued to publish, although less prolifically: his total number of poems from 1843 to 1848 was 143 (Robb 257). In his political life he made speeches before his fellow peers, championing the cause of the poor and oppressed.

The Revolution of 1848 saw Hugo being more caught up in political life and ceasing to work on his novel. Riots began in Paris in late February 1848 with protests against government economic policies. At first the National Guard tried to subdue the rioters, but on February 23 the guard went over to the people's side. By the morning of February 24 Paris was covered with barricades, Louis-Philippe had abandoned the Tuileries palace, and a provisional government was proclaimed. Hugo thought that a Regency should be established with the Duchess of Orléans as acting head of state, but most of Hugo's compatriots supported the premise of a new republic, as did another poet, Alphonse de Lamartine.

On February 25 Lamartine offered Hugo the post of Minister of Education in the provisional government. Hugo refused to accept, agreeing instead to serve as acting mayor of his section of Paris, the eighth arrondissement. He held the position for eight days, counseling moderation but also seeing that police were organized, barricades removed, and the streets repaired. Although Hugo was not an active candidate during the April elections in Paris, he received 59,446 votes and decided to participate in the June elections. He was elected a Paris representative to the National Assembly with 86,695 votes (Robb 267). Hugo did not belong to any particular political group and was conscious of the inconsistency of owing his first legislative seat to election by the king as a peer and his second to election by the people who had deposed the king.

In an effort to provide jobs for the many unemployed, national workshops had been established. Hugo felt it wrong to pay people for doing nothing although he was very sympathetic to the plight of the unemployed workers. When new revolts broke out in June after the workshops were closed, Hugo voted in favor of the decision to give full executive powers to General Cavaignac, thus supporting a temporary dictatorship. However, he accepted serving as one of the 60 representatives who were chosen to speak to the insurgents about the Assembly's decision. Backed up by National Guardsmen, the deputies, including Hugo, "harangued insurgents, stormed barricades, took prisoners, directed troops and cannon" (Robb 275). Hugo remained alive throughout the violence but troubled by what he had seen and experienced. His convictions were in a state of flux: he felt the people were a direct manifestation of God, but he believed also in order (Robb 277).

Martial law ended in November when the Assembly developed a new constitution. In December Louis-Napoléon Bonaparte, nephew of the emperor Napoléon, was elected president of the Second Republic. Hugo was hopeful that the new president would restore order but not try to conquer the world. He continued to serve in the Assembly and also had access to a newspaper, L'Evénement, run by his two sons and family friends. The paper often printed letters and speeches by Hugo.

During the elections for the new Assembly in May 1849, Hugo was again elected deputy. Continuing to position himself as middle of the road politically, Hugo made his moral positions very clear: opposition to the death penalty, defense of universal suffrage and funding for the arts, and belief that poverty could be eliminated (Robb 283–84). However, as the government began to act in nonrepublican ways, such as forbidding newspapers to say anything insulting about the president, Hugo denounced such actions. As part of the opposition he presented a speech during the debate on Louis-Napoléon's effort to extend his mandate beyond 1852. The one-hour speech extended to four hours because of interruptions by both supporters and detractors. In the speech Hugo left behind any royalist inclinations for complete support of the Republic. He compared Louis-Napoléon unfavorably with his uncle, saying, "What! Does Augustus have to be followed by Augustulus? Just because we had Napoléon le Grand, do we have to have Napoléon le Petit?" (quoted in Robb 290). The Assembly was in an uproar for several minutes, and Louis-Napoléon was not happy about being labeled the Little. As a deputy Victor was legally immune from prosecution, but his son Charles and the newspaper were both under fire. After a trial in June 1851, Charles was sentenced to six months in the Conciergerie, a prison in Paris. In September the second Hugo son, François-Victor, was sentenced to a nine-month prison stay, and *L'Evénement* was suspended. It was replaced by another newspaper, *L'Avénement du Peuple*, that was suspended six days later.

President Bonaparte's government continued to suppress various civil liberties, and many French, including Hugo, were expecting a coup. Paris awoke on the morning of December 2, 1851 to discover that a coup had taken place. The president accused the Assembly of plotting against him, vowed to protect all citizens, and promised to restore universal suffrage. Hugo and some other representatives went out to take stock of public opinion, but the prevailing opinion appeared to favor order and stability. Hugo wrote counter-proclamations to the president's messages and continued to be part of those in the Assembly opposing the coup. By December 5, the Assembly was dispersed and Hugo hid in Paris, unwilling to abandon his sons still in prison. By the evening of December 11, however, Hugo was in the train station, waiting to leave Paris for Brussels, Belgium. Posters of the so-called revolutionary leaders, including Hugo, were on display in the station (Robb 303–5).

Once in Brussels Hugo served as a focal point for other French republicans. He gathered others' stories together with his own and created a book about the coup that would not be published until 1877, although a short version of the story, titled *Napoléon-le-Petit*, was completed in June 1852. The Belgian government was under pressure to stop sheltering the revolutionaries, and Hugo made plans to find another refuge. Hugo and his family set sail for England in August 1852, passing through London, and settling first on the island of Jersey, located in the English Channel.

During the stay on Jersey Hugo continued to write and speak against the French government. He worked to assure the distribution of *Napoléon-le-Petit*, and by the end of 1852 some 38,500 copies were in circulation and being read in secret meetings in France (Robb 320). The book continued to be smuggled into France, much to Hugo's satisfaction. His antigovernment writings next focused on a volume of poetry called *Châtiments,* published in Brussels in November 1853, complete with missing words and blank spaces to show that the censor had been at work (Robb 326).

Other types of poetry occupied Hugo during his three years on Jersey, and he also became interested in table-turning, a method of communicating with spirits. Hugo entered into this type of communication with gusto, and it influenced his writing. It is impossible to tell how fully Hugo believed in these messages from those not present, and he stopped having table-turning sessions in autumn 1855.

Relations between England and France became much closer during the Crimean War in 1855, and Hugo was a vocal critic. He was expelled from Jersey in October 1855 and went to Guernsey, another island in the English Channel, but one more receptive to housing the French exile. He soon purchased a home in St. Peter Port and settled in Hauteville House with his household. He lived in Hauteville House until his return to France in 1870, following the defeat of Louis-Napoléon Bonaparte's Second Empire. He had refused the amnesty proposed by Napoléon III in 1859.

Poetry occupied Hugo's literary efforts until he decided in 1860 to begin again with *Les Misérables.* The final title change had been made in 1853 and confirmed in a letter to the British prime minister Lord Palmerston in 1854, but no new writing had been done (Guyard ix, x). From April 26 to May 12, 1860 the writer read what he had previously written. The original manuscript shows a certain number of marginal notes. Next, Hugo spent the period from May 12 to December 30 rewriting and making additions to his novel. At that point he had revised his original manuscript extensively and was ready to continue. He completed the fifth part of the novel on June 30, 1861, finishing near Waterloo, where he had gone to experience directly a pivotal location in the overall plan of *Les Misérables* (Guyard ix–x). Taking a break until September 16, 1861, Hugo completed his final revision over the following months and finished all the proofreading by June 14, 1862, after all but the final two sections of the novel had been published (Guyard x).

The novel was published by Hugo's Belgian publishers, Lecroix and Verboeckhoven. Hugo had signed a contract with the firm in 1861 since his long time publishers, the firm of Hetzel, would not give him the money he was asking, 300,000 francs (Robb 376). Hugo's contract negotiations helped establish serious writing as a respectable profession as well as his own financial security (Robb 377). Publication was preceded by a huge advertising campaign in many European cities. The novel was immediately successful and appealed to readers from across society's spectrum, but especially to the masses. Factory workers pooled resources in order to purchase a work of fiction otherwise beyond their means (Robb 378). Victor Hugo, author in exile, used his time away from France to create an unforgettable novel, one that has been transformed to the movie screen several times and inspired a 1980s musical, popular worldwide to the present day.

## PLOT DEVELOPMENT

A long novel in five acts, *Les Misérables* is tightly constructed, with all threads of plot, character, and theme becoming knotted together by the close of act three and resolving into a coherent conclusion at the end of act five. Each act is divided into books and the books into chapters. Hugo inserts books and chapters into each act that might appear as unrelated digressions, yet close reading reveals the relationship between the digression, the story Hugo is telling, and the ideas he wishes to leave with the reader. He places the digressions carefully, thus varying both the interest and the pace of the novel.

Act one is titled "Fantine," but this unfortunate woman is not introduced until book three of the section that bears her name. Book one presents Monseigneur Charles François Bienvenu de Myriel, bishop of Digne. Bienvenu translates as welcome, an apt name for a churchman more concerned with the well-being of his flock than the prerogatives of his office. After describing the bishop's way of life and his humanitarian as well as spiritual ideals, Hugo brings him to a confrontation with a dying man who was a former revolutionary. Following a discussion of ideals with this man, the bishop asks for his blessing. A man brought up with the privileges of aristocrats before the Revolution, the bishop is able to achieve reconciliation with one who represents a contrasting belief system. Concerned with human suffering more than with theological questions, "without trying to solve the enigma, he endeavored to staunch the wound" (57).

A well-worn traveler, seeking food and shelter, enters the story in book two. Rejected several times, he finds welcome at the bishop's home. The bishop shows respect to the unknown man, requesting that all the household silver be used to honor the stranger in their midst. When the stranger asks if the bishop is afraid that the new arrival might be a murderer, the bishop's response shows his faith: "God will take care of that" (82). Once everyone in the house has gone to bed, Hugo tells the stranger's story. He is a convict named Jean Valjean, bitter and dangerous, a victim of an unjust penal system. In spite of Monseigneur Bienvenu's remarks during dinner about repentance and charity, Valjean leaves the house during the night with the silverware. When he is brought back by the police, the bishop asks why Valjean did not take the silver candlesticks which were also part of the gift. He adds that he has bought Jean's soul and given it to God.

Jean Valjean continues on his way and toward evening is sitting by the side of the road when a young chimney sweep, Petit Gervais, passes by. The child drops one of the coins he is tossing in the air, and Valjean covers the coin with his foot. He scares the boy away. Shortly thereafter, Valjean realizes that, again, he is guilty of theft. He bursts into tears. Later that evening an unnamed man (undoubtedly Valjean) is seen kneeling in prayer in front of the bishop's door.

Book three of act one begins with a summary of the details of the happenings in 1817, from crimes to changes caused by the restoration of the monarchy. This book continues with the presentation of four young men, quite ordinary, and four young women, three quite experienced and the fourth who has kept her illusions about true love. This fourth young woman is Fantine, who is deeply in love with Félix Tholomyès, one of ordinary young men. The young men leave the young women at a restaurant one day. An hour later a letter is delivered, announcing that the young men are returning to respectable lives. Fantine is very sad; she has a small child and she loves Félix.

Fantine must find work and a way to care for her daughter Cosette. In book four, she discovers the Thénardier inn and arranges to have Cosette boarded there, thinking the Thénardiers will care for her. Fantine goes on in search of work, and Hugo describes the "dwarfish natures" of the couple who begin to abuse Cosette: "the poor lark never sang" (157).

Fantine's life intersects with Jean Valjean's in book five. She arrives in Montreuil-sur-mer, where a certain Father Madeleine has created a factory where the manufacture of jet beads has enabled both Madeleine and the town to prosper. He becomes mayor after having done much to benefit Montreuil-sur-mer. Meanwhile an Inspector Javert, assigned to the local police, thinks he recognizes Madeleine. When the mayor lifts an overturned cart off a driver named Fauchelevent, Javert is quite sure that the only man he ever knew strong enough to lift such a weight is a convict. Madeleine finds the injured Fauchelevent work as a gardener in Paris. Fantine is employed at the factory, and life goes well for her until it is discovered she has a child. She is fired, Thénardier increases the amount she must pay for Cosette, and her life spirals downward. She sells her hair, then her teeth, and finally herself. Hugo devotes a short chapter to denounce this European form of slavery, known as prostitution and affecting women. When Fantine attacks a local dandy who has stuffed snow down her neck, Javert arrests her for this criminal act. Madeleine arrives, and Fantine spits in his face because she believes he caused her dismissal from the factory. Appalled at what has happened to Fantine, Madeleine tells Javert to release her. The mayor assures Fantine that he will take charge of her and her child.

In book six, Fantine, ill, is in the infirmary. Madeleine sends money to the Thénardiers, telling them to bring Cosette to her mother. They stall and demand more money. Meanwhile Javert submits his resignation to the mayor, saying that he had denounced the mayor as the convict Jean Valjean. However, Javert has just learned that a man named Champmathieu has been arrested and recognized by former fellow convicts as Jean Valjean. Mayor Madeleine refuses to accept the resignation, but Javert is still fixated on the thought of his own wrongdoing.

In book seven the reader learns that Madeleine is indeed Jean Valjean, and he is torn between his ability to do good for others in his new identity and his conscience that tells him a man has been wrongly accused: "He could only enter into holiness in God's eyes, by returning to infamy in men's eyes" (227). After a long night of torment wrestling with his dilemma, Madeleine starts off to Arras where Champmathieu is on trial, still not knowing what he will do. Fantine, in the infirmary, awaits Madeleine's visit and the arrival of Cosette. In spite of accidents and breakdowns, Madeleine arrives in Arras, and because of his celebrity, is let into the court room. When Champmathieu is recognized by the fellow convicts, Madeleine speaks. He knows details that only Jean Valjean could know, and the court releases Champmathieu—who understands nothing of what has happened. Javert is overjoyed to receive an order to arrest Madeleine. Madeleine asks for three days to bring Cosette to her dying mother. When Javert only laughs, Madeleine threatens him with an iron bar wrenched from Fantine's bed. The town turns against Madeleine when he is in prison, but somehow he returns to his room and writes a note that he gives to Sister Supplice, the nun who has been caring for Fantine. When Javert arrives, seeking Valjean, Sister Supplice lies for the first time in her life, giving Valjean time to escape. Fantine dies and her body is thrown into the common grave. The priest decides that the money Valjean had left for Fantine's burial should be used for other charitable causes.

Act two, "Cosette," opens with a detailed account of Waterloo, what the area looks like when Hugo visits it in 1861, what it was like in 1815, the battle itself in all its aspects, and the meaning of Waterloo. The book closes with a battlefield scene after the fighting is over. A scavenger finds a living soldier, whom he robs. The soldier is a Colonel Pontmercy; the scavenger is Thénardier.

In book two, the reader learns that Jean Valjean has been captured. This event marks the end of the prosperity of Montreuil-sur-mer. In Montfermeil, where the Thénardiers still have their inn, some local residents are sure the devil is hiding his treasure in the woods near the village, as a mysterious figure has been seen going into the woods with a pick. In Toulon preparations are underway for a war against Spain. Hugo calls attention to the amount spent on cannon salutes that could have been used to feed the starving. A sailor falls from the main topsail of one of the battleships and is hanging by a line. A convict is seen climbing to the rescue. After the sailor is safe, the convict falls into the sea; no body is recovered.

Cosette enters the story in book three. It's Christmas Eve, and Cosette is knitting by the fire in the Thénardier inn. She is told to fetch water from the spring in the forest, a frightening task in the dark night. Even the sight of a wonderful doll at the street fair can't console her for long. At the spring she is staggering under the weight of the heavy bucket of water when a man takes it from her; Cosette is no longer afraid. The man asks her about her life and appears shocked to learn her name is Cosette. She asks for the bucket back as they are about to enter the inn; she wants to avoid a beating. The stranger observes the interactions at the inn and Cosette's lack of toys. He goes out and returns with the wonderful doll. The stranger negotiates with Thénardier, finally showing him a signed note from Fantine, authorizing this stranger to take charge of her daughter. The stranger leaves with Cosette, now dressed in new clothes, but black for mourning. This stranger is Jean Valjean. Hugo gives a brief summary of Jean's actions to this point, and the man and child return to Paris.

Their first lodging in Paris is described in book four. The two are very happy together. Virtue had entered Jean's life with his encounter with Bishop Bienvenu; love enters it with Cosette. But their landlady at the old Gorbeau House is suspicious as Jean goes out only when it's dark, and one evening, he thinks the beggar to whom he has been giving money is Javert. Next he sees Javert in the corridor outside his room in the Gorbeau house. That night Jean and Cosette leave.

Book five tells of the pursuit of Jean and Cosette by Javert and his men. Jean uses talents learned as a convict to stay ahead of the pursuers and eventually elude them. Jean and Cosette arrive in a dark garden. Jean needs help and finds it in the person of a man whose presence is signaled by a bell. It is Fauchelevent, now a gardener at the Convent of Petit-Picpus, who is delighted to help Father Madeleine as he had been helped. The book concludes with a summary of Javert's search for Jean since the latter's escape from the prison at Montreuil-sur-mer. Javert has had to give up, for the moment.

Books six and seven describe the convent, its history, and its present situation. Hugo also uses these books to outline his own ideas concerning the monastic or conventual life. He emphasizes that sincere prayer is always good but calls the convent "supreme egotism resulting in supreme self-denial" (520).

The problem in book eight is how to introduce Jean and Cosette into this convent where Fauchelevent works. Jean can be the gardener's helper and Cosette, called his granddaughter, can attend the convent school. She can be carried out of the garden in a basket and introduced properly at the convent door. Jean's exit and new entrance are more difficult to arrange. However, a nun has just died. She wants to be buried at the convent, which is against the law. The Mother Superior needs Fauchelevent's help to achieve this burial and is willing to accept the assistant Fauchelevent proposes. Jean is carried out in the coffin supposedly containing the deceased nun. After a certain amount of improvising, Fauchelevent is able to rescue Jean from the coffin before burial. Jean and Cosette have a new home. They can visit an hour each day, and Cosette learns to laugh. Jean reflects on different types of enclosures and his interactions with two houses of God, the bishop's and the convent's. Both had helped him, the first keeping him from falling back into crime and the second from falling into punishment.

Hugo introduces act three, "Marius," with a series of short chapters in book one, presenting the gamins of Paris, that is, street children. After developing the characteristics of these children in general, Hugo introduces Little Gavroche. This boy is free but unloved. His family, known by the name of Jondrette, has deserted him and now lives in the Gorbeau house where Jean and Cosette lived before finding refuge in the convent.

Book two introduces Monsieur Luc-Esprit Gillenormand, over 90 years old and a throwback to the eighteenth century, who regrets both the Revolution and Napoléon. His older daughter, unmarried and called both a prude and a bigot, lives with him, as does his grandson, Marius. The relationship between Marius and Monsieur Gillenormand is outlined in book three. Monsieur Gillenormand disapproved totally of his younger daughter's marriage to Colonel Pontmercy, a soldier in Napoléon's army. At the death of Marius's mother, the father agrees to a separation from his son so that the boy can inherit from his grandfather. The colonel lives a solitary life in Vernon, a town near Paris. Marius is brought up by his grandfather and absorbs the old man's attitudes: Marius is "royalist, fanatical, and austere" (624). However, when the colonel is dying, Monsieur Gillenormand sends Marius to see his father. Marius arrives too late, but he finds a note left by his father asking him to use the title baron (an inheritable title awarded to the colonel by Napoléon) and to help Thénardier, whom the colonel regarded as saving his life. After meeting Monsieur Mabeuf, a friend of the colonel, at church, Marius is stunned to hear from the old man of his father's concern for his son. Marius begins to study the history of the Napoleonic era, and soon he becomes enamored of the period. When his grandfather finds in Marius's room the note from the colonel and visiting cards listing Marius as the Baron Pontmercy, he is furious. Both men are adamant that their point of view is the correct one. Grandfather kicks Marius out of the house, and the latter leaves with only 30 francs, his watch, and a few clothes.

The title of book four, "The Friends of the A B C," is based on a play on words in French: *abaissé*, meaning the downtrodden, is pronounced phonetically the same as the first three letters of the alphabet. This group of young men meet in cafés to discuss their ideas concerning progress. Marius joins this group, and again, his ideas undergo change. When he defends Napoléon, Combeferre, one of the A B C, tells him that being free is greater than all of Napoléon's accomplishments. Marius decides, however, that he cannot reject Napoléon yet.

Marius learns about being poor in book five. Although his aunt sends him money from time to time, he always returns it. He finishes his legal studies, moves to the Gorbeau building, and earns small amounts by translating documents. Marius develops his friendship with Monsieur Mabeuf because of the ties with his father. Mabeuf, who has a passion for plants and books, is growing poorer and poorer as he has little income. Marius gives 25 of his remaining 30 francs to the landlady for the Jondrette family, who are about to be evicted for nonpayment of rent.

Book six is the story of Marius's discovery of a beautiful girl. For some months he has noticed a young girl accompanied by a white-haired man walking in the park, without paying much attention to either. However, one day he is overcome to notice that the girl has become a beautiful young lady. He is in love, starts dressing in his best suit for the trips to the park, and observes the young lady from behind trees. One day he follows the young lady and the man to their residence. The next day their visit to the park is very short, and the man stares at Marius. After a week Marius learns that they have left their lodging.

In book seven Hugo discusses crime in Paris. He says that at the depths of society there is evil, which comes from ignorance. He describes the four bandits that ruled the underworld of Paris between 1830 and 1835. Babet, Gueulemer, Claquesous, and Montparnasse, their helpers, and others like them are an ongoing scourge.

Action resumes in book eight. Marius is despondent throughout autumn and into winter because the young lady and the men have disappeared. One day, while he is out walking, two girls run by him and drop an envelope with four letters. Marius notes that these letters, signed with different names, all ask for money. Next, one of these girls knocks on his door and gives him a similar letter. It is from Jondrette. The girl chatters on about her life and appears very interested in Marius. After she leaves, he notices a hole in his wall, near the ceiling. Climbing on a chair he sees true misery, a filthy and sordid room. He watches the occupants, and when the girl returns, saying that the philanthropist is coming, the man damages more furniture and makes the second girl break a window. Marius is stunned to see that the philanthropist is the man from the park who arrives with the young lady. They bring clothes, and the man, Monsieur Leblanc, promises to return with money. Marius tries to follow, but the two take a cab and he has no money to pay for another cab. Returning home, he sees Jondrette speaking with a man identified as a criminal. The elder Jondrette girl sees Marius's distress and offers to help. He wants the address of the philanthropist. Meanwhile Jondrette makes certain preparations for the philanthropist's return. Marius is suspicious and decides to go to the police. The police officer gives him pistols to signal when the police should enter. This officer is Javert. When Monsieur Leblanc arrives, Jondrette starts his story, and four men enter the room silently. Marius is shocked to learn that Jondrette is really Thénardier. The four men subdue Monsieur Leblanc, and Thénardier tells him to write to his daughter, asking her to come. Madame Thénardier goes to deliver the letter but returns to say that the address is false. Leblanc bursts his bonds, grabs a chisel from the fireplace and holds it against his arm. Marius finds the note left by the Thénardier daughter that morning and throws it into the room. The message that the cops are there causes the men to flee, but they are met by Javert at the door. The accompanying police arrest the criminals, and Javert starts to write his report. When he looks up to talk to Leblanc, the latter has left by the window. A ragged boy comes by the next day, and the landlady tells him his family is in prison. He leaves, singing. It's Little Gavroche.

In "Saint-Denis and Idyll of the Rue Plumet," act four of this epic novel, the characters' various stories are developed in more detail. Hugo uses the first book of the section to give the reader background knowledge of the period between 1815 and 1832. Describing the Restoration and the beginnings of the July Monarchy under King Louis-Philippe, Hugo notes that the new monarchy was designed to protect the bourgeoisie, or the middle class, not the people, that is, the workers. By 1832 underlying unrest was visible in the gatherings of various groups; the ideal of a republic was not dead. According to Hugo, the goals of these groups centered on ending oppression and tyranny, providing work for men, educating children, giving women an amenable social climate, establishing fraternity for all: in one word, attaining progress (853). Concluding book one with a return to the personal story, Hugo shows Enjolras of the Friends of the A B C assigning tasks to his followers in preparation for what might come.

Marius has left the Gorbeau house following the episode with the Thénardiers, Monsieur Leblanc, and the police. In book two he is completely depressed about losing sight of his love and spends much of his time at a field on the outskirts of Paris called the Field of the Lark. Since Lark is the name the Thénardiers used for his love, he is sure he will learn where she lives by visiting this field. During the same time period, Javert is unhappy at the disappearance of Thénardier's prisoner and the escape of two of the most dangerous criminals. Mabeuf, meanwhile, is growing steadily more destitute. Even his garden suffers. One night a young girl appears and waters his garden. She asks for Marius's address and seeks him out. It is Eponine who tells Marius she can provide the address he wants. It is evident to the reader that Eponine loves Marius, who is too absorbed in his love for someone else to notice Eponine other than as a means to his goal.

In book three Hugo returns to Cosette's story. Going back in time, he details Jean's reasons for leaving the convent and the lodgings Jean finds. Cosette discovers one day that she has become beautiful. Jean realizes that she is growing up and her beauty will change her love for him. A short chapter retells the episodes in the park from Cosette's point of view. Jean senses Marius and feels his old ferocity awakening. He and Cosette are both sad but do not speak of their feelings. One morning they go out to watch the sunrise. They see wagons coming, then a crowd of people shouting. When the sun appears, those riding in the wagons, convicts being transported, begin their loud outcries and abusive language. Cosette and Jean are both terrified, Jean because of his memories and Cosette because of the violence.

As book four opens, Jean's and Cosette's life together grows darker. But after the visit to the Jondrettes/Thénardiers and Jean's injury from the red-hot chisel, Cosette is happier as she can devote her attention to her injured father. The coming of spring also lifts her spirits. When Jean is out one evening, he is attacked by the criminal Montparnasse. Jean overcomes him and gives him a lecture on the value of honest work. Gavroche, who happens to be watching, picks Montparnasse's pocket and takes the purse the criminal has stolen. He gives it, unseen, to Mabeuf, whose servant he has heard lamenting their lack of funds.

In book five Cosette has nearly forgotten Marius. He, however, is near death from sorrow. One evening when Jean is away, Cosette hears someone in the garden and sees a man's shadow. Jean reassures her by showing her the shadow cast by the stovepipe. A few days later Cosette finds a love letter under a stone on the garden bench. Immediately she is sure that it is from the man in the park and loves again. That evening this man is in the garden; it is Marius. They fall into each other's arms, kiss, and talk, finally telling each other their first names. Love has brought two kindred souls together, at least for the moment.

Book six is devoted to the actions of Little Gavroche, this sprightly, cynical yet compassionate street child. After Gavroche, Madame Thénardier had given birth to two more boys whom she didn't want. They were being cared for by Monsieur Gillenormand's former servant, Magnon, whose own two children had died. These children were supported financially by Gillenormand. Since Magnon didn't mention the death of her own two, the money kept coming. But the two little boys are left destitute when Magnon is arrested. Wandering the streets of Paris, they are taken under Gavroche's wing. He houses them in an immense hollow statue of an elephant located near la Place de la Bastille. After tucking in the children, Gavroche answers Montparnasse's call and goes to help his father escape from prison. Thénardier is indifferent to the fact that his son provided the rope that completes the escape.

Another Hugo discourse, this time on a linguistic phenomenon, is the subject of book seven. Hugo discusses *argot*, the French word for slang, especially that spoken by criminals, "the language of misery" (980). Hugo presents the background of *argot*, numerous examples, and concludes the book by noting that misery continues to exist.

Book eight carries forward the love story of Cosette and Marius. Their love is idealistic, dreamlike, and absorbs them totally. Jean suspects nothing, but complications approach. Eponine sees Marius, who has completely forgotten her, and follows him to the Rue Plumet. She sees her father and his criminal cohorts about to attack and persuades them to abort their plot or she will scream and call the police. Marius hears from Cosette that her father is planning to take her to England. Reality has entered their idyll. Marius tells Cosette he will return in two days and gives her his address. He goes to see his grandfather, who has been in despair about Marius's absence but still can't admit his love for his grandson. Instead, he insults Marius by saying that Cosette, since she has no fortune, should become Marius's mistress. Marius, outraged, leaves. Monsieur Gillenormand regrets his words, but it is too late.

Book nine puts Jean, Marius, and Father Mabeuf in motion. Jean is worried about Thénardier, whom he has seen prowling in the neighborhood. Also, while sitting near the Champs de Mars in Paris, he receives a paper with the words, move out. Marius is in despair and, with the pistols Javert gave him in his pocket, wanders the streets in a daze. Cosette is not in the usual place, and a voice tells him that his friends are waiting for him at the barricade, Rue de la Chanvrerie. Mabeuf is now completely without funds as he has sold his last book and given the money to his servant. He too is wandering in a daze.

In the tenth book of the act, Hugo talks about the differences between a riot and an insurrection. The spark for the happenings on June 5, 1832, was the death of General Lamarque, who had upheld the ideal of liberty. Men are arming themselves, the government is observing, the barricade is being constructed, and the National Guard is called out.

Gavroche is featured again in book eleven. He is marching through the streets, singing. As he has no money for food, he rips down posters to express himself, then throws a rock through a barber's window. He meets Enjolras and others from the Friends of the A B C. When they meet Mabeuf, Enjolras tells the old man to go home but he follows, because they're going to overthrow a government. Next to join the marchers is a girl in boy's clothes who asks about Marius.

The marchers arrive at the Rue de la Chanvrerie and the Corinth tavern in book twelve. Enjolras and friends decide to set up the barricade by the tavern because of its location on the narrow street. Gavroche is here, there, and everywhere as the construction proceeds. He keeps asking for a working musket. Gavroche is also the one who recognizes the new recruit as Inspector Javert. Javert is made a prisoner. One of the insurgents, a certain Le Cabuc, thinks they should shoot from the roof of the opposite building, and kills the porter who won't open the door. Enjolras executes Le Cabuc for the discipline of the insurrection.

Book thirteen brings the despairing Marius to the barricade, a black hole in the middle of the city. He pauses before entering, thinking of his father but also of the good reasons for the current insurrection.

The troops are approaching, warns Gavroche, in book fourteen. He grabs Javert's musket. With the first volley from the troops, the insurgents' red flag is shot down. There are no volunteers to hoist the flag until Mabeuf takes it and climbs the barricade. He is shot and killed, but the flag is flying. Marius shoots the guardsmen aiming at Gavroche and Courfeyrac, killing both attackers. With no more ammunition, he grabs the power keg and threatens to throw it if the troops don't fall back. They flee, and soon Marius hears a faint voice. Eponine, severely wounded, is crawling toward him. She dies in his arms after giving him a letter from Cosette that tells of her imminent departure from the Rue Plumet. Marius writes to Cosette and also a note saying where to carry his body when he is killed. He wants Gavroche to take the letter to Cosette while Gavroche wants to be at the barricade for the final assault. Gavroche decides to run quickly and return even more quickly.

The final scene of act four, book fifteen situates Jean and Cosette after their move. Both are absorbed in their private preoccupations. Jean is relieved to have removed Cosette from the Rue Plumet, but then he sees the reflection in a mirror from her blotter and is able to read her final note to Marius. Devastated, Jean's "self howled in the abyss of his soul" (1154). Their servant Toussaint reports that there is fighting near the church of Saint Merry. While sitting in front of his lodging, Jean sees Gavroche arrive and figures out the boy has a letter for Cosette. He takes the letter and learns from Gavroche the location of the barricade. Still in turmoil, Jean is joyful at the thought of Marius's probable death. He puts on his National Guard uniform and heads toward the barricade area. Gavroche returns to the barricade, singing.

Act five, "Jean Valjean," resolves the stories of the remaining characters, completes Jean's redemption, and creates a happy end for Cosette and Marius. In book one of act five, Hugo begins by telling the story of two immense barricades constructed in June 1848. The 1832 barricade was but a rough draft for 1848. But there is no more food for those at the barricade in 1832, and Enjolras says all that is left is to fight to the death. Combeferre wants the fathers of children to leave; they can escape wearing the four National Guard uniforms available. Five men are chosen and a fifth uniform appears. Jean Valjean has arrived, and Marius, recognizing the father of Cosette, vouches for him. The events of this last day unfold. The insurgents are able to drive back the attacking guardsmen at first but run out of ammunition. Gavroche goes over the barricade to retrieve ammunition from fallen guardsmen. He sings gaily as bullets fall around him. He is finally hit and cannot finish the last verse of his song. Marius brings back Gavroche's body.

In between the scenes at the barricade, Hugo returns to Cosette, dreaming in her room and not knowing what is happening not all that far away. He also shows the two little lost boys in the Luxembourg gardens, wandering hungry and ragged—a contrast to a well-dressed father and young son who are feeding the swans. Hearing more sounds of gunfire, the father takes his son away, and one of the little boys is able to grab a chunk of brioche before the swans. This is the reader's last glimpse of these lost children.

As the defenders rip up paving blocks to protect the bistro, Jean volunteers to dispose of Javert. Once out of sight Jean cuts Javert loose from his bounds, tells him to leave, and gives Javert his own address. He shoots into the air and returns to the barricade, calling "done." Marius, having recognized both men, feels chilled. Hugo digresses briefly to discuss why insurrections succeed or fail. This battle of the barricade is a lurch toward progress. The final attack by the National Guard succeeds. Enjolras is the only defender still standing. His audacity to die well impresses his executioner. Jean has left, carrying the wounded, unconscious Marius. His role in the battle has been to be silent and give aid. Uncertain what to do with Marius, Jean sees a grating in the street. Lifting it, he descends to an underground passage, still carrying Marius.

Book two is devoted to a history and description of the Paris sewer system. Book three chronicles Jean's journey through this dark and damp labyrinth. Dodging a police patrol who is searching the sewers for insurgents, Jean labors on. On the riverbank two men are shadowing each other. The first man disappears, and the second then notices an unlocked grating. He sets himself to watch. Jean, in the depths of the sewers, finds the note Marius had written concerning the disposal of his body. Hating Cosette's lover, he continues nevertheless, fighting quicksand, fatigue, mud, and darkness. He arrives at a locked grating but is accosted by a man whom he recognizes but who does not recognize him. It is Thénardier, who thinks this man is carrying the body of a person he has killed. He offers to let Jean out for half of the dead man's goods. Thénardier searches Marius's body, tears off a strip of his coat, and lets Jean out of the sewer. Javert is there. Jean, unrecognizable, covered as he is with the mud and grime of his journey, identifies himself, asking only that Javert allow Jean to take Marius home. "The corpse, the specter, and the statue" set off in the cab (1309). They deliver Marius to his grandfather's home. Jean has one last request, that he be allowed a brief stop to tell Cosette where Marius is. At the Rue de l'Homme armé, Javert pays the cabdriver and tells Jean to go in. As Jean climbs the stairs, he pauses on the second landing to look out the window. Javert is gone. The noise and bustle of taking care of Marius awaken his grandfather. Monsieur Gillenormand is certain Marius is dead and faints when Marius opens his eyes.

In book four the reader learns of Javert's inner torment. A convict has been his benefactor. He writes up his last report, leaves the police station, goes to the river, jumps in—only the night witnesses this conclusion.

At last Marius and Cosette will achieve happiness in marriage. In book five Marius is on his way to recovery. His one thought is of Cosette, and he fears a new confrontation with his grandfather. However, Monsieur Gillenormand is overjoyed with Marius's recovery and Cosette's beauty and goodness. He approves their marriage. Jean brings Cosette's dowry, the money that was buried in the woods near Montfermeil. He sees that Cosette's civil situation is regularized, saying that she is the last member of an extinct family and the dowry is from a legacy. Grandfather Gillenormand brings out presents of all sorts from his family treasures. Marius, in spite of his personal happiness, is worried because of his confused memories of Jean at the barricade. He also cannot locate Thénardier or the unknown man who carried him to safety.

Book six relates the events of the wedding day, February 16, 1833, Mardi Gras. Jean slips away from the wedding banquet, but his absence doesn't impinge for long on the general joy. Back in his room Jean takes out those things of Cosette's that he has saved and breaks down in tears. Once again he must fight with his conscience and decide whether to tell the truth about his life.

As book seven begins, Jean asks for a private interview with Marius and tells his story: "It's by degrading myself in your eyes that I raise myself in my own" (1397). His conscience has prevailed. Marius remains silent as Cosette enters, radiant in her happiness. After she leaves, Marius promises to keep Jean's secret and acquiesces to Jean's wish to visit Cosette. Marius now feels he understands his own latent antipathy to Jean, but he still wonders about the Jondrette affair, the barricade, and Javert.

In book eight Jean is detached bit by bit from Cosette. The visits take place in a basement room, and eventually the chairs are gone from this room. Jean does not return. When Cosette inquires about his absence, the servant returns with the news that Jean has gone on a trip. Cosette is so happy with Marius that she doesn't feel Jean's absence, but Jean slowly declines physically due to his sorrow.

The situation is resolved in book nine. Jean walks daily toward the couple's home but finally is so weak that he doesn't leave his bed. The caretaker calls a doctor, who understands Jean is dying of grief. Thénardier comes to visit Marius. He gives his explanation of Javert's suicide and the source of Jean's fortune. He also tries to prove that Jean murdered a young man in the sewers and brings out the piece of cloth from Marius's coat. Now Marius understands the entire story, refutes Thénardier's proof, but gives him 1,500 francs and says he won't turn him in because of Waterloo. Thénardier, with his remaining daughter, goes to America where he becomes a slave trader.

Marius calls Cosette and says they must immediately visit Jean who has been providence for both of them. On arriving, Cosette immediately shows her love for Jean, who is overjoyed to see and hear her. At the news that Marius and Cosette will take him home, Jean says he is dying. He tells them to love one another always and dies peacefully. As he had requested, he is buried in a quiet tomb. Even the inscription on the tombstone is written in pencil and fades away.

## CHARACTER DEVELOPMENT

Hugo is more interested in the ways his characters illustrate his ideas or are dominated by a single emotion than in their psychological subtleties. Many of them can be labeled with the name of their all-consuming passion: Javert is obsessed with law as he sees it, Marius with his love, Enjolras with the ideals of the Revolution. Jean Valjean himself becomes the epitome of charitable love toward others. With description and dialogue Hugo is able to make these characters and a huge supporting cast vivid for their time upon the stage.

Monseigneur Charles François-Bienvenu de Myriel is the saint who begins the novel and serves as the catalyst for Jean Valjean's eventual redemption. In order for readers to understand how the bishop became saintly, Hugo gives them his past history as an aristocrat before the Revolution of 1789. The events of this tumultuous period change his destiny, and Bienvenu becomes a priest, moving to the position of bishop. His past history is revealed through what people say about him; his present actions are shown through what he says to different people and how he says it. A letter written by his sister tells of his unpretentious and austere life. Although the bishop reveals prejudices typical of one brought up in privilege, he learns from the humble and shows the way of charitable love to his flock, and most particularly to Jean Valjean, the convict shunned and scorned by those whom he asks for food and shelter.

Similar techniques are used to introduce Jean. The reader sees him first as those he encounters see him. Hugo waits to tell the story of Jean's past and how an unjust penal system has condemned and brutalized this man, whose initial crime was to steal bread to feed his sister's children. He waits until Jean has been taken in and treated with respect by the bishop. This pause gives the reader the chance to develop empathy for this unfortunate and to applaud the generosity of the bishop, who includes the silver candlesticks to the items Jean took.

Jean's first transformation is into Monsieur Madeleine, the enlightened factory owner at Montreuil-sur-mer. Again the reader sees him through the comments of townspeople, as reported by Hugo. When Madeleine learns that another has been accused of being Jean Valjean, his struggle with his conscience is seen directly as he spends the night in uncertainty about what to do. He is never more human as he tries to use fate, accident, and his good works as mayor and businessman to avoid another downfall.

When Jean is able to fulfill his promise to Fantine and take over the care of Cosette, his character and, more importantly, his soul, gain a new dimension: love. His love for Cosette influences all his actions to the end. Hugo shows this love in action, how it becomes possessive and even jealous as Jean grows aware of Cosette's love for another. Although his goodness is tested, it is not found wanting. Jean suffers his final crisis of conscience when he determines to tell Marius the truth of his background. He knows he will die if he gives up Cosette, and he has always had a powerful instinct for survival. Yet he also knows that he must give way to Cosette's new happiness. Jean Valjean is a very human saint, as Hugo portrays him through his actions, his thoughts, and his turmoils. He has his happy ending as Cosette and Marius rush to his bedside, and he is able to die peacefully, surrounded by their love.

If Jean Valjean is an outcast because of his prison past, Fantine is also an outcast. In his description, Hugo emphasizes her essential innocence and the illusions that are slow to leave her. Because she loves Félix Tholomyès, he must love her. Even Tholomyès recognizes this love although he does not return it. He sums up Fantine's character: "she is visionary, dreamy, pensive, sensitive" (137). When Fantine is left alone with her child, she does the best she can. But society, according to Hugo, is against her. She cannot earn enough to support her daughter because she has entrusted the child to an unworthy couple. She must sell hair, her teeth, herself, and even these forced sales are not sufficient. Passive throughout most of her misfortunes, she flares up and attacks when the idle young man stuffs snow down her bodice. Then she rails at Javert and spits in Madeleine's face. Once Madeleine takes charge of Fantine's welfare, she reverts to her essential sweetness of character. Her last appearances in the story emphasize her concern for her child. But Fantine is doomed by all that has happened to her, and her health causes her death before Cosette can be brought to her. She is a symbol of innocence degraded by society and engages the reader's sympathy although she is more interesting for what she represents than for how she acts.

The woman is doomed, but the child's fate is more positive. The reader pities the abused Cosette, whom the Thénardiers treat as a slave. As she finds a loving father figure in Jean, she gives him the love that will help achieve his redemption. Cosette's feelings, as described by Hugo, are the only aspects of her character that are visible to the reader. What she believes or thinks is only hinted at; what she feels is all important, especially once she discovers the love of a young man. Her developing love for Marius and their eventual marriage show a young woman who will submerge her identify into that of her husband and be supremely happy. She follows Marius's lead in separating from Jean and is equally as willing to reconcile with the man who has enabled her to achieve this happiness.

There is a purity in Cosette that is reflected in the purity of Marius. He is the more interesting of the two, with a more active life and a more fully shown character. Marius is idealistic, reminiscent in his political development of the young Victor Hugo who was first a royalist and then a bonapartist, like Marius. Hugo, who had his own period of relative poverty, is able to show Marius's financial struggles in a believable manner. Marius is also idealistic in loving Cosette from afar. No Félix Tholomyès, Marius places his unknown beloved on a pedestal, horrified when the wind blows her skirt and her garter is visible. A person of integrity, Marius is concerned amidst his happiness with Cosette to pay his debt to Thénardier and especially to the unknown man who saved him after the fall of the barricade. Not a perfect young man, Marius is unconsciously cruel toward his grandfather and to Eponine, so caught up in his own love that their love for him doesn't register. Hugo brings out these traits through Marius's direct reflections and his actions, creating a memorable character whose happy end is depicted in a believable and sympathetic manner.

Inspector Javert, the incorruptible police officer obsessed with the law, comes alive through description of his physical presence, of his inner thoughts that never waver, and of his actions that never falter until the very end of his story. Javert blindly obeys legal authority and believes that all lawbreakers should be legally damned. He is incapable of going beyond the letter of the law. Yet his implacable pursuit of Jean Valjean, while it causes suffering, offers Jean the opportunity for spiritual strength. Jean refuses to kill Javert at the barricade and persuades his pursuer to let him take the unconscious Marius home. When he asks to pass by his own lodging to say farewell to Cosette, Javert grants the request—and then walks off into the night. Javert is so deeply shaken when he realizes that he has let Jean go free that he cannot cope with his breach of duty. For the first time it occurs to him that there may be a higher law than that created by man. However, he cannot accept this realization, so completes his report and disappears into the obscurity of the River Seine. His implacability is vividly portrayed throughout his appearances in the novel and makes him an unforgettable personification of an obsessive concept.

Monsieur and Madame Thénardier are presented first with details of their physical appearance, which suggest their inner being: both are hideous. Madame Thénardier fools the innocent Fantine into believing that here is a maternal woman when Fantine sees her affectionate manner with her two daughters. But this woman with her immense body and voice is at heart a brute, and Cosette suffers from her abuse. By the time the Thénardiers reappear in Paris, Madame's brutality has taken over her entire being. The reader can see she is a monster.

Monsieur Thénardier, although physically smaller than his wife, is well able to persuade her to follow his lead. The reader never learns what forces have created this man, but his actions speak for the crookedness of his soul and mind. Perverse is perhaps a more apt term than evil to characterize Thénardier. After being paid by Jean, he could have continued with his inn but appears in Paris with more conniving schemes to earn money. His den in the old Gorbeau house, a sordid, fetid room, shows his lack of success, and rather than be content with the contributions Valjean (as Monsieur Leblanc) promises him, Thénardier goes after Valjean's entire fortune. He fails and becomes even more embittered. His final failure with Marius caps his career—although he does receive enough money to leave for America. Hugo does not need to interject any pronouncements about Thénardier and his wife. Their actions speak for them.

One of the Thénardier daughters, Eponine, is more fully portrayed than her sister and illustrates again Hugo's belief that a child's misery is the most poignant of all. From the well-loved toddler of the inn, Eponine becomes the elder Jondrette girl, torn bodice and all, abetting the schemes of her criminal father. Yet Eponine, through her actions, reveals more than a harsh voice speaking *argot*. Her feelings about Marius show a desire for affection, quite possibly for respectability. She is humanly jealous of Marius's love for another girl and naturally resents his complete indifference to her, but her courage impels her to follow Marius to the barricade. Eponine's death in Marius's arms is a moving scene. With the story of this life and untimely death, Hugo shows one way a human life and its potential can be wasted.

Gavroche comes on the scene first as a representative of a certain type of child, the Paris gamin or street kid. Little by little Hugo develops this child's individuality, presenting specific details of behavior and speech. Gavroche steals soap but buys bread for hungry children. He helps criminals escape but gives a stolen wallet to a destitute old man. He mocks his own troubles but is sensitive to others' sufferings. Readers see directly, with little author commentary, the lively personality of this boy who meets all trials joyously, singing even as he is finally struck down by bullets.

Hugo reveals the personality of Monsieur Gillenormand in a similar way, showing this eighteenth-century throwback's feelings and attitudes through his actions and descriptions of his life. Gillenormand has the wit and elegance of the eighteenth-century salon but also its egotism. He refuses to admit strong feelings, such as love for his grandson, until he thinks the young man is dead. What Marius holds sacred, his grandfather treats in a flippant manner, for example, telling Marius to make Cosette his mistress. However, once forced into realizing how much his grandson means to him, Gillenormand bends all his efforts to making Marius and Cosette happy. He is a lively, believable old man, adding to the panorama of human life portrayed in *Les Misérables*.

A multitude of characters in the supporting cast are also portrayed through their words and deeds. Enjolras, the idealist of the Friends of the A B C, is motivated by a utopian view of a future where liberty, equality, and fraternity will transform the world. His compatriots in the group are differentiated with a brief description when Marius meets the group, and all die willingly at the barricade, perhaps not as committed to an ideal world as Enjolras is but meeting their end with dignity. An underlying dignity also characterizes Monsieur Mabeuf, this man whose intellectual interests and ever-increasing poverty don't keep him from befriending Colonel Pontmercy and then the colonel's son Marius. He is able to die with dignity intact as he raises the red flag over the barricade. Selfless women servants are also carefully drawn: Mother Plutarch who faithfully serves Mabeuf, Toussaint, devoted to Cosette and Jean. Even the criminals are differentiated from each other: for example, Gueulemer, the stupid strong man; Montparnasse, the handsome yet ruthless young man. Although all these characters illustrate the novel's themes, they come alive through Hugo's ability to describe and create a sense of those who illustrate the powerless and the unfortunate.

## THEMES

Preceding the first act of *Les Misérables* is Hugo's own statement of the essential idea of his novel: "so long as the three problems of the century—the degradation of man by the exploitation of his labor, the ruin of woman by starvation, and the atrophy of childhood by physical and spiritual night...so long as ignorance and misery remain on earth, there should be a need for books such as this" (*Les Misérables* n.p.). Hugo illustrates the three problems and shows through the theme of one man's redemption and rehabilitation how they could and should be solved.

Jean Valjean, unable to find enough work to live, is guilty of a petty crime, stealing a loaf of bread to feed his sister's starving children. Yet the penal system of early-nineteenth-century France makes him into a hardened criminal—potentially. Once his sentence has been served, he is forever marked by the ex-convict's passport. It is only through the act of a good (and godly) man that he is redeemed. When the bishop tells Jean he has bought Jean's soul and given it to God (106), Jean sets out on a new life of earning this redemption. In spite of crisis of conscience and personal trauma, he succeeds in doing the right thing: for example, he admits his identity to save Champmathieu, he refuses to kill at the barricade, he saves Marius, and he admits his past to Marius. Although he loses his direct connection with Cosette by telling Marius the stark truth and not revealing any of his good deeds, he is able to achieve complete redemption at his death and know that he still has Cosette's love when Marius learns the complete truth.

As a reformer, Hugo believes that man can be naturally good when he is not treated badly by society. In *Les Misérables* there are those Parisian criminals who illustrate innate evil, but in general Hugo holds to the ideal of human progress. He recognizes that the march toward progress is not without halts and deviations. He devotes several pages to explaining why the revolt of 1832 failed, in spite of all the high ideals of Enjolras and his friends. Its failure is an example of how humanity can put individual happiness above the collective welfare and choose individual comfort instead of repairing a broken system. Enjolras expresses Hugo's faith that progress will ultimately prevail when he explains the necessity of killing Le Cabuc. Le Cabuc's action was horrible and his own terrible, but an insurrection must have its discipline, and love for one's fellow men and women will ultimately prevail: "Fatality will vanish before Fraternity" (1116).

Hugo has changed his ideas concerning fatality since he published *The Hunchback of Notre-Dame* in 1831. Now fatality has become providence, and divine justice is almost supreme. Providence helps Jean Valjean avoid Javert and his men and find refuge in the convent where Fauchelevent is working. Fauchelevent, whom Jean had saved from being crushed by a cart, is now able to help his benefactor. Providence is not blind but uses human help to achieve looked-for goals. References to God's watching over all and knowing the hearts and souls of the unfortunate and the suffering occur throughout the novel, illustrating Hugo's belief that divine justice will perfect the human system of judgment.

Another illustration of Hugo's ideas concerning the role of poverty in creating the miserable ones is the disintegration of the family due to the burden of poverty. The Thénardiers as a family become a collection of individuals preying on others, following the paternal example of how to fight poverty. Gavroche is outcast, and the two younger sons are given away. Gavroche overcomes his background and situation and shows compassion to others. Eponine overcomes her jealousy of Marius's love for Cosette to follow him to the barricade, give him Cosette's message, and throw herself in the path of the bullet meant for Marius. However, the two younger boys are left wandering in the Luxembourg Gardens, their hunger met for the moment, but their fate unknown at the novel's end. Perhaps Hugo wanted readers to remember that little children are still left out in the cold, hungry and alone, with no one to protect and love them. As Gavroche said when he took the children to the elephant, he would hug his children more tightly if he had them (950).

It is through these direct examples of Gavroche, Jean Valjean himself, and the young men who form the Friends of the A B C that Hugo proposes solutions for improving the lives of the miserable ones. Jean as Monsieur Madeleine creates jobs and treats his workers fairly. Gavroche feeds the hungry children, although the insurrection keeps him from returning to them.

The Friends of the A B C demand laws that will create equal education and equal opportunities and eventual brotherhood among all, although their deaths at the barricades keep them for working to achieve such legislation. *Les misérables* are worth saving, says Hugo. One has only to see the transformation of an ex-convict into an enlightened employer, a loving foster father, and a savior of men at the barricade to understand the author's conviction that all men have the potential for doing great good. Rehabilitation will result in redemption, and the world will be better by emphasizing such transformation of those who suffer and are miserable.

## NARRATIVE STYLE

Victor Hugo's style in *Les Misérables* is characterized, like all his writing, by a deft use of language—language to describe, to narrate, to make a point, to interject ideas, and to create impressions. There is realism in this epic novel, but there is also what the author himself has felt (e.g., idyllic love), what he has observed (e.g., in prisons and on the street), and what he intuitively knows (e.g., the misery of the poor and forgotten). Hugo is not absent from his work, yet while presenting his own ideas and interpretations, he is not heavy-handed. Rather, his comments enhance the reader's understanding of actions, characters, and ideas.

In his use of language Hugo is at home in all registers, from the slang of the underworld to the intellectual discussions of students to the elegant conversation of a bourgeois salon. There are no restrictions on vocabulary in Hugo's mind; all words, intellectual or mundane, vulgar or refined, are appropriate in their own context. He uses any word that he feels will help him express meaning more effectively, even those words that are shocking in and of themselves. For Hugo, slang conveys both the courage and the misery of *les misérables* in the most authentic way possible and therefore is an essential tool in writing.

With his use of language, Hugo creates contrasting scenes of light and dark. Cosette's trip to the forest spring for water is marked by the sinister darkness, like her life to this point, but Cosette is able to escape into the moonlight when she meets Jean Valjean, and then into the firelight at the inn where Jean protects her. A contrasting scene is Jean's flight with Cosette from Javert's pursuit in Paris. Here it is the light that is the sinister element, for it reveals the pursuers, and the darkness of the convent garden represents safety. Finally, the dramatic journey through the Paris sewer system brings Jean from the intense darkness of his jealousy of Marius, and the dark depths of the underground, to the opening of the grate that lets him see the beauty of the sky at sunset. And Jean dies with the light of the candles on his face, while outside the night is dark.

As an example of Hugo's symbolic use of language, the reader will note reflections from the biblical story of Christ in the redemption of Jean Valjean. The picture of Jean struggling with his conscience the night before leaving for Arras reminds the reader of Christ in the garden of Gethsemane, knowing that his death is coming. Like Lazarus coming from his tomb, Jean is able to leave the coffin in the cemetery before he is permanently entombed. And once Jean has accepted that he must follow the path of redemption, he consorts with the dispossessed and the sinners, finding the good in their soul as he does with Fantine, telling her that she has remained pure in her soul in spite of having to sell her body. He also bears his burden to the end, carrying Marius through the sewers as Christ carried his cross to his crucifixion. And during his last crisis of conscience when he realizes he must tell Marius his story, he remains doubled over on the bed all night, in the position of one "taken down from the cross and thrown face to the ground" (1388).

In looking at Hugo's stylistic techniques it is also important to note how carefully he alternates narrative, description, and explanatory digression. He moves seamlessly between providing historical background and moving the story along. He uses flashbacks to effectively show how the lives of various characters intersect and explain their confrontations. For example, in the second act bearing Cosette's name, certain mysteries are not unraveled until after the action. How Javert has discovered that Jean Valjean is in Paris is revealed after the chase through Paris, in order not to break the dramatic suspense of the chase-escape adventure. This type of flashback enlivens the impression of life that Hugo creates and gives the novel a solid sense of place and time.

The 19 short chapters on the battle of Waterloo comprise perhaps the most famous digression in *Les Misérables*. Other digressions relate more closely to events in Jean Valjean's life, for example, the description of convents and the explication of the Paris sewer system, but Jean is in prison at the time of Waterloo and never visits the place. However, his real life begins also in 1815, some months after the definitive defeat of Napoléon at Waterloo. For Hugo it is necessary to explain Waterloo and its meaning for France, before he can show the rehabilitation of one of *les misérables*. Waterloo marks the end of the military epic yet it is not certain if it is the beginning of a new world or a return to the old way of doing things. The answer is not fully evident in 1832 when the uprising fails at the barricade, nor yet in 1862 when *Les Misérables* is published. However, Hugo continues his belief in human progress and the power of love. Jean's final admonition to Marius and Cosette is that they must love each other as there is scarcely anything else that matters (1461).

The chapters on Waterloo conclude with the ambiguous saving of Colonel Pontmercy by Thénardier, who is actually on the battlefield to steal what he can from the dead and dying. Good and evil interact continuously, and humankind cannot always anticipate the result. These two characters emerge from the collective mass engaged in the epic battle to play out their roles, directly and indirectly, in the ultimate redemption of one individual, Jean Valjean.

Victor Hugo, novelist, creates a visionary tale of good and evil, love and hate, progress and setbacks through a style that aims to create vivid, eloquent, dramatic, and lyric scenes. He meets his aim, for even readers who may be intimidated by the length and breadth of Les Misérables recognize the vitality of the themes and the characters created by the style of this writer who claimed to be the "sonorous echo of the universe" (quoted in Marsland, Klin 13).

## HISTORICAL CONTEXT

When Victor Hugo started work on Les Misérables in 1845, the constitutional monarchy of Louis-Philippe was in power. Although extreme poverty was the lot of many French, prosperity and stability characterized the country as a whole. However, there were calls for reform from many quarters, calls to broaden the number of men eligible to vote or to deny legislative representatives the right to also hold civil service jobs. An economic depression beginning in 1846–1847, fueled by bad weather and crop failures, led to factory closures and rising unemployment. Writers such as Hugo expressed sympathy for the common man and his sufferings. Opposition leaders, forbidden to hold political meetings, organized banquets in major French cities instead; political speeches that promoted reform served as entertainment between courses. Finally, the government reacted and ordered that a large banquet scheduled for February 22, 1848, in Paris be cancelled. On February 22 students and workers who opposed the government clashed with police in Paris. Louis-Philippe was confident that the rioting would be minor. However, the National Guard was no longer completely loyal to the monarchy, the army regiments stationed in Paris were commanded by less than competent generals, and Louis-Philippe himself did not want a blood bath in Paris (Wright 130–31). After dismissing Guizot, the prime minister whose removal was a goal of the opposition, the king hoped for an end to the rioting. He named Adolphe Thiers the new prime minister and a detested general, Marshal Bugeaud, head of the army in Paris. However, the rioting continued, and the king abdicated on February 23 in favor of his 10-year-old grandson in order to stop the violence. Although many deputies were willing to accept the continuation of the constitutional monarchy, rioters interrupted their meeting. When the poet Lamartine got the floor, he gave an impassioned speech in favor of a republic that ended the royalists' hope for a continuation of the regime (Wright 131). The grandson was taken into exile by his widowed mother, Louis-Philippe's daughter-in-law.

The provisional government put into place in late February 1848 was composed of members of the bourgeoisie, and two factions soon emerged: the radical wing wanted social experiments as well as political reform; the moderate wing wanted to concentrate on political reform. Both sides did agree to study ways and make recommendations for social experiments. A first attempt to provide work for the unemployed, the National Workshops, offered some relief but no lasting solutions to the economic crisis.

Lamartine became foreign minister in the provisional government. When radicals called for concrete support for revolutionary governments in central and eastern Europe, Lamartine gave only verbal support, fearing, perhaps, that overt support would cause a new anti-French coalition to be formed by other European powers, similar to that of the Napoléonic era (Wright 136–37).

The first election for the new republic was held in April 1848. Nine and a half million new voters were to choose deputies for the Constituent Assembly, and 84 percent of the eligible voters went to the polls. The results were in favor of the moderates: some 500 became members of the Assembly. Monarchists were represented by 300 members, and the radicals by 80 (Wright 137).

When the Assembly met in May to choose a five-man executive council to replace the provisional government, the moderates wanted no radicals. Lamartine, however, refused to accept a post unless the radical spokesman, Ledru-Rollin, was also elected to the council. Lamartine was unable to dominate the council or to provide an acceptable alternative for the National Workshops. When they were abolished, young men on the payroll were given the possibility of army enlistment and older men were offered work in the provinces draining swamps. A violent three-day civil insurrection followed in June. General Cavignac, in charge of defending Paris, refused to act immediately, and rebellious workers constructed barricades in the Paris streets. The General then ordered the troops to destroy the barricades. Estimates of those killed range from 1,500 to 3,000, and some 12,000 were arrested. Many of the arrested men were later sent to Algeria (Wright 138).

General Cavignac became the head of a temporary military dictatorship, replacing the five-man council. The euphoria that had marked the proclamation of the republic was gone, and by the end of the year conservative ideas were predominant. The constitution of 1848, finally completed by the Constituent Assembly, called for a unicameral legislature, elected for three-year terms by universal male suffrage. A president would be elected the same way for a four-year term. The constitution did not make clear the relationship between the president and the legislature (Wright 139).

Louis-Napoléon Bonaparte, nephew of Emperor Napoléon, had spent some years in prison and then exile for actions during Louis-Philippe's reign. He returned to France soon after the February revolution and was elected to the Constituent Assembly in June 1848. Named candidate for the presidency, he was elected by an overwhelming margin in December 1848. The magic of the Bonaparte name was still alive (Wright 140).

When the legislative elections were held in May 1849, the monarchists held a majority of seats; the moderate republicans were almost wiped out, and the radical left won a significant number of seats (Wright 140). Early in his mandate Louis-Napoléon seemed inclined to support the conservative majority, even signing a bill that modified universal suffrage and another that restricted the press and the right of assembling for political reasons. However, he was also interested in economic development and had even published a pamphlet entitled *The Extinction of Poverty* while he was in prison (Wright 141).

Victor Hugo was a member of the legislature with which President Bonaparte was trying to work. Although the president had worked to appease the conservative majority, by the summer of 1851, the relationship between president and legislature was at a stalemate. The legislature refused to grant the president a constitutional amendment to permit a second term, and it also would not vote for funds to enable him to pay personal debts (Wright 141). The president began planning a coup d'état, working closely with elements of the army, especially with those who wanted a return to the glory of the first Napoléon's empire.

The coup took place December 2, 1851, with the leading legislators being awakened in the early morning and arrested. The president also announced a drastic revision of the constitution of 1848 that would extend the president's term to 10 years and reduce the powers of the legislature. Through a plebiscite 92 percent of the voters voted to approve these changes. Protests did occur throughout the country. Their repression caused the death of several hundred protesters and the arrest of 26,000; 10,000 were deported to Algeria (Wright 144). Opposition leaders such as Hugo chose exile before they could be arrested. A year later, on December 2, 1852, Louis-Napoléon proclaimed himself Emperor Napoléon III (Napoléon I's son had died in 1832). There was no open resistance, and the transformation from republic to empire was ratified by 97 percent of the voters.

The first phase of the Second Empire was somewhat authoritarian in that opposition to the regime was restricted by controls on the press and on holding public meetings. Many of the most vocal critics, such as Hugo, had chosen exile; others were deported to French penal colonies in Algeria and Guiana. A limited political and legislative life took place within the confines of the Corps Législatif, but only summaries of its proceedings were made available to the public. Members of the legislative body were elected by universal male suffrage, but elections took place only every six years. Napoléon III and his ministers chose administrators from those already serving in such roles as well as from their close supporters. The Second Empire became an alliance of old and new forces (Wright 148–49).

After 1859, Napoléon III took the first measures to soften the authoritarian aspects of his regime. He offered amnesty to political exiles; Hugo was one exile who refused to return to France while Napoléon III was in power. The Corps Législatif's sessions were opened to the public, and the members were permitted to present formal resolutions to the emperor on an annual basis (Wright 150). More reforms followed during the years after the publication of *Les Misérables*.

The economic situation in France improved during the 1850s as it did in other parts of Europe. France's industrial production doubled between 1852 and 1870, and foreign trade tripled. The use of steam power and railroad transportation also increased markedly. Napoléon III also believed in stimulating economic growth and encouraged private investment and speculation as well as state-financed development, for example, the reconstruction of Paris. Private entrepreneurs established investment banks, department stores, and the first chain groceries; they modernized the iron and textile industries; they oversaw the completion of the network of telegraph and major railway lines (Wright 162–63).

When Hugo began his work on *Les Misérables*, conditions for the working population were characterized for the most part by long hours in unsafe surroundings for little money. Jean Valjean, as Monsieur Madeleine, creates a factory that encourages responsible work for living wages and, when he leaves, the economic situation in Montreuil-sur-mer reverts to its previous stagnation. Hugo set up a fictional model to counteract what he observed. The meager efforts of the labor reform of 1841, under Louis-Philippe, did little to improve the situation for working people, and their hopes for improvement in salary and conditions when the regime changed in 1848 were soon disappointed. Napoléon III was at first too dependent on the support of business leaders to encourage social reform. Labor did profit somewhat from the growing economic prosperity of the 1850s as wages increased somewhat faster than prices. Some factory owners anticipated Monsieur Madeleine's example; for example, textile manufacturers in Mulhouse in the 1850s provided model housing and began efforts to create safer working conditions. Others, however, felt that shorter hours and higher pay would only corrupt the inferior working class (Wright 174). Set in the 1830s, Hugo's novel criticized the long-standing social and economic conditions that were continuing in the 1850s.

During the time Hugo was writing *Les Misérables*, women were still subject to laws denying them equal roles in marriage. Divorce would remain illegal until 1884, and a double standard continued to exist concerning adultery with penalties being more severe for women than men. Education for girls was minimal. No state-supported secondary schools for girls existed until the 1860s. Like Cosette, most young girls were educated in convents. After 1850, communes of at least 800 people were required to establish schools for girls, and there was a lack of trained teachers for these schools. Women who worked outside the home were paid half of what men received and had no opportunity to enter most professional careers. Early French feminists were isolated, and their activities were chiefly seen in literature or journalism. The Revolution of 1848 saw the establishment of some women's clubs and newspapers, and there was a small group calling for voting rights for women (Zeldin, I 345–47).

Whatever the defects in the system of education during the 1840s and the 1850s, Hugo, and writers like Alexandre Dumas and Gustave Flaubert, benefited from the fact that more and more French were learning to read. With *Les Misérables*, Hugo put into an absorbing novel his thoughts and observations about people, places, and ideas. Going beyond the emphasis of Romanticism on individualism, Hugo portrayed the people, those who suffered the most from social and political injustice. He was also concerned with depicting reality as he saw it and observing his surroundings in minute detail. Objective in his descriptions he was not, but in his novel Hugo reflected the historical context in which he wrote it: a time of economic development that continued to ignore the needs of the poor and oppressed; a time of a political regime that attempted to shape a nation's role in the wider world and control the world at home; a time of literary efforts that were moving from lyrical outpourings of individual feelings to objective observations. Victor Hugo was a participant in the political changes from 1845 to 1851 and observer from exile of the France under Napoléon III as he worked on *Les Misérables*. Aware of his literary compatriots' works during the same period and the transition from romantic effusion to realistic observation, Victor Hugo was not swayed by trends but wrote in his own inimitable style for the widest possible public, diagnosing the ills of society and championing the individual.

# Antoine de Saint-Exupéry
## *The Little Prince*
### 1943

## BIOGRAPHICAL CONTEXT

Antoine de Saint-Exupéry is known worldwide for the slim volume telling the story of a small visitor to Earth from another place in the universe. *The Little Prince*, published first in New York City in 1943 in the midst of World War II, reflects its author's childhood; his discovery of flying, the stars, and the desert; and his musings about all these things.

Saint-Exupéry was born in Lyon, France, on June 29, 1900 into a family that could trace its ancestry back to the eleventh century (Robinson 2). With ties to the French aristocracy, Saint-Exupéry could use the title of count but did so rarely. His father, employed in the insurance industry, died in 1904, leaving Antoine's mother, Marie, a widow with five small children.

Early educational experiences included being taught at home and then studying in the Jesuit school in LeMans that Antoine's father had attended when Madame de Saint-Exupéry moved the family there. At school the boy wrote poetry and won the prize for the best French composition of the year when he was 14 (Robinson 8). Antoine's first trip in an airplane also took place during these school years, but with the outbreak of World War I, the family returned to the Lyon area. Madame de Saint-Exupéry worked as a nurse, and the two sons, Antoine and François, spent one term at another Jesuit school. In November 1915 the two, unhappy at school, were sent to school in Switzerland, the Villa Saint-Jean at Fribourg, where they spent two years. In 1917 at age 17, Antoine successfully passed the *baccalauréat*, the examination that marks the end of secondary education for French students planning to attend a university. However, François, his younger brother, had developed rheumatic fever and died only a month later, impressing Antoine with his dignity as he faced death (Robinson 9–10). And later recollections indicate that François died as quietly and gently as the Little Prince would later disappear bodily from the narrator's immediate world (Schiff 62).

The next several years were marked by Saint-Exupéry's efforts to find his place in the world around him. He first decided on a naval career, but to enter the Ecole navale he needed more training in mathematics. Enrolling in the Lycée Saint-Louis in Paris, he was a boarder at the Ecole Bossuet under the guidance of the Abbé Sudour, who would be a life-long mentor (Robinson 11). Saint-Exupéry did well on the final written examinations at the Lycée but did not pass the oral portion, failing on history and geography questions (Robinson 14). This experience, too, has its echoes in both the narrator's and the Little Prince's opinions concerning geography.

Saint-Exupéry was called to do his two years of compulsory military service in April 1921 and requested an air force regiment. Sent to a base located in Strasbourg and assigned to the ground personnel, Saint-Exupéry directed his efforts toward becoming a pilot. He took his first lessons with a civilian company and soon achieved his civilian license (Robinson 16–17). His next post was in Morocco, where he made his first contact with the desert that would play such an important role in his life and writings. Saint-Exupéry earned his military pilot's license in December 1921, and he completed his first military service at Le Bourget near Paris, reaching the rank of second lieutenant.

Once he had left military service in 1923, Saint-Exupéry had a difficult time finding his place in life. With no money, he needed a job, and being a pilot was the most attractive idea. However, he had fallen in love with Louise de Vilmorin, whom he had met while stationed at Le Bourget. When the two became engaged, her family was not at all favorable to having a son-in-law in such a profession. Saint-Exupéry first took a job as an inspector with a tile works. However, Louise broke off their engagement, and in 1924 Saint-Exupéry found part-time work in aviation and a position as a traveling salesman for the Saurer truck company. He did not sell many trucks in his 18 months with the company (Robinson 24–25).

In 1926 Saint-Exupéry obtained an interview with the general manager of the Compagnie Latécoère, an aviation company specializing in mail service. Abbé Sudour, his mentor from the days at the Ecole Bossuet, was instrumental in setting up this interview (Schiff 127). Saint-Exupéry's work with this company would provide him experiences in the desert, in the air, and with people and places that would then be reflected in his subsequent writings.

The same year, 1926, saw the writer's first publication, a short story, "L'Aviateur," which appeared in a short-lived magazine called *Le Navire d'argent*. Saint-Exupéry had been considering writing as a serious activity for some time, as letters to family and friends indicate (Robinson 26–27). This early story includes many ideas that would be developed more fully in later works.

Saint-Exupéry's first work for Latécoère involved ground training, learning the mechanical knowledge necessary for repairing a downed airplane, knowledge that would help him get through crash landings in the desert or elsewhere and knowledge that the narrator in *The Little Prince* would mention as important. Saint-Exupéry's first flight assignments were from Toulouse, the company's headquarters, to Spain and on to Africa. By 1927 he was spending much time in Dakar, Senegal and learning more about the desert. At the end of the year he was named *chef d'aéroplane*, or station manager, at Cape Juby, one of the company's ports of call between Casablanca in Morocco and Dakar, located in an area of western Africa controlled by Spain. The writer needed his skills as pilot, negotiator, and mechanic during his stay at Cap Juby, for his tasks included working to reconcile Spanish officials and local Arabs as well as finding downed planes, rescuing pilots, and keeping the mail running. The mail itself passed through Cap Juby only every eight days, which left Saint-Exupéry time for paperwork and flying the four planes left at the station every day to get rid of any buildup of condensation in the engines (Schiff 13). Like the Little Prince watering his rose and scrubbing out the volcanoes daily, he was faithful to his duty.

The next stage of Saint-Exupéry's commercial aviation career began in 1929 and took place in Argentina, where he served as director of the new Aeroposta Argentina. In the same year his first novel *Southern Mail* was published. In 1930 the writer received the *Légion d'honneur* for civilian aeronautics. He was also involved in the air and ground search for his friend and fellow pilot, Henri Guillaumet, lost in the Andes. Guillaumet walked for five days over mountains and through snow, ice, and storms to eventual safety, an exploit that Saint-Exupéry would chronicle in later writings.

Saint-Exupéry's next book, *Night Flight*, appeared in 1931, the same year he married Consuelo Suncin de Sandoval, whom he had met in Argentina. The book received the *Prix fémina*, Saint-Exupéry's first literary award. The rest of the 1930s saw Saint-Exupéry in several different positions after the Latécoère company collapsed. Among other work, he was a test pilot and nearly drowned in an accident, joined Air France in public relations, carried out some journalistic assignments including one in Moscow, and attempted a speed-record flight to Saigon. This flight resulted in a desert crash, and the pilot with his mechanic walked five days until rescued. Saint-Exupéry also did some reporting during the Spanish civil war, 1936–1937, and attempted another speed-record flight in 1938, this time from New York to Terra del Fuego in South America. The flight ended in a serious crash in Guatemala, and Saint-Exupéry convalesced in New York.

In 1939 Saint-Exupéry published *Terre des hommes*, or *Wind, Sand, and Stars* as it is known in English. The French version was awarded the Grand *Prix du Roman de l'Académie française*, and the English volume received the Book of the Month award. With the outbreak of World War II, Saint-Exupéry was mobilized as a captain. During 1940 he flew reconnaissance missions with the Group II/33 until the armistice with Germany was signed in June. The Group was evacuated to Algiers in North Africa, and Saint-Exupéry was demobilized on July 31.

Saint-Exupéry had fought hard to obtain an active assignment when the war broke out. Because of his age (39 in 1939) and physical condition affected by his several crashes, his friends wanted to see him in inactive postings, and he had been offered a position in the Ministry of Information early in the war (Robinson 96). Saint-Exupéry felt that one had to participate actively to be effective and did not want to be placed on the figurative shelf, with only a voice.

However, once France was out of the war, Saint-Exupéry again had to seek his own way and meaning for his existence. Members of the Vichy government tried to associate the writer with their efforts, even naming him to the National Council, an appointment that Saint-Exupéry rejected wholeheartedly. De Gaulle supporters urged him to join the Free French in London, and his exact reasons for not doing so have caused much speculation. In any case Saint-Exupéry made the decision to go to New York and traveled there via Algeria and then Portugal. While waiting to sail, he learned that his friend Guillaumet had been shot down over the Mediterranean. Saint-Exupéry was very much saddened by this death and felt that he had no more friends, being the last survivor of the group of pilots from the old Casablanca/Dakar run (Schiff 342).

Saint-Exupéry arrived in New York on December 31, 1940, beginning an exile from his homeland that would last two and a half years. His American publishers, Reynal and Hitchcock, found him a place to live, but bereft of country, family, comrades, and profession, the writer also had to navigate between the two groups of French exiles in New York City, Vichy partisans and De Gaulle supporters. When neither group could persuade Saint-Exupéry to join them, each one accused him of working for the other (Robinson 102). His publishers encouraged him to begin writing again, and Saint-Exupéry decided that he should speak for France and counter the American isolationist sentiments of early 1941. He began working on what would become *Pilote de guerre*, or *Flight to Arras* in English. His wife Consuelo arrived in New York in November 1940. Their relationship had always been tumultuous and continued to be so in the United States.

During 1941 Saint-Exupéry continued writing, but only published an article in *Harper's Bazaar*. *Flight to Arras* appeared in January 1942; it is a factual account of a reconnaissance flight as well as a philosophical meditation. American response was very positive, with *Time* calling it "most important book yet written about this war" (quoted in Robinson 111). The Nazis authorized the book's publication under the title *Pilote de guerre* in December 1942. The first edition in France of 2,000 copies sold out in a week, but shortly the book was banned in France because Saint-Exupéry had cited the heroic efforts of a Jewish member of his squadron. It circulated only clandestinely until the end of the war (Schiff 365–66).

*Lettre à un otage* was the next Saint-Exupéry book to be published, in early 1943 in New York. The next year it appeared in the magazine *L'Arche* in Algiers and was officially published by Gallimard, the French publishers, in December 1944, after France's liberation in August 1944 and Saint-Exupéry's disappearance during his last mission in July 1944. It was addressed to Léon Werth, a longtime friend living in occupied France.

But first and foremost during 1942 Saint-Exupéry was working on *The Little Prince*. Enjoying sketching since his youth, he had been drawing the little figure that would grace his new book since the 1930s. It appears that his American publishers, Reynal and Hitchcock, encouraged his putting the character into a children's story. Buying watercolors, Saint-Exupéry set to work, writing often late at night. Lewis Galentière, his American translator, said that Saint-Exupéry discarded 100 pages for every one he sent to the printer (Schiff 378). Madame de Saint-Exupéry located a house on Long Island so the couple could escape the summer heat in Manhattan. Saint-Exupéry finished the book in a 22-room mansion, reading his manuscript to visitors at any hour of the day or night (Schiff 379). The manuscript was finished by mid-October 1942, and the book itself appeared April 6, 1943.

Saint-Exupéry had never ceased wanting to return to action in France. With the Allied invasion of North Africa in November 1942, he redoubled his efforts to rejoin his squadron, sailing from New York in late April 1943 and arriving in Algiers on May 4. He finally received authorization to fly again, after making many appeals to friends and contacts, and joined the Group II/33 on June 4. He trained on the American-built Lightnings, planes new to him and more complicated than those he had flown before. Saint-Exupéry flew his first reconnaissance mission over occupied France on July

21, 1943. However, he overshot the landing after a mission on July 31; the plane was damaged and its pilot was grounded the next day. For nearly a year he would try to be reassigned to active flying, only succeeding after many despondent and uncomfortable months spent in Algeria. Finally Saint-Exupéry was permitted to join General Chassin as a staff officer on the general's posting to Sardinia. It is unclear exactly how Saint-Exupéry obtained his final permission from the American commander of the Allied air forces in the Mediterranean, General Eakers, but he was granted approval to fly five more reconnaissance missions on Lightnings with the II/33 (Robinson 134–35). Those missions completed, the pilot wanted to continue flying and did carry out three more assignments, in spite of friends' efforts to dissuade him. He was given an additional mission to fly reconnaissance over Annecy, France, on July 31. He never returned from that mission, and no definitive answer to his disappearance has yet been found. One year later a memorial service was held in Colmar, France. *The Little Prince*'s creator had vanished like his curly-haired creation, leaving no physical trace behind.

## PLOT DEVELOPMENT

*The Little Prince* is a sensitive portrayal of ideas and themes that come together in a story that appeals to children and adults, that resists a detailed analysis but leaves its essence in the minds and hearts of its readers. A narrator, Saint-Exupéry himself, relates the story through a series of vignettes; it concludes with the little prince's departure and the narrator's request to let him know if you, the reader, happen to be in the desert when the little prince returns. Each scene is illustrated by the writer's own drawings, which enhance the charm of his ideas and the words that express them.

The narrator begins his tale by recounting his misadventures as a six-year-old artist whose drawings were not understood by grown-ups. The boy grows up to be a pilot but never meets anyone to whom he can really talk until one day he crashes his plane in the desert. The next morning he is accosted by a small person who wants a sheep drawn for him. The narrator's artistic talent has not necessarily improved over the years, but at last his drawing of a sheep within a box is understood and is exactly what the small person wants.

This small person, called now the Little Prince, never answers any questions put to him, but little by little the narrator learns that he comes from a very small planet. The sheep can't wander off because there is no place to go. The narrator decides that the Little Prince is probably from asteroid B-612, seen once by a Turkish astronomer whom no one believed until he gave his speech in western clothes. This thought leads the narrator to reflect on the love of grown-ups for numbers, for concrete bits of information, such as salary, rather than for something more abstract such as a new friend's personality or the sound of his or her voice. He fears that his narration of his experiences with the Little Prince may not be as accurate as it should be because he has grown old and can no longer see a sheep inside of a box. Also, the Little Prince's visit took place six years before, and time dims details.

The next vignettes bring out information concerning the Little Prince's life on his tiny planet. It has good plants and bad plants; the Little Prince has had to pull up the baobabs each day so they won't take over the small area. He has had a sad life, with his only pleasure watching sunsets; one day he watched the sun set 44 times. The narrator realizes he has fallen into the typical grown-up response when he fails to answer with due seriousness the Little Prince's questions about the function of thorns. The Little Prince is furious, for his flower could be eaten by the sheep if the thorns are no use as protection; then something unique would be gone. The Little Prince is so angry at what the narrator has considered matters of consequence, that is, repairing the damaged airplane, that he bursts into sobs. The narrator, feeling blundering and useless, tries to comfort him.

More details are revealed about this unique flower, a rose. The Little Prince feels he should have been content to enjoy her company without worrying about what she said, or did not say. When he prepares to leave his planet, the rose asks his forgiveness. Of course she loves him and he should be happy.

The Little Prince visits six planets before arriving on Earth. The king on the first planet is delighted to have a subject and tries to make his orders reasonable. The conceited man on the next planet is pleased to have an admirer while the man who drinks on the following planet is drinking to forget that he is ashamed of drinking. The businessman on planet number four is only concerned with counting the stars, which all belong to him because he is the first to think of owning them. The fifth planet is the smallest of all and is inhabited by a lamplighter who lights and extinguishes his street light continuously. At least his work has some meaning, and the Little Prince is sorry to leave since there are so many sunsets on this planet. On the much larger sixth planet a geographer is so busy questioning explorers that he never leaves his desk. He won't accept their findings without inquiry concerning their moral character.

The Earth is the seventh planet, and the Little Prince is impressed by its size. A great many lamplighters are needed here. The narrator notes that man occupies a very small place on Earth, although grown-ups wouldn't believe this. The Little Prince meets the snake and comments that it is a bit lonely in the desert; the snake responds that it is lonely among men, but that he himself is very powerful and can send anyone back to the earth from whence he came. He offers to help the Little Prince should he wish to return to his planet.

Continuing his search for men, the Little Prince meets a three-petaled flower who thinks there may be a few men on earth; they're rootless, notes the flower. When the Little Prince climbs a mountain looking for men, he tries to talk and decides that these inhabitants don't converse but merely repeat what he says—he doesn't realize he is hearing an echo. Next he finds a garden full of roses. This saddens him, both because his rose had said she was the only one in existence and because he is not very important, given his tiny planet. His most significant meeting is with the fox, who explains the meaning of friendship. It is only with the heart that one sees rightly. Onward goes the Little Prince, arriving at a railway switchyard where he watches trains full of passengers rushing back and forth. The switchman says no one is satisfied with where he is. Humans want to save time, says the merchant who is selling pills to quench thirst.

The narrator continues working on his repairs while he learns about the Little Prince's travels. However, the narrator is worried, for his water is running out and the repairs aren't completed. The Little Prince points out the beauty of the desert. The two walk through the night, searching for water, and the narrator carries the little prince when he falls asleep. At daybreak they arrive at a well that is all ready for them, bucket and all. This water is good for the heart as well as the body. The Little Prince reminds the narrator to draw the promised muzzle for his sheep—so the sheep cannot eat the rose. The narrator's heart is torn because he senses that the Little Prince is preparing to leave.

The narrator overhears the Little Prince making plans with the snake and is very distressed at what he understands. The Little Prince reminds him what they have gained by knowing each other and they can both look at the stars and remember. The Little Prince explains why he must leave in such a fashion. There is a flash of yellow, and the Little Prince falls gently and quietly to the sand.

The narrator has never told this story in the six years since his return from the desert. He loves to listen to the stars, but he worries because he forgot to put the leather strap on the sheep's muzzle. It will always be a mystery: has the sheep eaten the rose? "And no grown-up will ever understand that this is a matter of so much importance" (111).

The last drawing shows "the loveliest and saddest landscape in the world" (113). The narrator hopes that those who might visit this place will recognize it and let him know if the Little Prince returns.

## CHARACTER DEVELOPMENT

The Little Prince and the narrator himself are the two main characters of this story of wonder. The inhabitants of the various planets are types who illustrate the grown-ups of the world, identified and characterized chiefly by their profession and their duties. They play their roles only for as long as it takes the Little Prince to determine what they represent. However, they are drawn deftly and remain in the reader's memory after the Little Prince travels on.

The Little Prince comes alive as the narrator sees and hears him that first morning in the desert. An "odd little voice," seemingly out of nowhere, asks for a drawing of a sheep (6). Between the drawings and the narrator's descriptions, the reader learns about the Little Prince: "It was from words dropped by chance that, little by little, everything was revealed to me" (11). Perhaps not everything was revealed, but the narrator learns enough from these words to understand that the Little Prince has a certain wisdom lacking in so many grown-ups. This little person has learned to recognize the value of love and friendship and responsibility through his experiences on his own planet and his travels through space. With his thatch of golden curls, his repetition of requests, his disregard of direct questions, and his ability to comfort and understand sadness, he comes alive to the reader as the narrator grows to understand him.

The narrator himself is developed as a believable human being through his own words. He sees his own foibles, recognizing that he has to force himself back to the sense of wonder he knew as a child in order to understand and appreciate the Little Prince. The narrator's irritation when he wants to get on with his repairs is a very human one: "Don't you see—I am very busy with matters of consequence" (28). Older readers can identify with his impatience, and younger ones can recognize the short-tempered reactions of the grown-ups in their lives. But the narrator's quick compassion for the Little Prince's frustrated tears caused by the obtuse grown-up makes him sympathetic: "I did not know how I could reach him. . . . It is such a secret place, the land of tears" (31). Saint-Exupéry succeeds in creating a character with whom the reader can identify, who doesn't hide his own shortcomings but who wants to connect with others and share their love.

The rose, the fox, and even the snake are given human characteristics. The Little Prince presents these three characters through what he tells the narrator. The rose, capricious yet appealing and lovable in her beauty and demands, teaches the Little Prince that beauty can be loved for itself. He decides later that he should have judged her by deeds, not her words, for the words made him unhappy. The fox explains to him what true friendship is and what responsibility means. Even the snake, although powerful enough to send any-one back "from whence he came," also knows of the loneliness among men (72). Because of Saint-Exupéry's ability to set up a world believable on its own terms, the plant and animals are very acceptable as characters.

## THEMES

Love and friendship, responsibility and usefulness, the important themes of *The Little Prince* are linked together in an encounter between a pilot who has crashed in the desert and a blond boy who has come from a small place among the stars—an encounter that enriches them both and all those who read about it.

Love, the Little Prince learns, is accepting the other as is. The rose is demanding; she seems to say one thing and mean another. The Little Prince, driven almost to despair, decides to leave her, this vain creature who tries to make the Little Prince feel that he is in the wrong. Once away, however, the Little Prince understands his rose more fully and recognizes that this love, which she confessed just before his departure, was real and needed to be accepted on its own terms: "She cast her fragrance and her radiance over me.... I ought to have guessed all the affection that lay behind her poor little stratagems. Flowers are so inconsistent!" (36–37). And love requires a return to the loved one at any cost, once the lover has accepted the responsibility to love: "You know—my flower...I am responsible for her. And she is so weak! She is so naïve!" (107).

Friendship, too, is a part of love. The little desert fox, an animal that Saint-Exupéry came to know and appreciate during a crash in the desert (an event related in *Wind, Sand and Stars*), reappears in this story to teach the Little Prince what friendship really means. Friends, says the fox, don't just happen; to become a friend, one must be tamed. The English word fails to indicate the nuance of the word Saint-Exupéry chose in French: *apprivoiser*, which means to create bonds of affection between the human being and the animal, or "to establish ties," as the fox says (80). The fox goes on to explain what he means: making friends takes patience; a friend should be dependable, arrive at the same time every day, and sit quietly while being tamed. Words can cause mis-understandings. The Little Prince returns to the field of roses and understands that while they are beautiful, it is an empty beauty because they have not been tamed and have no ties with anyone. He can now absorb the last lesson of the fox: "what is essential is invisible to the eye" (87).

Leaving one's friend is sad; the fox will cry, but he will also remember that the Little Prince's hair was the color of the wheat fields, and such memories bring happiness. The pilot will also shed tears when the Little Prince vanishes and when he worries about the sheep eating the rose. But he will be happy when he looks at the stars and hears in his memory the Little Prince's laugh, "like five hundred million little bells" (109).

Responsibility is indicated in two ways: the Little Prince is responsible for his rose, for he has tamed her; but he also recognizes the responsibility and usefulness of the work he does by keeping the baobab plant under control and the volcanoes swept out on his planet. He finds beauty as well as usefulness in the work of the lamplighter, who must light and extinguishes his lamps more and more often as his planet turns more and more quickly. A businessman or a king might find the lamplighter ridiculous, but the Little Prince sees each lamp as another star or flower brought to life. The lamplighter is faithful to his work.

The Little Prince will return faithfully to his work, to his responsibility, and to his planet. Because his body is too heavy for such a long journey, he will have to leave it behind, so he arranges his departure with the snake. The narrator does not find the Little Prince's body the next day, for the body is not the essential self. The Little Prince has learned this lesson and taught it to the narrator as they tamed each other. Their walk in search of water and the taste of this water sum up the Little Prince's philosophy. Men rush about looking for some unknown thing and never find it. The narrator recognizes what he has found in the water from the well: "Its sweetness was born of the walk under the stars, the song of the pulley, the effort of my arms. It was good for the heart, like a present" (96). And the Little Prince, knowing that what men seek could be found in a drop of water or in a single rose, adds, "But the eyes are blind. One must look with the heart..." (97).

## NARRATIVE STYLE

*The Little Prince* is unusual in that the written word is completed only through the illustrations. One cannot imagine reading the story without seeing the author's drawings. Saint-Exupéry had been drawing since he was a child, sketching caricatures and designs in the margins of his manuscripts and letters. He notes his own difficulties in creating drawings that others could recognize—but no one who reads *The Little Prince* ever forgets the boa swallowing the elephant or the sheep asleep in the box. Saint-Exupéry had special trouble with the baobab trees but was pleased with the result, finding his drawing both "magnificent and impressive" (24).

Saint-Exupéry chooses a first-person narrator to frame *The Little Prince*. The narrator comments, describes, and appeals at times directly to the readers. He combines his narration with direct dialogue involving the Little Prince, creating a more vivid reality for both characters. The narrator also recounts the visits to the various planets as if they are happening in the present, presenting them from the Little Prince's point of view.

Word pictures, that is, images, complement the visual illustrations in this book. Saint-Exupéry is able through his choice of words to create the beautiful yet mysterious world of the desert and the tender yet challenging world of friendship and love. The language is simple, able to be understood by a child, yet meaningful, able to stimulate the thinking and feeling of a grown-up. It moves quite well from French to English without losing its charm—*apprivoiser* is explained in French by the fox so the essential nuance is not lost although the English equivalent, tame, does not carry this meaning of establishing ties between persons. The language expresses beautifully the blending of fantasy and realism that is the hallmark of *The Little Prince*, a book that refuses a precise categorization as fairy tale or adult allegory but that reminds the reader of what should be essential in life: friendship, love, responsibility, and meaningful work.

## HISTORICAL CONTEXT

Saint-Exupéry wrote *The Little Prince* during one of the darkest years of World War II, 1942. Living in New York, he was still affected by the turmoil and suffering in his homeland of France. His dedication of *The Little Prince* to Léon Werth, his longtime friend, shows his realization of conditions in France. He notes that his friend is living in France and is hungry and cold.

World War II began in Europe with the German invasion of Poland on September 1, 1939; the government of France declared war on Germany on September 3, several hours after the British had done so. Mobilized along with the thousands of nonactive military personnel, Captain Saint-Exupéry was sent to the Toulouse airfield on September 4. Because of his age and physical condition as a result of the several plane crashes he had survived, the writer's friends tried to dissuade him from active service. He was urged to accept an appointment in the Ministry of Information to make a lecture tour to the United States, but refused all such urgent requests in order to remain with his squadron.

The war itself soon entered a period known as the phony war (*drôle de guerre*, in French), when not much happened on the European front. In May 1940 the German army overran Belgium and invaded northern France; the *drôle de guerre* was over. The French forces were not able to stop the German advance, and, during the next six weeks civilian refugees, the military forces, and even the government fled south. The collapse of France, traumatizing its citizens and shattering its allies, ended with the government's meeting in Bordeaux the night of June 16–17 to form a new cabinet in order to ask the Germans what peace terms might be. Paul Reynaud, the prime minister, proposed Marshall Philippe Pétain, the 84-year-old hero of World War I, as his successor. Some members of Reynaud's cabinet wanted to fight on, using Brittany in northwest France as a staging ground, but the German advance made this plan unworkable. The project to continue the war from French North Africa was more promising, and Saint-Exupéry's squadron along with all other air and naval forces that could reach Algeria arrived in an area still untouched physically by the war (Paxton 6).

On June 17, 1940, Pétain announced to the country via the radio that the government formed during the night was going to seek an armistice. The feeling among the majority of civilians and military personnel was one of relief. Convinced that the end of the war was only weeks or months away, most of the leading figures in France felt that fighting to the finish was futile (Paxton 9–11). France had lost millions of young men during World War I, as well as suffering materially from the intense fighting that took place on her territory over that four-year war. The prevailing mood of the populace in 1940 was to avoid the widespread death and destruction of 1914–1918 if at all possible.

However, there was some opposition to the armistice: those commanding France's overseas empire and the youngest general in the army, Charles de Gaulle. General Auguste Noguès in North Africa and General Mittelhauser in the Near East, both raised serious objections in the days before the armistice took effect, but both generals finally accepted the orders of the commander in chief of the defeated French army, General Weygand, to cease further armed resistance (Paxton 41).

General de Gaulle had made his way to London in June 1940 and made his famous radio address on June 18, calling on all the French who could to join him in London, in order to carry on the fight. Very few high-ranking military personnel or well-known civilians rallied to his call in 1940. Such a decision meant leaving country, family, and friends and choosing exile. De Gaulle and many of those who joined him faced criminal charges and were considered traitors to France by the Pétain government.

Once the armistice was signed on June 22 in a railway car located in Compiègne, near Paris, Germany occupied the eastern areas of France known as Alsace and Lorraine, all French territory north of the Loire River, and the entire Atlantic coast. Pétain's government decided on Vichy, located south of the Loire in central France, as its headquarters. Vichy, known for its many hot springs, had been hosting for years people coming for medical treatments and had numerous hotels that could be used to house government personnel.

Marshall Pétain called for a new order once the armistice had been signed. The slogan of *liberté, égalité, fraternité* (liberty, equality, fraternity) that had epitomized France since the Revolution of 1789 gave way to *travail, famille, patrie* (work, family, country). He saw his mission as instilling the right attitudes in the French citizens and creating social stability (Paxton 37). His cabinet supported the idea of working with Germany with the goal of being part of a new European order at the end of the war, which the Vichy government felt, in 1940, that Germany would win handily and quickly. Hitler, on the other hand, wanted first and foremost a quiet and subdued France that would provide both a base for his assault on England and a rich source of supplies for Germany, both food and war *matériel* (Paxton 51). The various negotiations between the two sides from 1940 to the liberation of France from its occupier in August 1944 are too complicated for discussion here, but the complexity of the situation shows the dilemma Saint-Exupéry was in when he tried to decide what to do after his demobilization in July 1940.

The writer spent some time at his sister's home in Agay, located on the Riviera, working on the manuscript that would be published as *Citadelle* (*The Wisdom of the Sands*, in English) after the war. Disillusioned about the defeat, Saint-Exupéry wanted to work for France but could not find an acceptable role in the postarmistice climate. He was not convinced of the relevance of either de Gaulle or the general's aspirations. The Vichy government had no more appeal, especially as it began to issue decrees that targeted French Jews, limiting them to certain professions. Saint-Exupéry finally decided that going to the United States might help him reach a perspective on his nation's situation.

During his decision making, the writer went to Vichy to collect the necessary papers for his journey. He was helped in this endeavor by Pierre Drieu La Rochelle, a writer who was also published by Gallimard, Saint-Exupéry's publisher. Drieu was working with the Germans on producing an acceptable literary journal. However, this effort was not generally known in October 1940, and Saint-Exupéry was probably pleased to have connections in Paris. He wanted to go there to collect his notebooks left behind when he joined his air group. Drieu La Rochelle drove Saint-Exupéry to Paris, saving him the uncomfortable trip in a crowded train. Saint-Exupéry collected his possessions, experienced the Paris curfew, and was confirmed in his decision that living in occupied France was not a viable option (Schiff 339–40).

Arriving in the United States for what he thought would be a stay of weeks, not years, Saint-Exupéry found the same fragmented state of mind among the French in exile as he had seen in France itself. Supporters of the Vichy government and those pro-de Gaulle and his Free French group barely spoke to one another, and subgroups in the two factions were also at odds.

Each side wanted to recruit Saint-Exupéry, a prestigious writer as well as a well-known aviator.

In January 1941 the Vichy government created a consultative assembly, called the National Council, in an attempt to have some form of representative body. Saint-Exupéry was named as a member of the group, according to a report whose source could not be documented. He called a press conference in New York to state that he had no political agenda and would have refused such an appointment if he had been asked (Schiff 350). The statement earned him no friends on either side; political neutrality is difficult at any time and especially hard during war and occupation.

Both sides continued their effort to convince Saint-Exupéry to join them. De Gaulle's representatives tried hard to convert the writer, but Saint-Exupéry thought he saw a potential dictator in de Gaulle, an opinion shared by many in the U. S. government in the early 1940s. He also did not feel that Pétain had saved France from total destruction by withdrawing the country from the war (Schiff 350–51).

While political storms raged about him, Saint-Exupéry finally finished *Flight to Arras* (*Pilote de guerre*, in French), and the book was published in the United States in February 1942, after the U.S. entry into the war. The thrust of the book was an attempt to make some sense of the experience of war (Schiff 363). Saint-Exupéry also wanted to affirm his belief in mankind and in the civilization of his origins (Robinson 105). The book changed some American perceptions of the French effort in the war, as it outlined the author's own experiences as a military pilot in 1939–1940, and readers could see the active participation of many French in the military effort. However, with this publication, Saint-Exupéry again became the center of controversy among his compatriots. Read initially by those supporting Vichy as an account of the war that surmounted politics, the book was seen by Gaullists as defeatist (Schiff 364). At the end of 1942 the book appeared in France, a country now completely occupied since the Allied landings in North Africa on November 8, 1942. Submitting a book for publication meant obtaining approval from censors. Initially the Germans saw the book as an example of the best type of French literature and censored only one line. However, *Pilote de guerre* was recalled after a short time because certain Frenchmen could not accept that Saint-Exupéry's praises of his squadron included references to the heroics of a Jewish member of the group, Jean Israel (Schiff 365–66). Soon the book was available only clandestinely, and Gallimard, Saint-Exupéry's publisher, was not allowed to publish any reprints of the writer's earlier works (Schiff 366).

As the Allies were planning the invasion of North Africa, a high official in American military aviation visited Saint-Exupéry to tap his knowledge of the area, its landing fields and flying conditions (Robinson 113). Saint-Exupéry published an "Open Letter to Frenchmen" in the *New York Times Magazine* following the invasion. This letter called on Frenchmen to forget partisan spirit and to unite (Robinson 114). He even telegraphed Cordell Hull, secretary of state under President Franklin Roosevelt, concerning his willingness to serve in any capacity and calling for the military mobilization of all the French in the United States (Robinson 114).

Very much part of the historical context of France during World War II, Saint-Exupéry was separated by his residence in New York and his attitude toward the political factions from direct participation while he was writing *The Little Prince*. Yet, he wanted to serve, as emphasized in his telegram, and just before the book's publication Saint-Exupéry received his sailing orders and became an official part of General Béthouard's mission. The General had come to the United States on mission from General Henri Giraud to obtain weapons. General Giraud, who had escaped from a German prison in May 1942, had been smuggled out of France by the Americans and sent to French North Africa to serve as the French leader supporting the Allied invasion. After negotiations, the Allies and the Free French factions agreed that de Gaulle should also be sent to Algeria, and that he and Giraud would serve as co-presidents of a new French Committee of National Liberation. By the end of 1943, however, de Gaulle had succeeded in relegating Giraud to an obscure role and established his own leadership of the French resistance movement. De Gaulle had more ability as a political leader and more popular support (Wright 416).

Affected directly by the historical context in which he lived, Saint-Exupéry wanted to remain true to his own conception of mankind. He wrote *The Little Prince* in the midst of war and let it express his happiness at the memory of childhood faith and imagination. Friendship and simple joys evoked by the smile of a loved one or the beauty of the desert are always present at some point in Saint-Exupéry's writings. Even in *Letter to a Hostage* (*Lettre à un otage*, in French), also published in 1943, he reiterates the idea that friendship and joy are formed when human beings forge ties. This short book reflects its writer's concern for those left behind in France, hostages to cold and hunger and an occupying force. With his active life as an aviator Saint-Exupéry did not often meditate on social and political problems, but during the years of World War II especially, concerns for humanity preoccupied him. Faced with death many times as an aviator, he never lost his intellectual lucidity and his sense of hope. Even in the midst of war he could write about friendship, beauty, joy, and individual sadness while striving always to serve actively. World War II as it involved France and Saint-Exupéry was a period of complexity, factions, death, and destruction. Saint-Exupéry, who tried to serve his country and illustrate its values as he perceived them, remains part of this historical context, yet separate from its direct turmoil as he tells the story of the small person who journeys from his tiny planet to discover the important values of friendship, love, and responsibility.

# Bibliography

Page numbers from the eight novels discussed in this volume are from the following editions.

Camus, Albert. *The Plague*. Trans. Stuart Gilbert. New York: Random House, Inc., 1972.
————. *The Stranger*. Trans. Matthew Ward. New York: Alfred A. Knopf, Inc., 1988.
Dumas, Alexandre. *The Three Musketeers*. Trans. Eleanor Hochman. New York: Signet Classics, 1991.
————. *The Count of Monte Cristo*. Trans. Robin Buss. New York: Penguin Books, 1996.
Flaubert, Gustave. *Madame Bovary*. Trans. Geoffrey Wall. New York: Penguin Books, 1992.
Hugo, Victor. *The Hunchback of Notre-Dame*. Trans. Walter J. Cobb. New York: Signet Classics, 1964.
————. *Les Misérables*. Trans. Lee Fahnestock and Norman MacAfee. New York: Signet Classics, 1987.
Saint-Exupéry, Antoine de. *The Little Prince*. Trans. Katherine Woods. New York: Harcourt Brace Jovanovich, 1943.

## SELECTED NOVELS AND ESSAYS BY ALBERT CAMUS

The works in this list have been published in both French and English. The dates are those of the original publication and its first translation.

*L'Etranger*. Paris: Librairie Gallimard, 1942. (*The Stranger*. Trans. Stuart Gilbert. New York: Alfred A. Knopf, Inc., 1946.)
*La Peste*. Paris: Librairie Gallimard, 1947. (*The Plague*. Trans. Stuart Gilbert. New York: Alfred A. Knopf, Inc., 1948.)

*La Chute*. Paris: Librairie Gallimard, 1956. (*The Fall*. Trans. Justin O'Brien. New York: Alfred A. Knopf, Inc., 1957.)

*L'Exil et le royaume*. Paris: Librairie Gaillimard, 1957. (*Exile and the Kingdom* [short stories]. Trans. Justin O'Brien. New York: Alfred A. Knopf, Inc., 1957)

*Le Premier Homme*. Ed. Catherine Camus. Paris: Librairie Gallimard, 1994. (*The First Man*. Trans. David Hapgood. New York: Alfred A. Knopf, Inc., 1995. The manuscript was incomplete and unpublished at the time of Camus's death in a 1960 auto accident.)

*Le Mythe de Sisyphe*. Paris: Librairie Gallimard, 1943. (*The Myth of Sisyphus*. Trans. Justin O'Brien. New York: Alfred A. Knopf, Inc., 1955.)

*L'Homme révolté*. Paris: Librairie Gallimard, 1951. (*The Rebel*. Trans. Anthony Bower. New York: Alfred A. Knopf, Inc., 1954.)

*Carnets: Mai 1935–février 1942*. Paris: Librairie Gallimard, 1962. (*Notebooks, 1935–1942*. Trans. Philip Thody. New York: Alfred A. Knopf, Inc., 1969.)

*Carnets II: Janvier 1942–mars 1951*. Paris: Librairie Gallimard, 1964. (*Notebooks, 1942–1951*. Trans. Justin O'Brien. New York: Alfred A. Knopf, Inc., 1966.)

## SELECTED BIOGRAPHICAL AND CRITICAL WORKS IN ENGLISH ABOUT CAMUS

Brée, Germaine. *Camus*. New Brunswick, N.J.: Rutgers University Press, 1961.

———, ed. *Camus: A Collection of Critical Essays*. Englewood Cliffs, N.J.: Prentice-Hall, Inc., 1962.

Kellman, Steven G., ed. *Approaches to Teaching Camus's The Plague*. New York: The Modern Language Association of America, 1985.

Lottman, Herbert R. *Albert Camus*. Garden City, N.Y.: Doubleday & Company, Inc., 1979.

McCarthy, Patrick. *Albert Camus: The Stranger*. Cambridge, U.K.: Cambridge University Press, 1988.

Quilliot, Roger. *The Sea and Prisons*. Trans. Emmett Parker. University, Ala.: The University of Alabama Press, 1970.

Rhein, Phillip H. *Albert Camus*. New York: Twayne Publishers, Inc., 1969.

Thiher, Allen. "Teaching the Historical Context of *The Plague*." *Approaches to Teaching Camus's The Plague*. Ed. Steven G. Kellman. New York: The Modern Language Association of America, 1985: 90–101.

Thody, Philip. *Albert Camus*. New York: The Macmillan Company, 1961.

Todd, Olivier. *Albert Camus*. Trans. Benjamin Ivry. New York: Alfred A. Knopf, Inc., 1997.

## CONTEMPORARY REVIEWS OF *THE STRANGER*

Chiaromonte, Nicola. "Albert Camus." *New Republic* 29 April 1946: 630–33.

O'Brien, Justin. "Presenting a New French Writer." *New York Herald Tribune Weekly Book Review* 14 April 1946: 10.

Plant, Richard. "Benign Indifference." *Saturday Review of Literature* 18 May 1946: 10.

Wilson, Edmund. "Albert Camus—Charles Dickens—Lafcadio Hearn." *New Yorker* 13 April 1946: 113–14.

## CONTEMPORARY REVIEWS OF *THE PLAGUE*

Kee, Robert. *The Plague. Spectator* 3 Sept. 1948: 314.

McLaughlin, Richard. "Battle Against the Forces of Darkness." *Saturday Review of Literature* 31 July 1948: 10–11.

O'Brien, Justin. "World Contagion. The Plague." *New Republic* 16 Aug. 1948: 23–24.

Prescott, Orville. "Outstanding Novels." *Yale Review* Sept. 1948: 189–92.

Rugoff, Milton. "Parable of Our World Seen in a Stricken City." *New York Herald Tribune Weekly Book Review* 1 Aug. 1948: 1.

Spender, Stephen. "Albert Camus, Citizen of the World." *New York Times Book Review* 1 Aug. 1948: 1, 20.

## SELECTED NOVELS AND PLAYS BY ALEXANDRE DUMAS

The works in this list have been published in both French and English. The dates are those of the original publication and its first translation.

*Henri III et sa cour.* 1829. (*Henri III and His Court* [play] published in *Nineteenth Century French Plays*, 1931.)

*La tour de Nesle.* 1832. (*The Tower of Nesle* [play], 1906.)

*Les trois mousquetaires.* 1844. (*The Three Musketeers; or, The Feats and Fortunes of a Gascon Adventurer*, 1846.)

*Le comte de Monte-Cristo.* 1845. (*The Count of Monte Cristo*, 1846.)

*Le vicomte de Bragelonne; ou, Dix ans plus tard.* 26 vols. 1848–50. (*The Vicomte de Bragelonne; or, Ten Years Later*, 1857. Portions of this work also translated and published as *The Man in the Iron Mask*, cf. Signet Edition, Trans. Jacqueline Rogers, 1998.)

## SELECTED BIOGRAPHICAL AND CRITICAL WORKS IN ENGLISH ABOUT DUMAS

Gorman, Herbert. *The Incredible Marquis Alexandre Dumas.* New York: Farrar & Rinehart, 1929.

Hemmings, F. W. J. *The King of Romance: A Portrait of Alexandre Dumas.* London: Hamish Hamilton, 1979.

Marinetti, Amelita. "Death, Resurrection, and Fall in Dumas' *Comte de Monte-Cristo*." *The French Review* L (1976): 260–69.

Maurois, André. *The Titans.* Trans. Gerard Hopkins. New York: Harper & Brothers, 1957.

Schopp, Claude. *Alexandre Dumas Genius of Life*. Trans. A. J. Koch. New York: Franklin Watts, 1988.

Stowe, Richard S. *Alexandre Dumas, père*. Boston: Twayne Publishers, 1976.

## CONTEMPORARY REVIEWS OF *THE THREE MUSKETEERS* AND *THE COUNT OF MONTE CRISTO*

"Historical Romance—Alexandre Dumas." *The British Quarterly Review* Feb. 1848: 181–204.

"Literary Impostures: Alexandre Dumas." *The North American Review* April 1854: 305–45.

## SELECTED NOVELS BY GUSTAVE FLAUBERT

The works in this list have been published in both French and English. The dates are those of the original publication and its first translation.

*Madame Bovary*. 1857. (*Madame Bovary*. Trans. Peterson, 1881. Also noteworthy is the translation of Eleanor Marx Aveling first published in 1886 which was updated by Paul de Man and published in a Norton Critical Edition of the novel in 1965.)

*Salammbô*. Michel Levy frères, 1862. (*Salammbô*. Trans. Lovell, Coryell, 1885.)

*L'Education sentimentale*. Michel Levy frères, 1869. (*Sentimental Education: A Young Man's History*. Trans. D. F. Hannigan, 1898.)

*La Tentation de Saint-Antoine*. Charpentier, 1874. (*The Temptation of Saint Anthony*. Trans. D. F. Hannigan, 1895.)

*Trois contes*. Charpentier, 1877. (*Three Tales*. Trans. Arthur McDowell, 1923.)

*Bouvard et Pécuchet*. Alphonse Lemerre, 1881 (posthumous). (*Bouvard and Pécuchet*. Trans. D. F. Hannigan, 1896.)

## SELECTED BIOGRAPHICAL AND CRITICAL WORKS IN ENGLISH ABOUT FLAUBERT

Bart, Benjamin F. *Flaubert*. Syracuse, N.Y.: Syracuse University Press, 1967.

Berg, William J., and Laurey K. Martin. *Gustave Flaubert*. New York: Twayne Publishers, 1997.

Brombert, Victor. *The Novels of Flaubert*. Princeton, N.J.: Princeton University Press, 1966.

Giraud, Raymond, ed. *Flaubert: A Collection of Critical Essays*. Englewood Cliffs, N.J.: Prentice-Hall, Inc., 1964.

Levin, Harry. *The Gates of Horn*. New York: Oxford University Press, 1963.

Porter, Laurence M., and Eugene F. Gray, eds. *Approches to Teaching Flaubert's Madame Bovary*. Ed. Laurence M. Porter and Eugene F. Gray. New York: The Modern Language Association of America, 1995.

Schlossman, Beryl. "Flaubert's Moving Sidewalk." *Approaches to Teaching Flaubert's Madame Bovary*. Ed. Laurence M. Porter and Eugene F. Gray. New York: The Modern Language Association of America, 1995: 69–76.
Steegmuller, Francis. *Flaubert and Madame Bovary*. London: Macmillan, 1968.

## CONTEMPORARY REVIEWS OF *MADAME BOVARY*

Baudelaire, Charles. "*Madame Bovary*, by Gustave Flaubert." First published in *L'artiste*, October 18, 1857. Available in English in the *Norton Critical Edition of Madame Bovary*. Trans. Paul de Man. New York: W. W. Norton & Company, 1965: 336–43.
Morras, W. P. "Gustave Flaubert, the Realist." *Lipincott's Magazine of Literature, Science and Education* 1 Oct. 1870: 439–46.
Sainte-Beuve, Charles Augustin. "*Madame Bovary*, by Gustave Flaubert." First published May 4, 1857. Available in English in the *Norton Critical Edition of Madame Bovary*. Trans. Paul de Man. New York: W. W. Norton & Company, 1965: 325–36.

## SELECTED NOVELS BY VICTOR HUGO

The works in this list have been published in both French and English. The dates are those of the original publication and its first translation.

*Han d'Islande*. 1823. (*Hans of Iceland*, 1845.)
*Bug-Jargal*. 1826. (*The Slave King*, 1833.)
*Le dernier jour d'un condamné*. 1829. (*The Last Day of a Condemned*, 1840.)
*Notre-Dame de Paris*. 1831. (*The Hunchback of Notre-Dame*. Trans. F. Shoberl Galignani. London: Richard Bentley, 1833.)
*Les Misérables*. 1862. (*Les Misérables*. Trans. Lascelles Wraxall. London: Hurst and Blackett, 1862.)
*Les travailleurs de la mer*. 1866. (*The Toilers of the Sea*, 1866.)
*L'homme qui rit*. 1869. (*The Man Who Laughs*, 1869.)
*Quatre-vingt-treize*. 1874. (*Ninety-three*, 1874.)

## SELECTED BIOGRAPHICAL AND CRITICAL WORKS IN ENGLISH AND FRENCH ABOUT HUGO

Barrère, Jean Bertrand. *Victor Hugo*. Paris: Hatier, 1967.
Brombert, Victor. *Victor Hugo and the Visionary Novel*. Cambridge, Mass.: Harvard University Press, 1984.
Edwards, Samuel. *Victor Hugo: A Tumultuous Life*. New York: David McKay Company, 1971.
Guyard, M. F. Introduction. *Les Misérables*. By Victor Hugo. Paris: Garnier, 1963: i–xxvii.

Houston, John Porter. *Victor Hugo*. Rev. ed. Boston: Twayne Publishers, 1988.
Marsland, Amy L. and George Klin. *Les Misérables*. Lincoln, Nebr.: Cliffs Notes, 1993.
Robb, Graham. *Victor Hugo*. London: Picador, 1997.

## CONTEMPORARY REVIEWS IN ENGLISH OF *THE HUNCHBACK OF NOTRE DAME*

"French Literature—Recent Novelists." *The Edinburgh Review* LVII, July 1833, 330–57.
Janin, Jules. "Literature of the Nineteenth Century: France. *The Athenaeum* 8 July 1837: 466, 499–506.
"Notre Dame: A Tale of the Ancient Regime." *The Examiner* 25 Aug. 1833: 533–34.

## CONTEMPORARY REVIEWS IN ENGLISH OF *LES MISÉRABLES*

de Peyronnet, Caroline. "Victor Hugo's 'Les Misérables.'" *The Edinburgh Review* Jan. 1863: 208–40.
Lewes, G.H. "Victor Hugo's Last Romance." *Blackwood's Magazine* XVII, August 1862: 172–82.
"Literature of Victor Hugo." *Eclectic Magazine* LVII, December 1862: 489–94.
"Reviews and Literary Notices: 'Les Misérables.'" *The Atlantic Monthly* X, July 1862: 124–25.
Swinbourne, Algernon Charles. "Victor Hugo's New Novel." *The Spectator* 12 April 1862: 410–11.
"Victor Hugo and 'Les Misérables.'" *The New Englander* XXIII, July 1864: 454–81.
"Victor Hugo's 'Les Misérables.'" *The Boston Review* Jan. 1863: 52–68.
Watson, C. Knight. "'Les Misérables.'" *The Quarterly Review* Oct. 1862: 271–306.

## SELECTED WORKS BY ANTOINE DE SAINT-EXUPÉRY

The works in this list have been published in both French and English. The dates are those of the original publication and its first translation.

*Courrier sud*. Paris: Gallimard, 1929. (*Southern Mail*. Trans. Stuart Gilbert. New York: Smith & Hass, 1933.)
*Vol de nuit*. Paris: Gallimard, 1931. (*Night Flight*. Trans. Stuart Gilbert. New York: Century Co., 1932.)
*Terre des hommes*. Paris: Gallimard, 1939. (*Wind, Sand, and Stars*. Trans. Lewis Galentière. New York: Reynal & Hitchcock, 1939.)
*Pilote de guerre*. Paris: Gallimard, 1942. (*Flight to Arras*. Trans. Lewis Galentière. New York: Reynal & Hitchcock, 1942.)

*Lettre à un otage*. Paris: Gallimard, 1945. (*Letter to a Hostage*. Trans. John Rodker. In
    *French Short Stories*. New York: New Directions, 1948.)
*Le Petit Prince*. Paris: Gallimard, 1948. (*The Little Prince*. Trans. Katherine Woods.
    New York: Reynal & Hitchcock, 1943.)
*Citadelle*. Paris: Gallimard, 1948. (*The Wisdom of the Sands*. Trans. Stuart Gilbert.
    New York: Harcourt Brace, 1949.)


## SELECTED BIOGRAPHICAL AND CRITICAL WORKS IN ENGLISH ABOUT SAINT-EXUPÉRY

Robinson, Joy D. Marie. *Antoine de Saint-Exupéry*. Boston: Twayne Publishers, 1984.
Schiff, Stacy. *Saint-Exupéry: A Biography*. New York: Alfred A. Knopf, Inc., 1994.


## CONTEMPORARY REVIEWS OF *THE LITTLE PRINCE*

Cimino, Maria. Rev. of *The Little Prince*. *Saturday Review of Literature* 17 April
    1943: 50.
Garner, P. A. Rev. of *The Little Prince*. *Book Week* 2 May 1943: 3.
Moore, A. C. Rev. of *The Little Prince*. *Horn Book* May 1943: 164–66.
Sherman, Beatrice. Rev. of *The Little Prince*. *New York Times* 11 April 1943: 3.
Travers, P. L. Rev. of *The Little Prince*. *Weekly Book Review* 11 April 1943: 5.
Willis, K. T. Rev. of *The Little Prince*. *Library Journal* 15 Mar. 1943: 248.


## RELATED SECONDARY SOURCES

Ageron, Charles-Robert. *Modern Algeria*. Trans. Michael Brett. London: Hurst &
    Company, 1991.
Gordon, David C. *The Passing of French Algeria*. London: Oxford University Press,
    1966.
Paxton, Robert O. *Vichy France, Old Guard and New Order, 1940–1944*. New York:
    Alfred A. Knopf, Inc., 1972.
Wright, Gordon. *France in Modern Times*. 3rd ed. New York: W. W. Norton & Com-
    pany, 1981.
Zeldin, Theodore. *France, 1848–1945*. 2 vols. London: Oxford University Press,
    1973–77.

# Index

## About the Author

MARILYN S. SEVERSON is a Professor of European Studies specializing in French in the Department of Foreign Languages and Literature at Seattle Pacific University. She is the author of *James A. Michener: A Critical Companion* (Greenwood, 1996).